The Complete Book of

Woodworking

The Complete Book of
Woodworking

An Illustrated Guide to Tools and Techniques

Consultant Declan O'Donoghue

Photographers Colin Bowling and Paul Forrester

THE LYONS PRESS

All you need to know about...
The Complete Book of
Woodworking

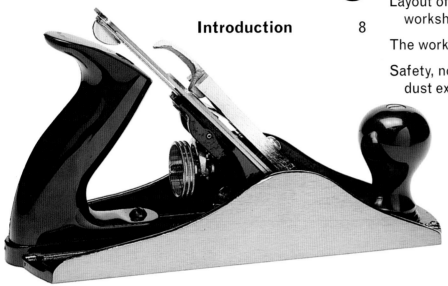

Introduction   8

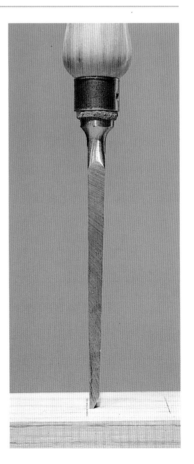

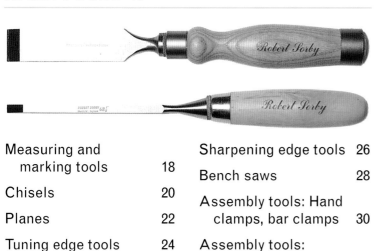

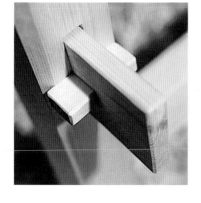

TEN
WOODTURNING 177

THIRTEEN
PLANS 209

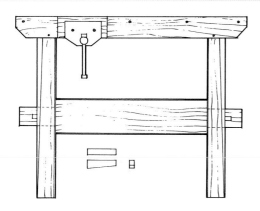

First Lyons Press edition, 2001

Lyons Press is an imprint of The Globe Pequot Press

First published in Great Britain in 1997 by Hamlyn, a division of Octopus Publishing Group Limited, 2-4 Heron Quays, London E14 4JP

ISBN 1-58574-332-1

In describing all the woodworking practices and projects in this book, every care has been taken to recommend the safest methods of working. Before starting any task, you should be confident that you know what you are doing, and that you know how to use all tools and equipment safely. The Publishers cannot accept any legal responsibility or liability for any direct or consequential accidents or damage arising from the use of any items mentioned, or in the carrying out of any of the projects described.

Imperial/metric conversions
For the sake of consistency exact imperial/metric conversions have been used throughout the book (1 in.: 25.4 mm). This sometimes results in measurements that, for practical reasons, you may find easier to round up or down. This will make your work easier without altering the proportions of a piece. This does not apply to generic measurements as in tool sizes, however, where the imperial/metric conversions relate to the tool size as it is likely to be sold.

Contributors: Christian Gaze (Chapter 6); Ben Harms (Chapter 11); peter Hoggard (Chapter 9); Declan O'Donoghue (Chapter 8); Dave Regester (Chapter 10); Mark Ripley (Chapter 7); David Savage (Chapters 1-5 and 7); Chris Simpson (Glossary and captions); Andrew Varah (Chapter 12)

Executive Editor: Simon Tuite
Editor: Jo Lethaby
Executive Art Editor: Mark Stevens
Designer: Les Needham
Design Assistant: Julian Keeble
Illustrators: Jane Hughes and Mark Ripley (plans)
Picture Researcher: Maria Gibbs
Production Controller: Mark Walker

Produced by Toppan Printing Company Ltd
Printed in China

10 9 8 7 6 5 4 3 2

INTRODUCTION

It was in the late 1970s that I picked up my first new tool kit, as I was about to embark on an affair with one of the most beautiful and versatile materials known to man, namely wood. My preconceptions, as an impressionable teenager, of starting to make fine furniture that very week were soon firmly quashed! We were to spend the next two weeks tuning and preparing our new tools. And so ensued a grueling and messy experience with carborundum powder, mineral spirits, and plate glass. It only reinforced the frustration of not being able to get at the real material—wood, which varies not only in color and texture but also in smell, and is a warm and forgiving material to work with.

However, this experience did imbue a sense of the importance of overall excellence, not only in the making of a piece of furniture but also in the way that we approach all aspects of our work, from tuning and familiarizing ourselves with the tools we become intimate with, to the way we store and sharpen them, select our raw material, present our ideas, and finally make the projects.

When I look back at how much I learned in a very short space of time, and the rocketing improvements in standards, I feel there is no reason why you, the reader, cannot aspire to do the same, albeit at a gentler pace!

When I was first approached to be involved in this book, I initially thought "I'm too busy," but as someone who has always preached positive and sharing attitudes to work and ideas, I could not refuse!

We live in an age where leisure time is on the increase, and many people would wish to spend that time constructively. What better way than by making useful items for oneself or for others? Woodworking is a challenge that can be as rewarding as any, but which leaves a tangible trail of one's mistakes and achievements which can be continually learned from as well as enjoyed.

The Complete Book of Woodworking is comprehensive. It covers not only techniques and the safe use of hand and power tools and machines, but also gives full plans and instructions for making a variety of well-designed items. There is a feature putting furniture in a visual context, showing what has been achieved already and inspiring you to develop your own ideas. The book covers all the important areas, so you can undertake with confidence the projects described within and more.

All the contributors are professional woodworkers at various stages of their careers. They have generously responded with the weight of their experience which, thankfully, is an ever-increasing trait against a historical precedent of near secrecy!

Finally, I hope that this fine book and the ever-improving availability of equipment for the small workshop will act as a catalyst for an ongoing adventure with wood, and be a fulfilling journey for all who undertake its projects and beyond!

Declan O' Donoghue FSDC MSDI

ONE **THE HOME WORKSHOP**

If you wish to achieve fine workmanship, it is possible to attain this working in the garage or on the kitchen table, but it is far easier to set aside a place for concentrated work. Your workshop is somewhere special, somewhere that reflects the standards you aim to achieve. It is a place where your tools are always kept sharp and are stored in racks adjacent to your bench; where your bench is set up true and level in good working light; and where your components, half-completed, are stacked ready for you to take them up and complete the job. A workshop is a place of reflection, a place of planning, and of executing new projects to even higher standards.

LOCATION AND SIZE

The size and location of your workshop is determined first by your own personal conditions, and second, by the kind of work you intend to do there. Someone working with hand tools making small pieces of furniture can create a workshop out of a large broom closet and work there very successfully. A great deal of space is not required if you plan to get your lumber machined to your specifications by a local supplier or cabinet shop and complete the job using hand tools and one or two small power tools. If, however, you are working with machines and you intend to make large structures, then the size of the space required would be considerably more. Single bedrooms, single garages, garden sheds, and basements are all popular home workshop locations.

Planning your workshop

When selecting your workspace, spare a thought for the following considerations. First, do you need to have your own machines or could you get the time-saving lumber preparation done by a local lumber yard or cabinet shop? If you are prepared to acquire skills with a relatively small group of hand tools—perhaps with the assistance of a weekend course or evening class—you can manage without the noise, dust, expense, and general unpleasant working conditions created by woodworking machines and power tools.

Second, consider the heating and humidity control of your workshop. Wood is very sensitive to changes in humidity, and an unheated workshop will invariably be damp and encourage not only your lumber to warp, but your tools and machines to rust. Garage workshops should be insulated not only on the walls and the ceiling but also on the large garage door. Outdoor workshops should be carefully heated with a form of dry heat: some mobile gas heaters are cheap to run but give out gallons of moisture. Consider the benefits of putting in a low-output background heater that runs all the time, together with a dehumidifier that extracts moisture from the air but also keeps the air warm. The humidity and warmth of the average centrally heated home should be your aim.

RIGHT *A typical home workshop showing a range of benches and tables and tools stored on walls and shelves*

LEFT *For safe and accurate work, it is important to have machinery and work surfaces well illuminated*

BELOW *If you plan to undertake large projects, you need to consider layout carefully: how to bring materials in and take finished pieces out*

Lighting and electricity

Good lighting within a workshop is very important, but direct sunlight through a window landing on partly finished components can cause them to warp and twist. If you can, situate your bench adjacent to a window and hang plenty of inexpensive fluorescent shop lights from the ceiling. Be especially careful to ensure that your machines are well lit. To certain machines, such as a bandsaw or a radial-arm saw, you may want to add a swing-arm desk lamp.

Electric sockets should be positioned around the workshop so that you can avoid trailing cords across your work area.

LAYOUT OF THE WORKSHOP

Planning a workshop is best done first on paper by drawing a floor plan to scale, and then placing within that plan pieces of paper cut to size to represent the machines, benches, and storage cupboards that you intend to use in the workshop.

Machines

If you are using machines, imagine what it would be like processing boards for a 6 ft. (1829 mm) or 8 ft. (2438 mm) long dining table. Make the best use you can of diagonals and doors and openings. Determine if you can afford to bring full-sized 4 x 8 ft. (2438 x 1219 mm) plywood into your workshop, or whether these boards will have to be sawn into smaller sizes by your supplier. Remember that a small pile of components can take up very little room but that, once assembled, the resulting batch of six dining chairs can take up a lot of space!

Using a machining table that can be adapted to hold an inverted circular saw, a router, or a jigsaw provides the advantage, besides economical machining, of not taking up a great deal of space. There are also small bench-mounted machines such as mortisers, drill presses, and bench grinders that require only a work surface to support them. Old kitchen cabinets carefully anchored to the wall to provide rigidity can be used very satisfactorily to support these types of machines and also to provide storage underneath for power tools, abrasives, and blades.

Make use of the fact that a bandsaw has a much higher table than most other small machines, such as a table saw or a planer. If you are stuck for space you can position your bandsaw so that lumber is fed across, above, and over an adjacent machine. You can also use doors and windows to your advantage. If your windows are low enough, lumber can be fed across a bandsaw or planer table and out through the adjacent window. Remember that although the ideal is to have a place for everything, most small machines are light enough to move around, should you need to plane an extraordinarily long piece of lumber.

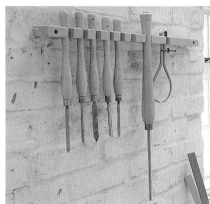

TOP *A light, airy workshop. This placing of the table saw and bandsaw best uses the space*

ABOVE LEFT *A drill press is useful for straight drilling and cutting mortises*

ABOVE RIGHT *Turning tools neatly and conveniently placed in a wall rack*

LEFT *A router table turns the hand-held router into a small spindle shaper*

Storage

Racks and storage cabinets are a great way of keeping tools and blades in an orderly fashion, especially around the bench. Here the professional will go to great lengths to store and arrange tools so that they can be picked up and put away again quickly and easily. There is nothing so frustrating as rummaging around in a pile of sawdust and shavings looking for a small but essential hand tool. Router bits, for example, can be kept in a block of wood drilled to accept their different shank sizes. Clamps can be kept either

ABOVE *A grinder being used to sharpen turning tools*

LEFT *The powered router, showing some of the cutters available for this machine*

vertically or horizontally in racks, as can saws and chisels. It is useful to put tools and blades specific to one machine on an adjacent shelf or cupboard. If you are using sanding machines, and even if you have a dust extractor, open cupboards or racks are dust traps that are best avoided: sooner or later everything will be covered in pale brown snow. In this case, the only answer is to put everything away in closed cupboards and cabinets.

Plan a special place for your project. The space requirement will change as the project develops: first a pile of rough boards, followed by sawn and planed components, then jointed sub-assemblies and, finally, the finished piece of work.

Care should be taken when planning a workshop to deal with the issue of fire risk. Lumber components, scrap wood, sawdust, shavings, oils, and polishes are all potential fire hazards that need to be controlled and kept away from flame. Your insurance company may need to be informed if you change the use of a part of your home in this way.

Sharpening bench

You will need an auxiliary bench that can be set up as a sharpening bench. This would house a small grinder and also provide a surface for your sharpening stones. The sharpening bench can be placed reasonably near your main bench so that within a few moments a new edge can be honed on a dull tool. Set up good lighting on this bench since sharpening needs a good light to enable you to examine the new cutting edge. Also make sure that this bench is of the correct working height to be used comfortably when standing. In a very small workshop, the sharpening area may have to be one end of the main workbench.

LEFT *An ideal way to store bar clamps and other similar tools*

BELOW *A plan of a small workshop, indicating where machines might be placed and how usage can be improved by moving particular machines for specific operations*

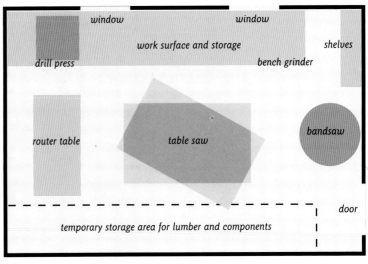

THE WORKBENCH

The true cabinetmaker's workbench has been described as a craftsman's "altar." Although it is possible to make good things without a workbench, it is considerably easier to do good work on a good workbench than it is without it. A first-class workbench should be one of the first things an aspiring cabinetmaker either makes or buys for him or herself. Certainly it will cost a great deal, in both time and materials, but your bench is the foundation stone upon which everything else, quite literally, is made, and so it will be a worthy investment.

The functions of a workbench

The essence of a good bench is that it is an enormous clamping device that enables you to hold the job in position while you work upon it. The very act of holding the job for you enables you, the craftsperson, to get yourself into exactly the correct position to do the particular operation you are considering, rather than being compromised by holding the job down and attempting to work on it at the same time. A good bench should be very heavy; it should not vibrate when moved or nudged, and it should be exactly flat.

Flatness is important because a cabinetmaker uses a bench like an engineer uses a surface plate—as a reference surface, as well as a surface upon which to plane true and flat components. It is therefore important to keep the surface of your bench clean and free of damage. Check it periodically for flatness, and after every major job take a bench plane and clean and resurface the bench top to provide a clean start for the next job.

When positioning a new bench it is important to set it up level and true so that you can use the end or back surface of the bench to sight against when setting your job in either of the bench vises.

ABOVE *A really sturdy bench provides a fine platform for precision work. This shows a piece of work that is held by bench dogs and an end vise*

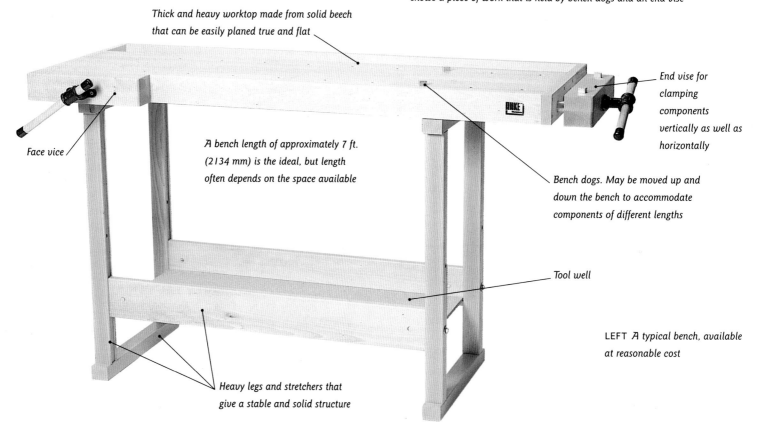

Thick and heavy worktop made from solid beech that can be easily planed true and flat

End vise for clamping components vertically as well as horizontally

Face vice

A bench length of approximately 7 ft. (2134 mm) is the ideal, but length often depends on the space available

Bench dogs. May be moved up and down the bench to accommodate components of different lengths

Tool well

LEFT *A typical bench, available at reasonable cost*

Heavy legs and stretchers that give a stable and solid structure

It is far easier to saw straight if your job is set vertically in the bench vise.

Two clamping methods are available: the face or front vise, usually placed on the left-hand end of the bench, and the end or tail vice, placed on the right-hand end of the bench. Both vices are used for clamping work in the conventional way, but the end vise can also be used in conjunction with two movable pegs called bench dogs, to hold work flat on the surface of the bench while you plane or work in some other way on the surface of a board or small component. It is this vise that enables you to hold even the

LEFT *A very substantial bench with a Scandinavian vice system that gives a wide variety of holding alternatives*

ABOVE *A simple folding table that is very useful as an occasional work area*

BELOW *A neat arrangement of some of the tools and materials that you will need to store in your workshop*

smallest component for jointing or for the final stroke of a plane.

An additional holding device for use in conjunction with a bench is a bench hook. This is a simple tool that enables you to hold a piece of wood while retaining your balance and sawing at the same time.

Other work surfaces

Auxiliary benches can take the form of Workmates, folding trestles, or carpenters' sawhorses, which can be put up and dismantled as necessary. A folding bench attached to the wall, which can be dropped down, can also provide useful assembly space when needed.

A "drop-on" top made of particle board with a Formica face that can be placed on top of your bench is useful for finishing work. This avoids marking either your bench surface with finishing materials or your finished work with wood shavings or chips.

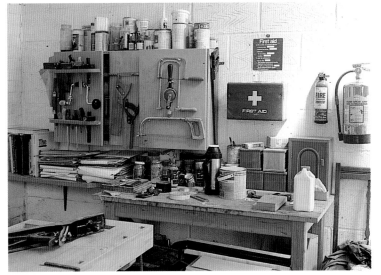

The workbench   15

SAFETY, NOISE, AND DUST EXTRACTION

For your own health and the comfort of your friends and neighbors you should always consider how the dust and noise being created by your workshop is going to be managed.

RIGHT *For the sake of your health, especially the eyes, it is important to wear the appropriate protective gear at all times*

LEFT *A workshop showing a portable extractor linked to the bandsaw while in use*

Safety in the workshop

Consider also your personal safety within your workshop. Sharp-edged tools can easily slip and cut you very badly. Woodworking machines and power tools can remove fingers faster than the speed of light. Always consider how an accident of this nature would be dealt with. Make sure there is a first aid box at hand and that you never use machinery unless there is somebody nearby who can drive you to a hospital. (Remember, if you are unfortunate enough to cut off a finger, pack it in ice and take it with you. It is a gruesome thought, but a separated digit can be sewn back on.)

Hearing loss due to prolonged exposure to the noise of power tools is common in the industry. Avoid this by always wearing ear protection, in the form of either ear muffs or the more comfortable ear plugs, when using any power tool. You should also consider the risks to your eyes, especially when using saws and routers. Clear plastic face masks are easy to put on and comfortable to wear.

Power tools and machines, especially if being used with man-made boards such as MDF, can create an extremely uncomfortable and potentially unhealthy level of dust. Not only for your own health but for your increased enjoyment of the craft, you should install some kind of dust-extraction equipment if you propose to use machines and power tools. A "wet-and-dry" shop vacuum is adequate for use around the bench and can be attached to some small power tools. This is good practice, since it is collecting the dust before it has had a chance to get into the air and down your lungs. When using routers it is advisable to wear some form of dust mask to protect yourself from the potentially serious health hazards associated with prolonged exposure to the exceptionally fine dust particles produced by these very useful and popular power tools. Larger portable extractors are needed for machines and need to be ducted to each machine in turn as you use it.

LEFT *Machines of this type can either be connected to one machine at a time, or linked up to several smaller machines*

FURTHER INFORMATION

TWO

HAND TOOLS

The home woodworker will frequently step over using hand tools and move straight to the promise of the quick accurate result given by power tools and machines. In so doing, however, the amateur is casting away the pleasure of working in a calm, quiet, dust-free workshop, creating silky plane shavings and controlling joints created accurately with razor-sharp hand tools guided by a skilled craftsperson. The skills required to tune, sharpen, and use planes, chisels, and saws are relatively easily acquired. They take a little patience, and perhaps a little tuition and time, but the rewards are immeasurable.

MEASURING AND MARKING TOOLS

Accuracy is really a very simple matter. Taking great care, mark your components exactly to size and then, again taking great care, cut to your marking line. This way your components cannot help but fit exactly together. This process begins with accurate, clean, marking—starting first with striking knives.

Striking knives

These are used in preference to pencils for marking because, whereas a pencil line has a thickness, a striking knife is beveled on one side only and is therefore capable of giving a mark of absolute accuracy. Sharpen your striking knife as carefully as you would a chisel and buy the best available. The steel should be of exceptional quality as it has to be constantly rubbed against the blades of steel squares.

Gauges

Marking and cutting gauges are used to scribe dimensions with the grain and across the grain, respectively. A marking gauge is fitted with a small sharp pin, while a cutting gauge is fitted with a small scribing knife, again sharpened with a bevel on one side only like a striking knife. You may need two or three gauges, since occasionally it may be required to leave a gauge set up to a particular dimension for a period of time. You may choose to have both types of gauge, but standard marking gauges can work well both with the grain and across it.

Mortise gauges are fitted with two pins, one of which is adjustable to enable parallel lines to scribe the position of mortise-and-tenon joints. You will find you need a mortise gauge—it is an important tool and it is worth getting the more expensive but easier-to-use versions of this tool where the second, movable, pin is controlled by a screw thread.

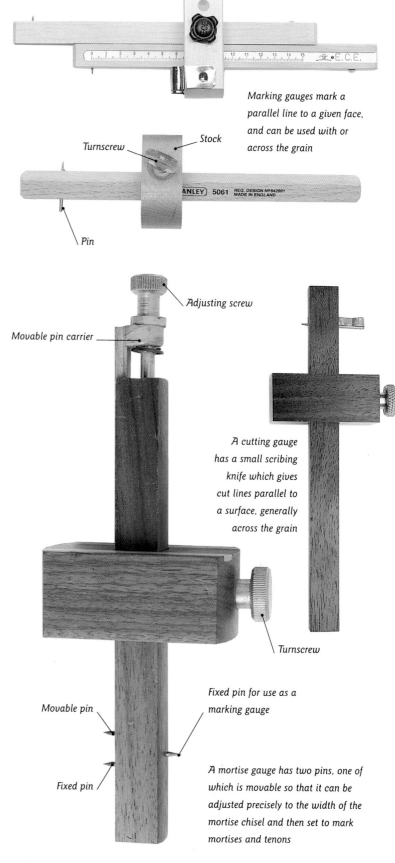

Marking gauges mark a parallel line to a given face, and can be used with or across the grain

Turnscrew — Stock

Pin

Adjusting screw

Movable pin carrier

A cutting gauge has a small scribing knife which gives cut lines parallel to a surface, generally across the grain

Turnscrew

Fixed pin for use as a marking gauge

Movable pin

Fixed pin

A mortise gauge has two pins, one of which is movable so that it can be adjusted precisely to the width of the mortise chisel and then set to mark mortises and tenons

Different types of striking knives; craftsmen's preferences vary greatly and selection is a personal choice

24 in. (600 mm) steel rule

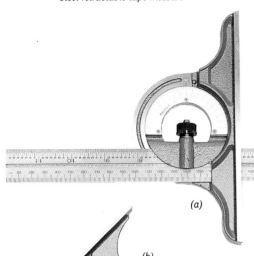

Steel retractable tape measure

Combination square—a rule (normally 12 in./300 mm) which accepts a number of different heads: (a) protractor head, (b) 90°, 45°, and spirit level, and (c) 90° center head

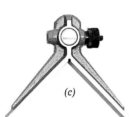

(a)

(b)

(c)

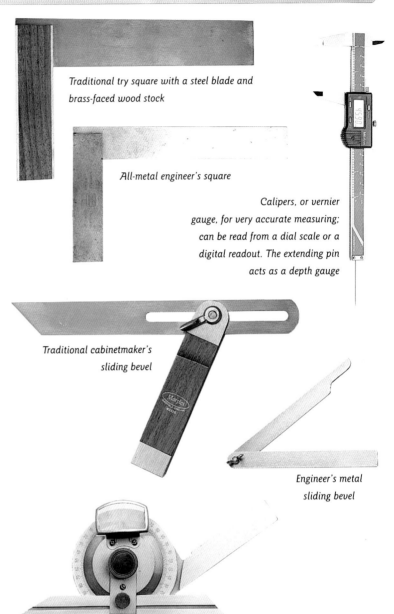

Traditional try square with a steel blade and brass-faced wood stock

All-metal engineer's square

Calipers, or vernier gauge, for very accurate measuring; can be read from a dial scale or a digital readout. The extending pin acts as a depth gauge

Traditional cabinetmaker's sliding bevel

Engineer's metal sliding bevel

Protractor head

Miter or 45° square

Rules and edges

The dimensions of your projects are checked against workshop rules. A steel rule with $\frac{1}{32}$ in. (1 mm) graduations is usually easier to read than one marked with $\frac{1}{64}$ in. (0.5 mm) graduations. It is useful to have a 24 in. (600 mm) rule kept by the bench and a 6 in. (150 mm) rule which can fit in an apron pocket. A tape measure is often used for larger components but is much less accurate than a big steel rule.

Another essential piece of equipment is a straight edge of about 39 in. (1000 mm) in length. This is used to check components and other tools for flatness. Do not rely on the edge of a rule to do this job as it may not be as straight as you need it to be.

Dial calipers are wonderful tools and have many uses within the workshop—principally checking the thickness of components. A less expensive, plastic dial caliper measuring to $\frac{1}{100}$ in. (0.25 mm) is easily accurate enough for woodwork and has the benefit of not suffering unduly if dropped.

Squares and sliding bevels

Combination squares are very useful but tend to be heavy and cumbersome and, unless they are quite expensive ones, can lead to inaccurate work. Sliding bevels are used for marking angles. Where possible, an all-metal engineer's sliding bevel should be used. Marking templates for dovetail joints can also be used.

Attractive brass templates should be avoided, however, as the steel striking knife can wear the brass template very quickly.

A square that is not quite square is a traitorous implement in the workshop. Where possible, use good-quality all-steel engineer's squares. A small 6 in. (150 mm) square and a 2 in. (50 mm) square are perfectly adequate for most work. Wooden-handled, steel-bladed squares are perfectly adequate for rough large-scale work where accuracy is less critical.

Measuring and marking tools

CHISELS

Bevel-edged chisels will be some of the most important hand tools you possess. About 80% of your work with chisels will be done with chisels ranging between ¼ in. (6 mm) and ¾ in. (19 mm). There are undoubtedly occasions when you will need wider bench chisels and occasions when you will need paring chisels, but they are few and far between. So if you are buying chisels for the very first time get yourself a beautiful set of small chisels and get the feel of using them and sharpening them before moving on to larger, more expensive tools. It is not necessary to have a complete set of chisels; indeed, many craftsmen rely on a fairly complete collection of small chisels less than ½ in. (12 mm) wide. Unless they are regularly working on large projects they will have maybe only three other larger chisels of differing widths up to about 1¼ in. (30 mm).

Tool selection

Choose a range of chisels that fits and becomes an extension of your hands. The handles should balance the weight of the blade, i.e., small handles for small sizes and larger handles on wider chisels. This, together with the way the blade is shaped, is more important than the hardness of the steel that forms the cutting edge. Although there are immense benefits to be gained from purchasing Japanese chisels in the larger sizes, many craftsmen prefer European chisels in the smaller, more delicate sizes. European tools are lighter, easier, and quicker to sharpen than Japanese tools. The latter have laminated cutting edges, which means harder steel at the cutting edge and, therefore, used properly, they hold their edges several times longer than European tools. The larger Japanese chisels benefit from the Japanese practice of hollow grinding chisels—this allows the user to get the back of the chisel perfectly flat and mirror polished.

Heavier, square-sided, firmer chisels and mortise chisels are also available but are not really widely used by the modern woodworker. Bevel-edged paring chisels of ⅝ in. (15 mm) and 1¼ in. (30 mm) widths are useful for fine, delicate work and should never be struck with a mallet or hammer. There are two or three other chisels that you may need to find a budget for. The first would be a matched pair of left- and right-handed skew ground chisels. These are essential tools for clearing out the corners of lapped dovetails—most commonly found on the front of drawers. You can clear those few corner fibers away with a bench knife, but a skew ground chisel is a much better tool. It is possible to buy both left-

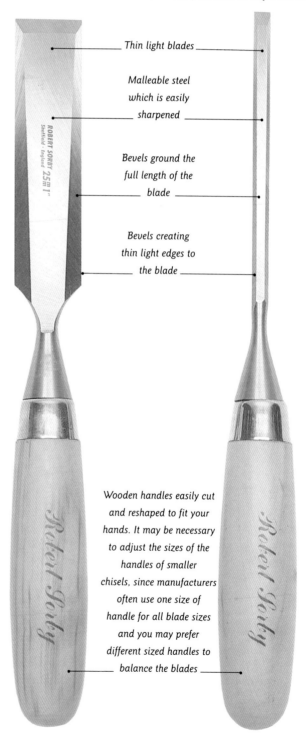

Thin light blades

Malleable steel which is easily sharpened

Bevels ground the full length of the blade

Bevels creating thin light edges to the blade

RIGHT *Two bevel-edged chisels of superior manufacture. Note the way the blade joins the handle*

Wooden handles easily cut and reshaped to fit your hands. It may be necessary to adjust the sizes of the handles of smaller chisels, since manufacturers often use one size of handle for all blade sizes and you may prefer different sized handles to balance the blades

and right-handed skew ground chisels from a good tool supplier, but you could take the opportunity of finding a useful purpose for one or two of your spare chisels (or buy some from a second-hand shop) and grinding them for yourself.

Lastly, a cranked paring chisel is very useful for cleaning out the inside of assembled carcasses. It is almost impossible to slice off those tiny knobs of half-dried glue that squeeze out of a joint without the assistance of a cranked paring chisel.

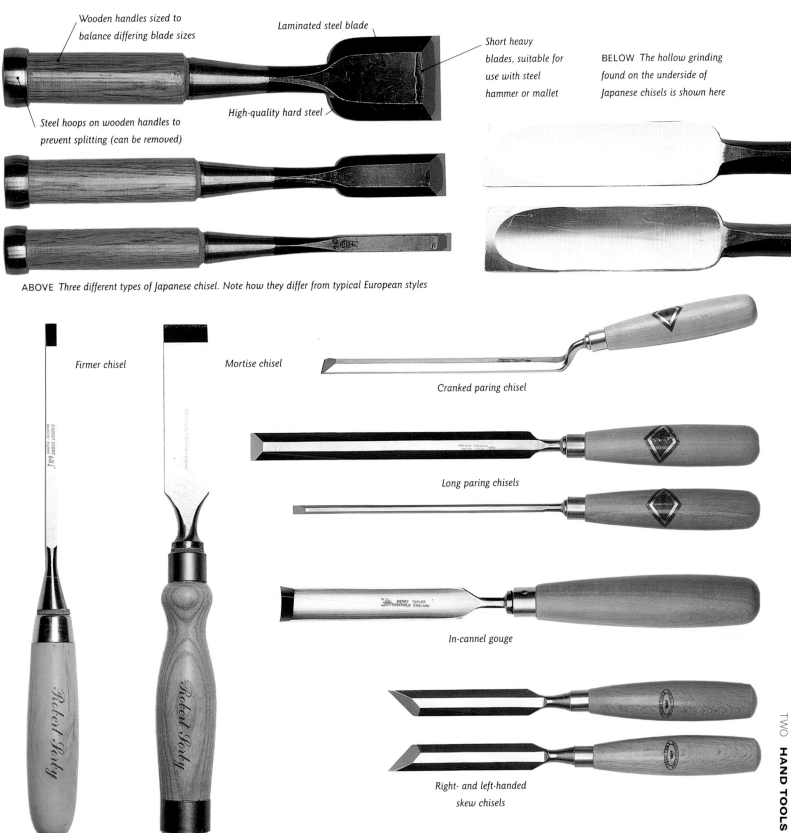

Wooden handles sized to balance differing blade sizes

Laminated steel blade

Short heavy blades, suitable for use with steel hammer or mallet

BELOW *The hollow grinding found on the underside of Japanese chisels is shown here*

Steel hoops on wooden handles to prevent splitting (can be removed)

High-quality hard steel

ABOVE *Three different types of Japanese chisel. Note how they differ from typical European styles*

Firmer chisel

Mortise chisel

Cranked paring chisel

Long paring chisels

In-cannel gouge

Right- and left-handed skew chisels

PLANES

One of the most essential operations in furniture-making is ensuring the surface is flat, straight, and true. This is carried out by planing, which is in itself a skill in woodworking that is a pleasure to develop and very satisfying when competence has been achieved.

Bench planes

Bench planes are used by most woodworkers to prepare surfaces prior to final finishing and to trim and fit joints. There is enormous satisfaction to be gained from using a well-adjusted plane to accurately take off those one or two shavings that turn a tight uncomfortable joint into a perfect fit. In some cases a hand-planed surface is itself alive and tactile and needs no further finishing except for a little burnishing with wax polish. Bench planes are generally available in three or four lengths: the short smoothing plane or "smoother," the intermediate jack and fore planes, and the long jointer, or try, plane. Planes developed this way in order to perform different functions. Before machines took over the laborious task of planing rough boards into flat dimensioned lumber, a craftsman would have needed a full set of planes: a jack plane for initial preparation, a fore plane for final truing up, a jointer plane for straight-edged joints, and finally a smoothing plane to true off assembled carcasses. Most woodworkers today manage with one jack plane of medium length and a smoothing plane. Wooden planes are very popular, being easier to tune and set up, and lighter and nicer to use than their metal counterparts.

Specialized planes

Specialized planes such as block planes and shoulder planes are a distinct category of tools different from the bench planes but nonetheless very useful small planes. Block planes can be used both with and across the grain. They have a low cutting angle and an adjustable throat, making them very versatile tools. Unlike the larger bench planes described above, block planes and some other specialized planes have their blades set at a low cutting angle in

the body of the plane, probably between 10° and 20°. This low cutting angle is combined with setting the blade in the body of the plane with the bevel up (unlike bench planes which have a cutting angle of 45° and the blade bevel facing down). This bevel-up configuration gives a similar overall cutting angle to the bench planes of 45° because the 15° that the iron is set in the body of the

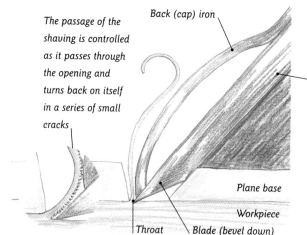

Note the position of the cap iron close to the cutting edge

The passage of the shaving is controlled as it passes through the opening and turns back on itself in a series of small cracks

Back (cap) iron

Front face of frog. Adjusting the frog forward or backward allows control of the position of the cutting edge in relation to the throat, i.e., a wide setting for coarse work and a narrow setting for fine work and interlocking grain

Plane base

Workpiece

Throat   *Blade (bevel down)*

Cross-section of a hand plane in use

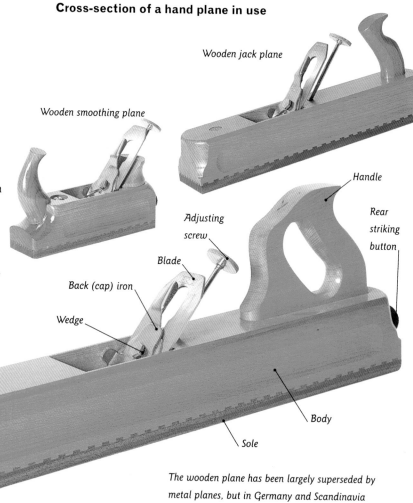

Wooden jack plane

Wooden smoothing plane

Handle

Rear striking button

Adjusting screw

Blade

Back (cap) iron

Wedge

Front striking button

Body

Sole

Wooden jointer plane

The wooden plane has been largely superseded by metal planes, but in Germany and Scandinavia wooden planes are still made and used

plane is added to the blade sharpening angle of 30°. The benefit of this is that it enables you to modify planes designed in this way (with the bevel of the cutting iron facing upward) to change their overall cutting angle by simply grinding and honing the cutter to a different angle. This is especially useful when planing wood with wild grain configurations.

Shoulder or rabbet planes are designed similarly but in addition have a blade the full width of the body, enabling them to cut right into the corner of a joint such as a rabbet or the shoulder of a tenon. Many woodworkers find that owning a large and a small shoulder plane will enable them to do most kinds of work.

The side rabbet plane is one that you would only need perhaps once every two years, to enlarge just fractionally a groove to accept the edge of a panel, for example; but on that one occasion it will be impossible to do the job with anything else.

Plane blades

Plane blades come in two distinct forms. Block and shoulder planes come with the blade set at a low cutting angle but with the bevel of the blade facing upward. Conventional bench planes come with a high 45° cutting angle but with the bevel of the blade facing downward and a cap iron fitted to the rear of the blade. The cap iron is there to help control the path of the shaving through the throat of the plane and prevent tears and splits in that shaving. It is very important that the cap iron is carefully fitted to the blade to enable it to function properly.

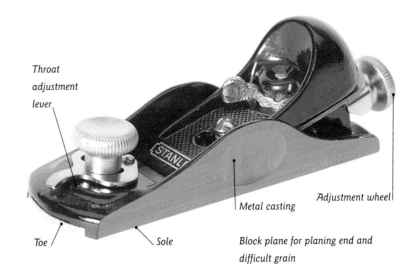

Throat adjustment lever

Metal casting

Adjustment wheel

Toe

Sole

Block plane for planing end and difficult grain

Wooden block plane

Small shoulder plane

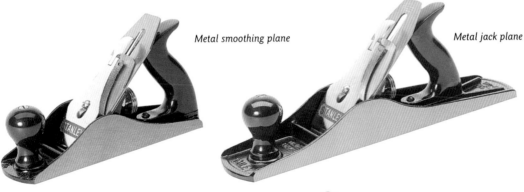

Metal smoothing plane

Metal jack plane

Metal planes such as these are in general use in many countries

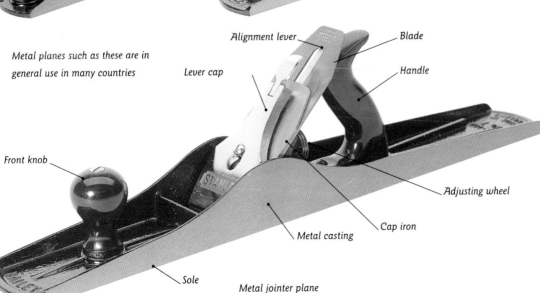

Alignment lever

Blade

Lever cap

Handle

Front knob

Adjusting wheel

Cap iron

Metal casting

Sole

Metal jointer plane

ABOVE AND BELOW *Two different standard shoulder planes*

Side rabbet plane

TUNING EDGE TOOLS

Tuning is the process of preparing a tool prior to sharpening. Usually tuning is only done once in the lifetime of the tool and it is a process of upgrading the tool to a level of precision and function that the manufacturer cannot economically provide. In the case of chisels, this is done by working on the back of the blade to provide a flat, true surface that has been worked up to a high mirror polish. This work, though laborious, is only ever done once and, when completed, the back of your chisel should only ever touch your finest polishing stone.

Preparing chisels for sharpening

First your blade must be checked for flatness. This is important because a truly flat blade is easier to sharpen. This process is achieved by using a piece of plate glass with ground edges and carborundum powder, lubricated with either water or oil. Rub the back of the chisel on the glass with this abrasive to check for an even gray color right out to the edges and corners of the chisel. Be careful to incorporate all of the carborundum as you work, since this abrasive breaks down with use to give a finer and finer finish, and any coarser grains left will scratch the surface of the blade you are trying to set true. Once a true surface has been created—this takes about 15 minutes with a ½ in. (12 mm) chisel—you can check your work by polishing the back of the chisel first on a 1000 grit Japanese water stone, lubricated with water, and finally on a 6000 grit polishing stone. If an even polish does not come up very quickly, go back to the glass plate. There is no point in attempting to use a water stone to flatten your edge tools—these are polishing and sharpening stones and will not alone produce a flat surface. Be very careful not to get carborundum paste on the Japanese water stones. Your objective should be a finely polished surface right across the cutting edge and right out to the corners of the chisel—bear in mind that it is

the corners of the chisel that do the most effective work.

You should note that the Japanese chisel has a hollow ground back that makes the preparation of these wide and extremely hard chisels much easier. Without this hollow grind the preparation of these chisels would take a very long time indeed.

Tuning planes

Steel planes must also be prepared before they will work effectively. The sole of a plane is almost never flat and true when new. Use a roll of 60 grit abrasive on a flat machine table to lap the sole of your plane true and flat. This can be checked by using a straight edge and looking against a strong light source. This process may have to be repeated once or twice in the first year while the casting continues to move; after some time it eventually settles down.

Having flattened the sole, adjust the frog of the plane. This is the steel block upon which the blade assembly sits. Check the fit of the frog to the plane body and, if necessary, file the frog to fit tightly. Next check that the blade assembly is similarly fitting closely to the frog. Finally, slide the frog and blade assembly backward and forward until the gap in front of the cutting edge is approximately ¹⁄₁₆ in. (2 mm) wide, then locate the frog and tighten the adjustment screws. This will help the plane cut more effectively, preventing tears with "difficult" species of dry hardwood.

For a bench plane to function properly the blade must be slightly curved across its width. This helps the blade to cut a

Tuning a plane

1 Securely tape a length of 60 grit abrasive paper to a protected flat surface ready for tuning your plane.

2 Rub the sole of the plane along the abrasive paper.

3 To ensure that the sole is perfectly flat, check it against a straight edge.

4 Holding the plane up to the light will also show if the polished surface is precisely flat.

5 It is essential to ensure that the cap iron is adjusted to fit closely behind the cutting edge so that no shavings pass underneath the cap iron.

A Japanese water stone, used to polish the backs of chisels and plane blades

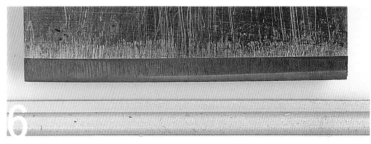

shaving with a width of only approximately 1–1⅜ in. (25–35 mm) in the center of the blade. The cap iron that fits on the back of the blade should be filed and adjusted to fit cleanly upon its mate. There should be no gap between these two pieces of steel; otherwise shavings will get jammed between them. The front surface of the cap iron should also be polished to present a smooth surface to any shaving.

6 When properly ground, the plane blade is slightly curved across its width.

Preparing a chisel

7 Rubbing the back of a chisel on a polishing stone to develop an even polish.

SHARPENING EDGE TOOLS

Sharpness is essential in order to achieve control over the cutting edge. It is a means of reducing the force or power required to push that edge through the wood. The more power you require to shove your plane across or push your chisel through the wood, the less control you have. If your edge is sharp it will slice through with the minimum of effort—if it is blunt, you are going to have to shove and push and force and struggle your way through the wood. So keep your chisel sharp and be sensitive as to how the edge is performing. If you sense any slight increasing resistance, hone the cutting edge. Never let a chisel become blunt; always touch it up before it reaches that stage.

Grinding

Sharpening, or honing, is achieved first by using a water-cooled grinder to create a bevel of 25°. Water-cooled grinders are easier to use and the coolant prevents the cutting edge from becoming overheated and burnt in the grinding process. Burning the cutting edge "draws the temper" or changes the hardness of the cutting edge, and in this way a good and expensive tool can be ruined in less than a moment. It is important to be able to regrind your tools easily, so it is worth spending a good portion of your budget on a good water-cooled grinder. It is possible to buy relatively inexpensive edge tools and chisels; sharpen them frequently and always hone them before they lose their edge and they will function for you as well as the most expensive hand-made laminated edge.

Honing chisels

Once the chisel is ground, you can turn to the honing stones. These are synthetic stones made in Japan and lubricated with water. There are other systems available, but Japanese water stones are cheaper, quicker to use, and produce a superlative edge. You will need two stones—one of 1000 grit and the other is a polishing stone of 6000 grit. To hone an edge, rest the chisel on the honing stone with the bevel side down. Press down on the back of the chisel so the cutting edge is in contact with the stone and the chisel is also supported on the flat surface of the stone by the

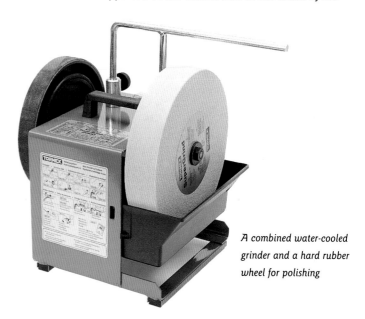

A combined water-cooled grinder and a hard rubber wheel for polishing

A small combination grinding machine, with a carborundum wheel one side and an abrasive belt finisher on the other

Japanese water stones in a unit that lubricates and stores the stones

other end of the hollow ground surface created on the grinder. Having settled the chisel on the surface of the stone, carefully pull your chisel back toward you. Use a honing guide for this if you wish, but the technique is not difficult to master. Your objective is to hone the front ¾₄ in. (1 mm) of the cutting edge.

After two or three strokes on the honing stone you will feel a small burr created along the cutting edge. Now move to the polishing stone and by working on alternate sides of the chisel, polish the edge until that burr falls away. Watch for the burr to fall away completely; do not strop it or remove it with your finger. Polish it away and you will then have a perfect sharp cutting edge.

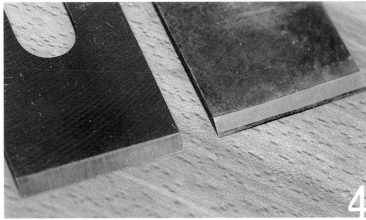

3 Honing a plane blade on the stone.

4 Plane blades before honing (left) and after honing (right).

Chisel blades
5 This shows the burr that has developed on a chisel that is being honed.

6 Here the burr has been polished away to produce a cutting edge which is very sharp.

Honing plane blades
1 It is possible to use a honing guide when honing a chisel or a plane blade.

2 The honing guide holds the blade at the correct angle in relation to the stone. However, with practice you will find that you can master this process without needing the guide.

Using a grinder
7 Grinding a high-speed steel turning gouge on the grinding wheel. Note that it is not recommended to grind carbon steel cutting tools on a bench grinder.

Sharpening edge tools 27

BENCH SAWS

Crosscut and ripsaws have their teeth sharpened in two different ways. The leading edge of a crosscut tooth slopes away from the vertical, while a rip-tooth leading edge is vertical. In addition, a crosscut tooth is filed at an angle to its face and a rip tooth is at 90° to its face. The teeth of the crosscut saw act like knives severing the wooden fibers, whereas the teeth of a ripsaw act like tiny chisels paring material away in their progress down the grain of the wood. A crosscut saw is essential for work on damp softwoods, but the rip-tooth is more useful with dry hardwoods, and many cabinetmakers reset their fine-tooth panel saws with a rip-tooth configuration. Man-made boards such as particle board and chipboard will dull a handsaw very quickly, so for these use an inexpensive hardpoint saw that cannot be resharpened. A high-quality bench saw will have a taper ground blade that is thicker near the teeth and thinner near the top. This gives relief to the cut and helps to guide the saw. A small panel saw with 10 TPI (teeth per inch) would be a useful bench saw if you were not using many machines.

Backsaws

Another commonly used saw is the backsaw. This has a stiff brass back and comes in two sizes: the tenon saw and the dovetail saw. In common with most new tools supplied today, backsaws invariably need some tuning in order to perform properly. In this case, the layer of varnish that is usually applied to the blade must be removed and some of the set applied to the saw teeth must also be removed, using either a small slip stone or a tiny hammer, tapping very gently against a small anvil. The set is applied to the teeth to make the saw cut a groove or "kerf" that is wider than the plate of the saw. This is a good reason to make sure that your saw has some set, but quite often this kerf is wider than necessary. By reducing the kerf of the new saw you are reducing the energy and work required to use the saw and thereby increasing your control over that saw. Most craftspeople have two or three backsaws: a tenon saw for general work and larger joints, a small 8 in. (200 mm) dovetail saw with very little set on it for small joinery, and a 10 in. (250 mm) dovetail saw or a smaller tenon saw for larger carcasses.

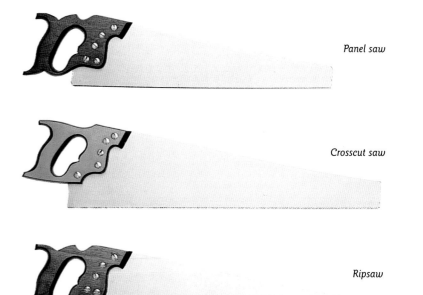

Panel saw

Crosscut saw

Ripsaw

ABOVE *A set of three bench saws, the longest sharpened as a ripsaw to cut along the grain; the medium one as a crosscut saw for cutting across the grain, and the smaller a general-purpose panel saw*

Crosscut saw teeth

Ripsaw teeth

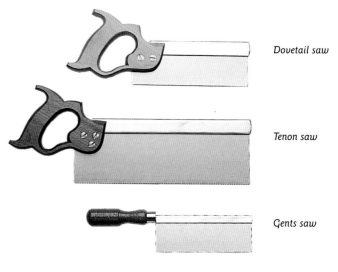

Dovetail saw

Tenon saw

Gents saw

ABOVE *A set of three backsaws: a dovetail saw, a tenon saw, and a very fine gents saw*

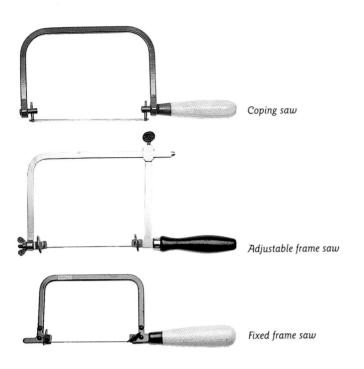

Coping saw

Adjustable frame saw

Fixed frame saw

ABOVE *A set of fine saws for sawing curves. The coping saw is the most common and is used for cutting dovetails; the others are used for fine piercing work*

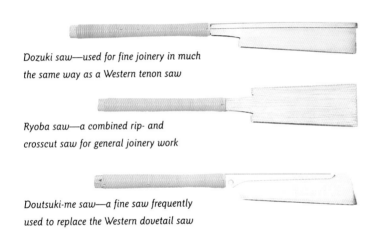

Dozuki saw—used for fine joinery in much the same way as a Western tenon saw

Ryoba saw—a combined rip- and crosscut saw for general joinery work

Doutsuki-me saw—a fine saw frequently used to replace the Western dovetail saw

ABOVE *Japanese saws have become popular additions to the woodworker's tool kit. They have very fine blades and generally cut on the pulling action*

Modern frame miter saw

Other types of saw

Japanese saws are very popular as they are beautifully sharpened from new and cut a very thin and fine kerf. Their most unusual feature is that, unlike most Western saws, they cut on the pull stroke rather than on the push stroke.

Piercing saws and coping saws are popular for some small curved work, and the gents saw, named after the Victorian gentleman woodworker, can be used for small delicate work. It is, however, no substitute for a well set-up dovetail saw. Finally, the miter saw is a modern frame saw set in a jig to cut at predetermined angles. This is popular for picture-framing and for cutting small components true and square.

Sharpening saws

It is possible to sharpen all your saws in-house, though it is not to be recommended. "Saw doctors" have the equipment and expertise to sharpen bench saws much more accurately than even a skilled hand can do. What you can do, however, is sharpen the very small saws. Dovetail saws are best sharpened using a 4 in. (100 mm) Swiss precision saw file at right angles to the blade. The technique is to settle the file into the gullet of each tooth and to give one stroke to each tooth. Sharpen saws like this little and often, rather than waiting for them to get dull and useless.

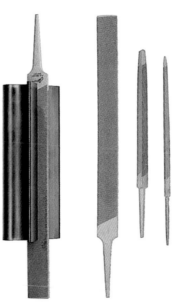

A set of files for sharpening saws and a jig designed to hold a file at 90° for sharpening

Sawtooth setter

ASSEMBLY TOOLS:
HAND CLAMPS, BAR CLAMPS

It is one of the secrets of woodworking that when two or more pieces of wood are glued together in a good tight joint, it is necessary to apply only a little bit of pressure and hold the job there while the glue sets. This is done by applying either hand clamps for smaller jobs or bar clamps for large components such as doors and windows.

The different types available

All-metal C-clamps are available in several sizes and depths and can be used to apply enormous amounts of pressure. Invariably you do not need so much pressure. A well-made joint simply needs a little bit of glue and a little bit of squeeze. What you do need is consistent pressure all along the joint, which may mean that you need 10 or 12 clamps for one small assembly job.

One of the benefits of the wooden cam clamps is that although they are not suitable for applying high pressure, they are easy to use and very light in weight. This type of clamp is also relatively inexpensive.

The main type of workshop clamp is, however, the short bar clamp, an all-metal clamp sometimes referred to as an "F-clamp." Although these clamps are the best available for fast assembly work in a busy workshop, they can be expensive.

Single-handed clamps are useful in situations in which it is necessary to get the pressure on while holding the work in one hand and tightening the clamp with the other. Apart from this undoubted advantage, this type of clamp is not really robust enough to withstand heavy use.

Long bar clamps or pipe clamps are the most widely used method of jointing boards together to form panels. Sometimes

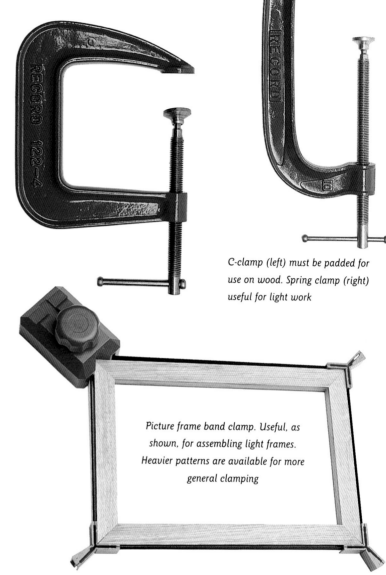

C-clamp (left) must be padded for use on wood. Spring clamp (right) useful for light work

Picture frame band clamp. Useful, as shown, for assembling light frames. Heavier patterns are available for more general clamping

FURTHER INFORMATION

Board clamp. Ideal for clamping of large boards, but for general work bar clamps are more versatile and useful (see Availability p.232)

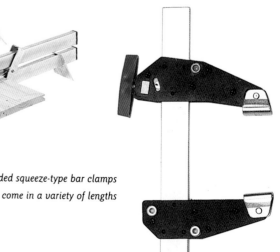

Single-handed squeeze-type bar clamps come in a variety of lengths

Wooden clamps. These have either a movable cam head or hand screws (right). They are useful where light holding is needed (see Availability p.232)

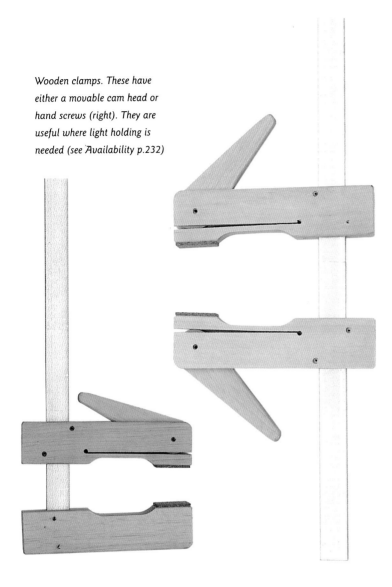

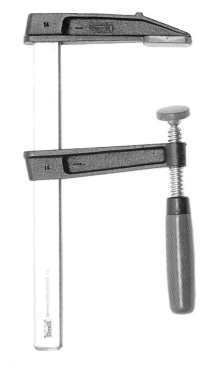

F-clamp. Useful clamps, but buy good-quality ones since they can easily be over-tightened and spoiled if sub-standard or abused

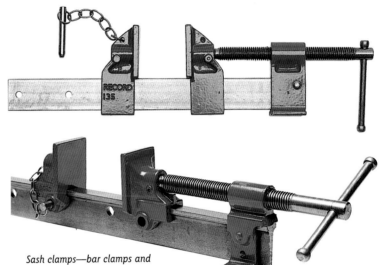

Sash clamps—bar clamps and pipe clamps. The traditional clamp for cabinet assembly work and still one of the best. Buy bar clamps in various lengths, or use pipe clamp fixtures and supply your own pipe

called sash clamps because of their original use in the clamping of windows and door frames, these would typically be used with two, maybe three clamps underneath the panel and two or three clamps above, placed at distances of 4–6 in. (102–152 mm) apart. Always keep the bars or pipes well waxed and free of any glue that might squeeze out, and protect the job from the jaws of the clamp by using plastic jaw pads or wooden spacers. Again, when clamping any work, remember the maxim: a well-made joint requires only a small amount of pressure and a small amount of glue. If you have to apply excess pressure to bring the joint together then something is wrong.

You can never really have enough clamps. Start off with perhaps six hand clamps and four sash clamps and buy more as the need arises. Amateur woodworkers may find the new single-handed clamps very useful. There are some very cheap cramps available that may do the job if your budget is limited, but assembly tools are important tools, so get the best you can afford.

Japanese miniature bar clamps. These are made of solid brass and are useful for a variety of jobs (see Availability p.232)

Assembly tools: Hand clamps, bar clamps

ASSEMBLY TOOLS: HAMMERS AND SCREWDRIVERS

Screwdrivers and hammers are also types of assembly tools. There are many aspects of cabinetmaking in which clamps should not be used; for example, assembling a drawer. This would be accomplished using either a small nylon hammer or even a small steel-faced hammer. The size of the hammer would be chosen to fit the size of the job.

Hammers

One of the most useful tools for assembling large dovetail carcasses is a 4 lb. (2 kg) club hammer, frequently used for demolition. This tool is used to drive the joint together and expel the last bit of partially dried glue left in the corner of the joint. Remember, however, that a good joint never has to be "bashed" together.

Nylon-faced or rubber-faced hammers are frequently used in preassembly work because they do not mark the surface of the job. These soft-faced hammers are, however, often replaced in the final glue-up with a steel-faced hammer because the ringing sound of a steel hammer will change as the joint is knocked home, thus giving a skilled craftsman greater control.

Screwdrivers

It is important to use screwdrivers that exactly fit the slot in your screw heads. This can be achieved by taking a full set of screwdrivers and, if necessary, grinding the ends of the blades to suit the heads of your screws. Screws have the benefit of actually pulling components together without the need for clamps. So where it is difficult to apply a clamp to a curved component or where you do not have a clamp of the right size, consider fitting screws and covering the heads of the screws with wooden plugs.

Phillips-head drywall screws have finely cut threads that have superior holding power in end grain lumber. Where it is necessary to hold components together using screws, drywall screws are effective, readily available, and inexpensive. They do break, however, so never over-tighten drywall screws. Phillips screwdrivers should be chosen carefully to fit the type and brand of screw used.

FURTHER INFORMATION

Compact ratchet screwdriver with six interchangeable bits

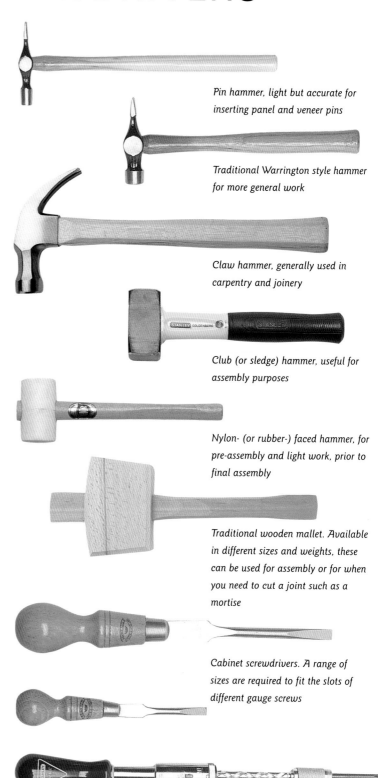

Pin hammer, light but accurate for inserting panel and veneer pins

Traditional Warrington style hammer for more general work

Claw hammer, generally used in carpentry and joinery

Club (or sledge) hammer, useful for assembly purposes

Nylon- (or rubber-) faced hammer, for pre-assembly and light work, prior to final assembly

Traditional wooden mallet. Available in different sizes and weights, these can be used for assembly or for when you need to cut a joint such as a mortise

Cabinet screwdrivers. A range of sizes are required to fit the slots of different gauge screws

Spiral or pump-action screwdriver with interchangeable screwdriver bits which allow it to be used with any type of screw

In a home workshop there are two distinct categories of power tools: hand-held or portable power tools such as finishing sanders, drills, and routers, and fixed power tools or machines. There are also some tools that fall into both categories; for example, the portable circular saw that can, if turned upside down and fitted beneath a machine table, be turned into a stationary machine.

Always remember that when you use a power tool or machine in your home workshop, you are not protected by the benefit of any health and safety legislation. It is your responsibility alone to ensure your safety, and you would be well advised to either seek advice on the subject from a competent professional woodworker or attend a short course on the subject.

BANDSAWS

Of all the small woodworking machines on the market, the bandsaw is perhaps one of the most versatile, as well as one of the most misused. Provided that the blade is changed regularly—the smaller the bandsaw, the more frequently this needs to be done—and the blade is kept properly tensioned and adjusted within its guides, then a small bandsaw is capable of accurate ripsawing, crosscutting, and, unlike the table saw, doing curved work and deep ripsawing or resawing. If you let the blade become dull and fail to keep it properly adjusted, you will fight to make the bandsaw maintain a cut somewhere near the line that you intended to cut.

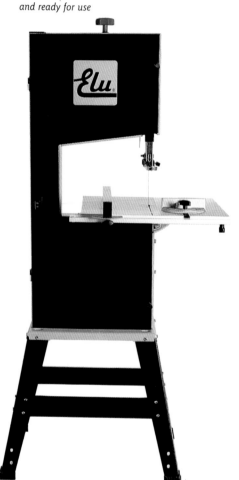

The machine with doors closed and ready for use

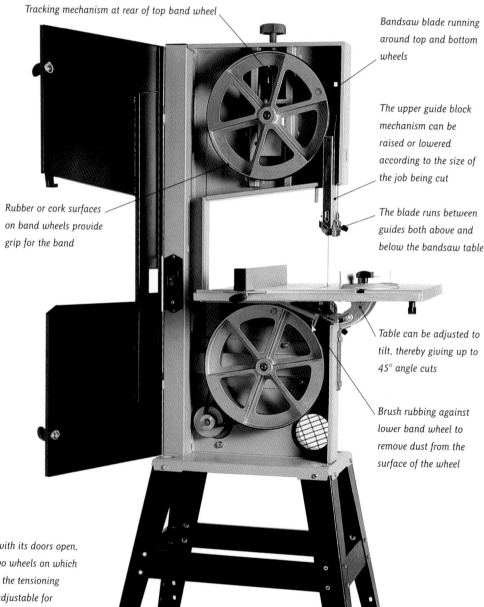

Tracking mechanism at rear of top band wheel

Bandsaw blade running around top and bottom wheels

The upper guide block mechanism can be raised or lowered according to the size of the job being cut

The blade runs between guides both above and below the bandsaw table

Rubber or cork surfaces on band wheels provide grip for the band

Table can be adjusted to tilt, thereby giving up to 45° angle cuts

Brush rubbing against lower band wheel to remove dust from the surface of the wheel

The bandsaw with its doors open, showing the two wheels on which the blade runs, the tensioning device that is adjustable for different sized blades, the table with a straight fence, and the sliding protractor head. The drive pulley from the motor can be seen bottom left

FURTHER INFORMATION

Critical dimensions on a bandsaw include the height under the guides once they are raised—this is the theoretical limit of the thickness of the piece of wood the saw can cut. Most small bandsaws should really be restricted to cutting lumber of no thicker than about 4–6 in. (102–152 mm). It is, however, possible to resaw boards of up to 10 in. (254 mm), but this requires a more powerful bandsaw than is normally used in the home workshop. The second major critical dimension on the bandsaw is the throat. This is the distance from the blade to the pillar of the bandsaw. A throat of about 15 in. (381 mm) is usually perfectly adequate for most work in a small workshop.

The band

The essence of the bandsaw is the band itself—the blade. Blades are generally available in two types: normal and skip tooth. The skip tooth pattern makes a rougher but faster cut. Blades are usually available in two types of steel: standard or bimetal. Bimetal means that the front section of the blade has been hardened by heat treatment to produce teeth with harder cutting edges and longer life. The rear section of the blade is not treated and consequently is still left in a softer, flexible condition, hence the name bimetal. These blades are preferable to the standard blades and can be resharpened by a competent saw doctor perhaps two or three times before being discarded. This is because it is not possible to reset the teeth of the blade, and, as the blade is resharpened, the set is reduced and the kerf (width) of the cut is reduced.

The blade is placed on the band wheels and tensioned, and should run in approximately the center of the width of the band wheel, which can be adjusted by turning the tracking knob at the rear of the upper band wheel. Once the blade is tracking correctly the blade guides should be set around the blade, both above and below the bandsaw table. The blade guides are adjusted so that they give support to the blade but are no closer to the blade than the thickness of a piece of paper, and not actually touching or rubbing against the stationary blade.

Various widths of bandsaw blade are available, depending upon the size of your machine. The narrower blades can be used for cutting tighter and tighter curved work. Blades as narrow as ¼ in. (6 mm) wide can be used on some small bandsaws.

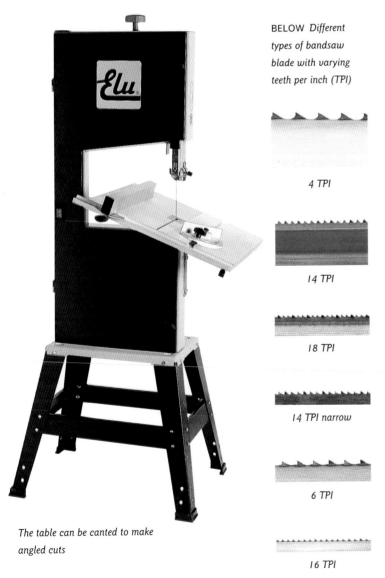

The table can be canted to make angled cuts

BELOW *Different types of bandsaw blade with varying teeth per inch (TPI)*

4 TPI

14 TPI

18 TPI

14 TPI narrow

6 TPI

16 TPI

ABOVE *A detail of the guide mechanism for the saw blade. The two guide pads are positioned on either side of the blade to keep it running in line; the thrust wheel behind the blade rotates so as to take up the pressure when sawing*

TABLE SAWS

One of the most useful machine tools for the furniture-maker's workshop, the table saw enables cuts to be made with precision, either ripping along the grain or cross-cutting (dimensioning) to length. There are a variety of different models on the market, with a range of sizes and useful features.

Circular saws

Table saws are favorite machines in cabinetmaking and joinery workshops, having the flexibility of ripping components to widths as well as crosscutting or dimensioning components to length. Modern carbide tipped circular saw blades have the capacity to produce a cut that is almost as smooth as that produced by a plane. For this reason they are frequently favored over high-speed steel blades, which produce a slightly coarser cut. A 10 in. (250 mm) table saw is capable of a depth of cut that enables it to do most of the work required in a small workshop. Saws can also be used for cutting dados and tapered components. One of the most endearing qualities of the table saw for the beginner, however, is the accuracy with which a line can be sawn straight and square.

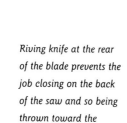

A typical saw blade

Riving knife at the rear of the blade prevents the job closing on the back of the saw and so being thrown toward the operator

Removable table insert around the blade can be replaced with wooden inserts and the saw raised through it to give greater support to the job

Miter gauge

The blade is fitted on a rise-and-fall arbor, which enables the height of the blade above the table to be altered. The arbor also allows the blade to tilt up to 45° in relation to the table

Heavy cast-metal table absorbs vibration and is resistant to rust

A table saw mounted on a dust extraction stand showing the fixed table on the right with an adjustable ripping fence, the saw with a guard and extractor pipe, and the moving table on the left, which enables crosscutting (on some models this facility is not available and the protractor has a slide in a groove). The controls on the front enable the blade to be raised or lowered and to be canted from 90° to 45°

(see Availability p.232)

The saw can be canted to make angled cuts

The saw can be turned through 90° so that it is in line with the fence and can be used for ripping

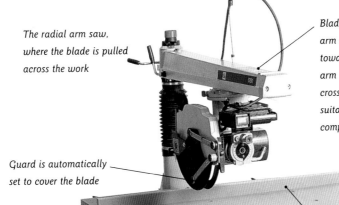

The radial arm saw, where the blade is pulled across the work

Blade is pulled along radial arm across the job and toward the operator. Radial arm is very good for crosscutting but not very suitable for ripping components with the grain

Guard is automatically set to cover the blade

The saw arm can be angled to cut angles other than 90° to the fence

Rear fence and table give support to the job for an accurate clean cut as head of saw tilts for 45° and compound and miter cuts

ABOVE The miter or cut-off saw, dedicated to crosscutting square or at an angle

LEFT The contractor's saw, a lighter and less expensive table saw, more suitable for taking to a job site (see Availability p.232)

Other bench saws

A radial arm saw is a much more specialized piece of equipment, and particularly good at crosscutting. Although there are other tasks that the radial arm saw can do, such as cutting moldings and miter joints and, in some cases, providing the platform for the addition of a router, by and large the radial arm saw is only used as a crosscut saw. Given that a saw of this type often needs a large supporting table to the left and right of the saw, the space it occupies in a small workshop frequently cannot be justified. One variation of the radial arm saw is the miter, or cut-off, saw. This is a circular saw hinged to a table and fence which is dedicated to crosscutting or miter cutting relatively small components. Although a stationary machine, it is usually light enough to be carried to a location and used on-site.

A more common kind of site saw is the light, portable table saw or "contractor's saw." This can be anything from a full-size table saw on legs to an "upside-down-skill-saw-in-a-box."

The final type of sawing machine common in small workshops is a scroll saw. This is a motorized frame saw usually with a very thin blade, and is useful for sawing thin, tightly curved components. Modern versions of this machine are so accurate now that the cuts produced, while often slightly blackened, are smooth and clean and frequently need no other finishing work prior to assembly.

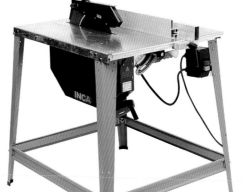

RIGHT The scroll or fret saw, which gives very fine cuts with fairly tight turns; in shapes such as those found in jigsaw puzzles

JOINTERS AND PLANERS

A jointer is used for preparing the initial reference surface on lumber because, in the process of drying, wood tends to cup and twist after it has been sawn into planks. To deal with this, these machines need to have a relatively long table both in front and at the back of the cutter head in order to take out that twist or cup and leave a dead flat surface. Such machines need to produce not only a smooth planed surface but also a flat one. Jointers have a relatively narrow cutter head, and accommodate boards of 8–12 in. (203–305 mm) in width. Since it is poor practice to joint lumber much wider than 10 in. (254 mm)—because of possible warping—it would be false economy to buy a jointer with a cutter head much wider than this. There are narrower machines available that can be used for small components or for edge jointing wider boards.

The planer

The planer has a cutter head above an adjustable machine bed and is used to plane a parallel surface to your first or face side. The bed is set at a predetermined distance from the underside of the cutter block. Planers function by having two or three cutter knives set in a head that revolves at high speed. The depth of cut of these knives is affected by the setting of the table, or bed, of the machine.

Both jointers and planers, but most particularly the planer, should be used in conjunction with a dust extractor, since they produce large quantities of shavings and wood dust. If not

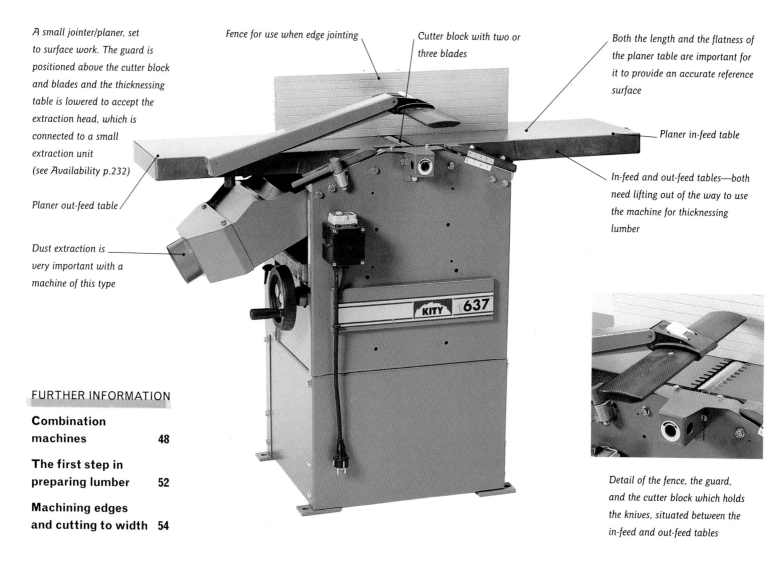

A small jointer/planer, set to surface work. The guard is positioned above the cutter block and blades and the thicknessing table is lowered to accept the extraction head, which is connected to a small extraction unit (see Availability p.232)

Planer out-feed table

Dust extraction is very important with a machine of this type

Fence for use when edge jointing

Cutter block with two or three blades

Both the length and the flatness of the planer table are important for it to provide an accurate reference surface

Planer in-feed table

In-feed and out-feed tables—both need lifting out of the way to use the machine for thicknessing lumber

KITY 637

Detail of the fence, the guard, and the cutter block which holds the knives, situated between the in-feed and out-feed tables

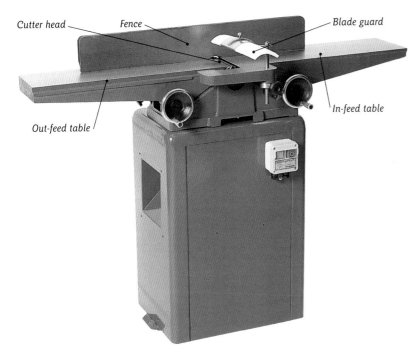

Cutter head Fence Blade guard

Out-feed table In-feed table

collected, the shavings are a fire risk and the dust is a health hazard. A further type of planer is a hand-held electric planer. This is largely used as a site tool by joiners and carpenters (often for trimming doors) and has very little use in the workshop.

Leaving lumber preparation to the experts

While every woodworker has to go through the process of preparing lumber for each and every job, you may decide that this initial preparation, which after all is only a small part of the overall process of completing your project, could best be done by sub-contracting it to a local cabinet shop or lumber yard. In this way you have no need to install expensive machines that take up a considerable amount of space in your workshop and are used for only a very small proportion of the time. Should you adopt this approach, you may find it useful to have a small jointer like the one shown here for use after your lumber has been prepared and when you are working with much smaller components.

ABOVE *The jointer is a simple machine made primarily for surfacing narrow components and trueing the edges of boards. The two hand wheels on the front adjust the in-feed and out-feed tables*

RIGHT *Planers cut from the top of the board, feed automatically, and are used to reduce the thickness of a board as well as plane its surface smooth*

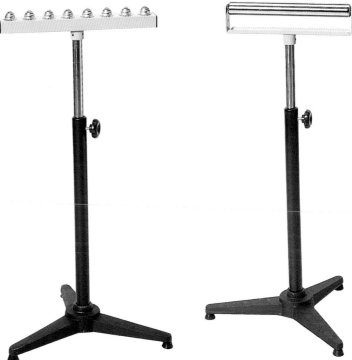

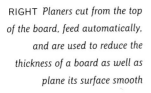

Hand-held electric planer

ABOVE *When working on one's own with long stock, it is often helpful to have the work supported when it comes off the saw or planer. These stands give such support, using either a series of ball bearings or rollers*

ROUTERS

A "plunge" router consists of a powerful motor, sometimes fitted with a variable speed setting, which is mounted on top of two columns attached to a router base plate. The motor moves up and down on these columns against two springs. At the base of the motor is a collet which accepts interchangeable cutters called router bits. The machine functions by spinning the cutter at a very high speed, as high as 27000 rpm. The cutter can be either lowered into the job by pressing down on the motor against the springs in the two columns, or set at a predetermined position and then entered into the job sideways. Alternatively, the router can be set upside down in a small table with the cutter protruding above the table and the job fed across the table.

In many smaller routers, the motor slides into a cylindrical housing, rather than on posts. These routers provide depth-of-cut adjustment, but lack plunge capability. The fact that a router can accept so many differently shaped router bits gives this power tool exceptional versatility. It would probably be true to say that the invention of the router has revolutionized woodworking, making it possible for even a relatively unskilled person to cut moldings, shape components, rout square and clean rabbets, cut mortises, and do many other operations that would otherwise have required a large number of hand tools. The modern router is in effect a small, versatile machining center that will enable you to undertake a wide range of machining operations without high capital cost.

Small routers use a ¼ in. (6 mm) collet capable of taking a wide variety of smaller router bits, and larger routers as shown below use a ½ in. (13 mm) collet, capable of taking not only the small ¼ in. (6 mm) router bits but also the larger router bits with ½ in. (13 mm) shanks. Many woodworkers find that the smaller router is more comfortable and pleasant to use, being lighter and more manageable. There may be occasions, however, when one cannot avoid using a cutter with a ½ in. (13 mm) shank. Such router bits are used for producing large moldings; for example, a raised panel for a door.

RIGHT A hand-held heavy-duty router and guide rail, showing the arrangement of the fence and the collet that accepts the router cutters

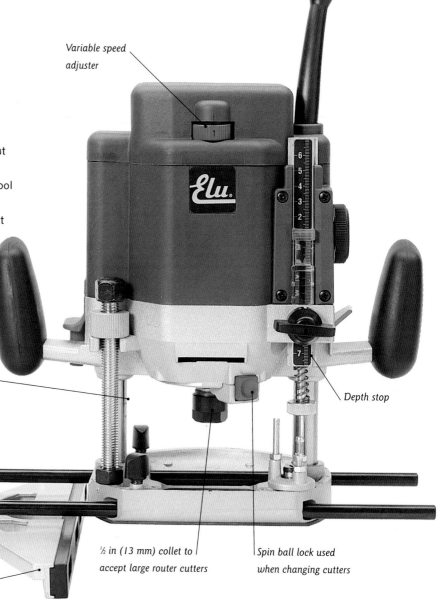

Variable speed adjuster

Motor and cutter assembly plunges up and down on the two columns

Depth stop

½ in (13 mm) collet to accept large router cutters

Spin ball lock used when changing cutters

Side fence attached to router base plate

Noise and dust

A worthwhile feature on some routers is the variable speed setting. This enables the speed of the motor to be adjusted to suit the size of the cutter being used. Because routers are extremely noisy, emitting a high-pitched scream, it is considerably beneficial, even when using a relatively small router bit, to be able to turn the speed down without affecting the performance of the cutter. Electronic speed controllers can also be purchased as separate accessories.

Besides the noise of these machines, another disadvantage is the dust. The dust particles produced by routers, especially when milling man-made boards, are micron fine, and a short session with a router not attached to a dust extractor can cover both the workshop and the operator in a shower of fine, lung-clogging dust. Many modern routers are becoming better designed and enable the operator to fix a dust extractor outlet to the machine without greatly impairing the visibility of the cutter head or the depth of cut. When purchasing, consider this feature very carefully and always use a router with a dust extractor, even for short runs.

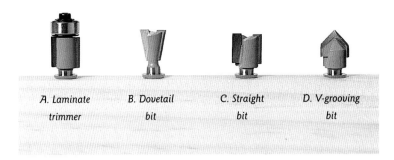

A. Laminate trimmer   B. Dovetail bit   C. Straight bit   D. V-grooving bit

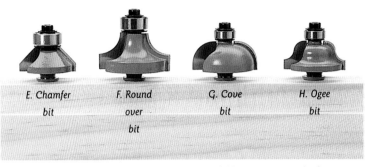

E. Chamfer bit   F. Round over bit   G. Cove bit   H. Ogee bit

ABOVE *Examples of the range of router bits available: A, E, F, G, and H have ball bearings which run along the edge of the work while the bit makes the appropriate cut on the edge of the work; B, C, and D require guiding by a fence*

Router bits

It is the ability to change router bits quickly and without incurring great expense that makes routers so versatile. Router bits are available in a wide variety of shapes and sizes. They basically fall into two categories: bits that are used for dimensioning lumber or cutting joints, such as straight bits or rabbet bits, and bits that are involved with creating decorative moldings. Router bits are available in high-speed steel (HSS) or tungsten carbide tipped (TCT). HSS bits are less expensive and can produce an acceptable cut, but they hold their edge for a relatively short time. TCT bits have the ability to hold their edge for longer but they are much more expensive. TCT bits can be resharpened by a saw or tool-sharpening service. It is also possible to "touch up" a dull HSS bit using a small hand-held abrasive stone.

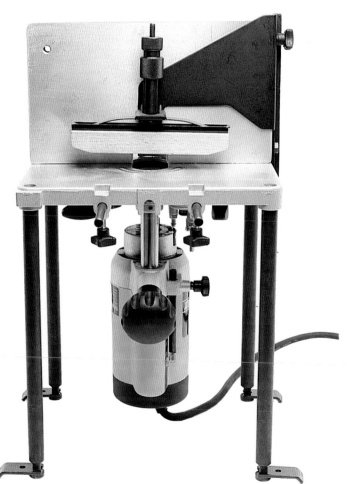

ABOVE *A large router inverted and fitted to a special table which allows it to be used as a small spindle shaper*

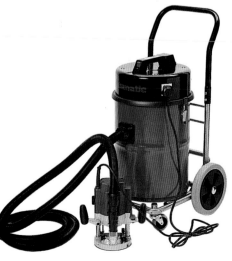

Router connected to a small shop vac

PORTABLE SAWS

More useful on site than in the workshop, portable saws are useful for a variety of tasks and can also be used mounted in a machine table as described below.

Circular saw blades come in various blade patterns and tooth types. Tungsten carbide tipped (TCT) blades are common and are recommended for use on man-made boards, especially particle board. Both rip and crosscut pattern blades are available for special applications, but generally most saws are fitted with combination blades that function relatively well in either situation.

Circular saws

The circular saw is the power tool highly favored for carpentry and site work. In this situation it can be taken to the job and used to trim components to length or to rip large sheets of man-made boards into smaller component sizes. Two types of saw are available. On the more standard saw, the handle is mounted approximately above the motor. The second type, called a worm-drive saw, is often preferred by professional carpenters. More powerful, more rugged, this saw is also more expensive.

A new development in the circular saw market has been the cordless saw. This useful tool is small and light and can be used anywhere to trim or to dimension components.

A small portable circular saw, shown here as a cordless version

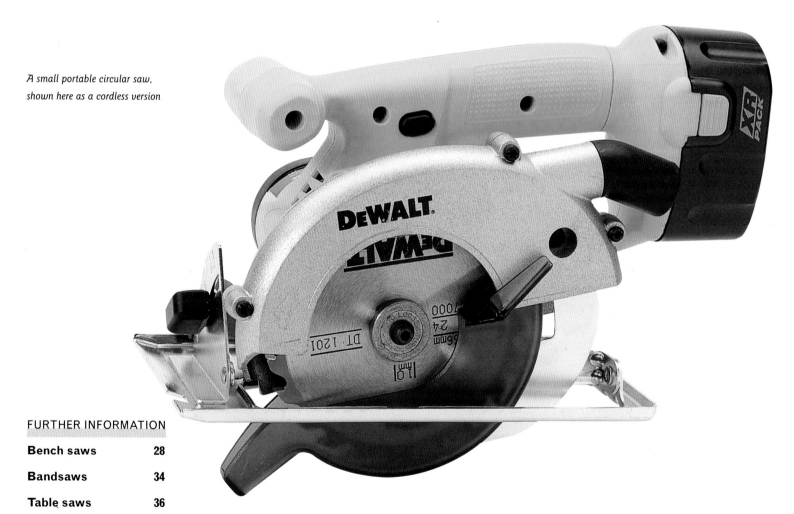

A small hand-held jigsaw

A basic biscuit jointer uses plunge action and a small circular saw to cut slots for biscuits

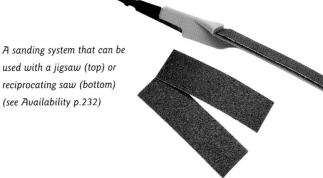

A sanding system that can be used with a jigsaw (top) or reciprocating saw (bottom) (see Availability p.232)

A glue dispenser with biscuits (see Availability p.232)

Jigsaws

Jigsaws are hand-held power tools with a small, narrow reciprocating blade. Because of the narrowness of the blade, a jigsaw is most at home when used for cutting curved components. Although new, stiffer blades are available for some makes, which are more accurate when used for ripping to a straight line, the jigsaw is not generally favored as a very accurate saw for dimensioning lumber. It could, however, be a useful saw for cutting up large sheet material into more easily handled sizes, or large boards into small pieces. A similar type of saw is the reciprocating saw. This is a tool that will hold a blade similar to, though more sturdy than, a jigsaw blade and is generally used by carpenters for freehand cutting.

The reciprocating saw: most useful for rough freehand cutting and remodel work

Biscuit jointers

Biscuit jointers are among the more useful power tools in the small furniture workshop. These are essentially commercial tools that enable strong and quick joints to be made, using a flat "biscuit." The biscuits are specially shaped to fit into a slot created by a small saw in both of the components being joined. The strength of the joint is due, first, to the close-fitting nature of the biscuit in the slot and second, to the fact that the biscuit is of compressed beech which swells slightly when it comes in contact with the glue. Edge joints can very quickly be jointed together and accurately glued up with a biscuit jointer.

DRILLS AND MORTISING MACHINES

The simplest method of making a hole in a piece of wood is to use an old-fashioned hand-cranked brace and bit with lip-and-spur, or auger, drill bits. Their main advantage is that the small screw in the center of the drill bit holds the drill in the wood, making it extremely controllable.

Hand-held electric drills—mostly used with what are known as twist, or jobbers drill bits—are really designed for use with metal, but they can do a fairly good job in woodwork. In a power drill, the best bit to use on wood is either the brad point bit or the Forstner bit. Both have a brad point at the center which locates the drill at the start of its cut, and the Forstner bit has an outer cutter that scribes the circumference of the hole.

Hand-held cordless electric drill with rechargeable battery

Cordless drills and screwdrivers

Cordless power drills, originally invented for use on-site, are gaining popularity in the home workshop simply because of their convenience. The disadvantage of many cordless drills, however, is that they are slower and less powerful unless fitted with a fairly large and heavy battery. Besides drilling holes, cordless drills may be used to drive in screws, but care must be taken not to drive the head too deep under the surface. A better option is to use a cordless screwdriver. This is fitted with a clutch which has a number of different settings that can be set on the drive so that the screw is only driven flush with the surface. The cordless screwdriver will also function perfectly well as a conventional hand-held drill, making it the more useful tool.

Drill stands and drill presses

The benefit of the drill stand is the ability to set the drill up so that it is always going to function at 90° to the job. As most holes are drilled at 90°, the drill stand or the machine equivalent, the drill press, is a very popular workshop tool.

Drill presses come in two forms. Both normally have a ½ in. (13 mm) chuck and a movable table that can be slid up or down a column or cranked using a small handle working on a rack and pinion. One version is the bench-mounted drill press, and the other is a floor-standing model that allows you to drill longer objects. On the top of the drill press, inside a casing, is a series of pulleys that enable the position of the belt on them to be changed, so changing the speed of the drill. This allows the drill to be slowed down when using large drill bits or sanding wheels. The depth of cut taken by the drill is controlled by a depth stop on the quill of the machine. This is the part of the machine that holds the drill chuck and moves up and down when the drill is driven into the job.

Drill presses are extremely versatile and can be used as sanding machines with the addition of flap wheels or small sanding drums, as mortising machines with the addition of a mortising attachment, and as milling machines with the addition of a cross vise. They enable a job to be clamped under a cutter and moved sideways, left or right, or forward or backward.

Although a drill press is an easy machine to learn how to use,

Standard twist drill

Brad point bit

Twist drill, available in larger sizes

Flat or spade bit

Two types of Forstner bit, one with a smooth edge (left), the other with a saw edge (right)

Adjustable bit: normally used in a hand brace

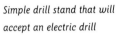

Simple drill stand that will accept an electric drill

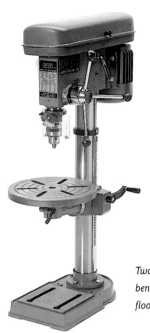

Two drill presses, one for bench mounting and the other floor standing

Dedicated mortising machine

always make sure that the chuck key is removed from the chuck and that the cutter is free to move before the machine is switched on; remove any loose clothing, ties, cuffs, or necklaces.

Mortising machines

A drill press can be modified to function as a mortiser, but this is practical for only very modest use. The purpose-made mortising machines are far more efficient and far easier to use. Mortising is the practice of creating a square hole, which is done by setting up a tool called a mortising bit. Mortising bits have an auger bit fitted inside a square hollowed chisel. The drill bit cuts slightly in front of the chisel, and the sharpened points of the hollowed chisel cut out the square corners around the drill bit. A mortising machine holds the mortise tool, enabling it to be driven down into the job, and holds the job in place while the tool is lifted out. The mortising machine also allows the job to travel sideways, left and right, thereby enabling the mortise tool to cut several square cuts side by side, thus creating a deep slot or mortise.

Drill bits

Flat spade-type drill bits are very useful for drilling large holes; make sure that the point of the bit is engaged with the job before starting the drill. Brad point bits are most widely used by woodworkers; they locate easily in the start position with a central point and do not deflect when the power is turned on.

Forstner bits are unlike most other types of boring bits in that they are guided by their rims and not just by the center point. Holes bored with Forstner bits are clean and accurate, and flatter bottomed. Only a Forstner bit can bore half a hole on the edge of a board or overlapping holes. They are completely unaffected by grain or knots. Sawtooth bits, with saw teeth around the rim as well as a cutting edge, are better in end grain work.

Plug cutter

Hole cutter

Combination auger bit

Jennings auger bit

Irwin auger bit

Ridgeway center bit

Countersink bit

Hollow mortising chisel with center auger

Drills and mortising machines

SANDERS

The invention of electrically powered sanding machines has certainly taken the backache out of the process of shaping and finish sanding.

Belt sanders

One of the most common electric sanders is the belt sander. Because a belt sander is so aggressively efficient at removing wood, many woodworkers hesitate before using a belt sander for fine surface finishing. It is a relatively cumbersome machine and, as it moves around over the surface to be sanded, it is very possible to sand unevenly and create digs and gouges in an otherwise relatively smooth surface. This is because the sanding plate is relatively small. The platen on a 3 in. (75 mm) belt sander would probably be no larger than 3 in. (75 mm) square. Belt sanders are more useful for sanding narrow components such as rails and stiles. Some belt sanders have a sanding frame that fits around the machine and effectively enlarges the area upon which the belt sander is sitting. This is a considerable improvement and is a worthwhile accessory if you are thinking of sanding a large area such as a table top using a small belt sander. Small stands are available, too, which enable the belt sander to be turned upside down and converted into a small stationary sanding machine. This is another worthwhile accessory. A stationary sanding machine is often more useful in the workshop than a portable power tool.

Random orbital sanders

For finishing large areas, the orbital sander was a popular power tool for many years. This had a flat rectangular pad that oscillated in small circles and was effective, but could leave small circular marks on the finished job. This has been greatly improved upon by the introduction of the random orbital sander. Random orbital sanders, as the name suggests, sand in a circular action but without leaving the tell-tale sanding marks left by a conventional orbital sander. The random action gives a smooth, clean surface without any sanding marks. It is not, however, a flattening sander and should be used only on work that has already been made flat with either a hand plane or a machine. Random orbital sanders have self-adhesive and velcro-adhesive pads that make changing the sanding discs very quick and efficient. Where possible, always use dust extraction with sanding machines of this kind as the dust and abrasive particles can cause further scratches on the work and should be ducted away to your dust extractor.

A basic hand-held belt sander

Random orbital sander

Orbital sander

Other types of sander

The detail sander is another comparatively recent addition to the range of power tools. It features a delta-shaped sanding pad that is capable of reaching into the corners of preassembled cabinets. As it is good practice to presand and prefinish before assembling those parts of the job that cannot be reached after assembly, detail sanders have a limited use in the home workshop but would be useful for some jobs, such as detail sanding around carvings.

Sanding machines come in many forms but the most useful in the small workshop is a combined belt and disc sander. A small machine of this type is invaluable for either shaping, using a coarse paper, or finishing small components. The disc sander can

Detail sander

be used to round off corners and sand end grain true and flush; the belt sander can be used for edge sanding against a fence or surface sanding small components.

Whereas a disc sander is perfectly good for creating and finish sanding convex edges, a separate sanding machine is needed for sanding concave curves. To do this it would be possible to set up a small drum in the drill press or, alternatively, consider a small spindle sander. This is a machine designed especially for this purpose, which moves the sanding drum up and down slightly during the sanding process. This has the benefit of preventing the abrasive from becoming clogged and burnt, as can happen without this oscillation.

Disc sanders

A disc sander is one of the most useful pieces of equipment in this category. It is important that the disc should be relatively large, since it cuts by virtue of its weight rather than its speed. If a sanding disc is run too fast, the chances are that the abrasive will actually burn the job rather than cut it. The disc sander is most effective for sanding end grain true and square. It can also be used to shape and polish end grain to a very high luster. A good sanding machine has a rigid table which ensures that the job remains square with the sanding wheel, but which can also be adjusted to sand compound angles and complex shapes.

Combined sanding machine with a small disc sander and a belt sander

It is often useful to mount the belt sander vertically

Small dedicated disc sander

Spindle sander: the drum reciprocates up and down as it turns. Drums are available in a range of sizes

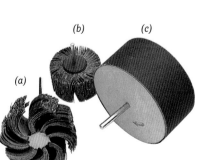

(b) (c)

(a)

(a) Contour sander
(b) Rotary flap sander
(c) Foam drum sander

Drum sander set

COMBINATION MACHINES

The small workshop can be efficiently served by a combination machine that combines in one machine all the operations of a table saw, disc sander, horizontal boring machine, vertical drill press, and lathe. This single machine can save space where it is at a premium and can save money when compared with the cost of separate machines.

Combos *versus* separates

All these machines can be bought separately but they are available in a combined, or combo, machine. The benefits of a combo is that it can be more economical to buy all of these machines combined in one than it is to buy them separately. A combo will also occupy considerably less space than three or four separate machines.

Many combination machines are exceptionally well made, with heavy cast-iron tables and well-engineered fences and guidance systems.

The disadvantage of a combo machine is one of inconvenience. That inconvenience is variable according to the design of the particular combination machine. The ability to change from one operation to another is undoubtedly less efficient on a combination machine than it would be using separate machines. But in a home workshop efficiency is not always the objective. You may have other considerations such as space or cost that would outweigh this.

A second factor that largely confines these machines to the amateur market is the difficulty for more than one person to work on a combination machine at once. For this reason most commercial workshops tend to buy separate machines, which reduces the potential retail market for a combination machine.

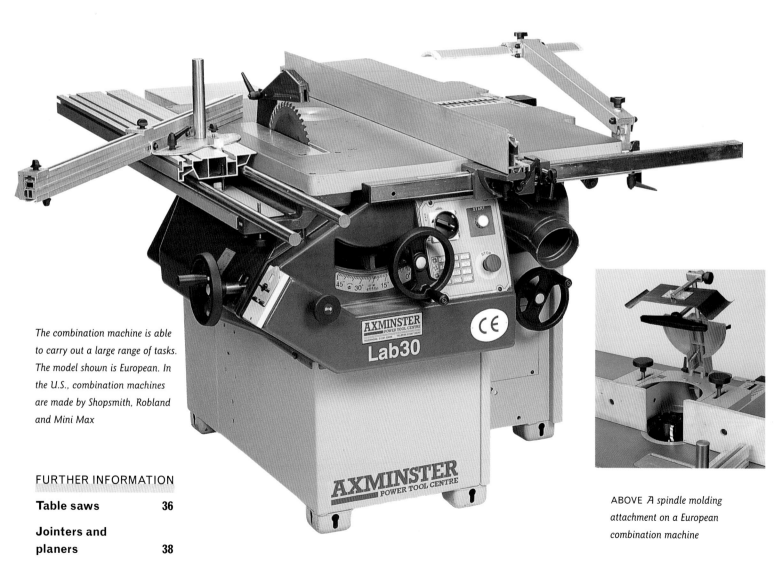

The combination machine is able to carry out a large range of tasks. The model shown is European. In the U.S., combination machines are made by Shopsmith, Robland and Mini Max

ABOVE *A spindle molding attachment on a European combination machine*

FOUR **BASIC TECHNIQUES**

This section covers the basic techniques required to prepare lumber for woodworking projects, using both hand tools and small machines. Starting with an unplaned rough board, the whole process is covered, from sawing the board into smaller components and planing it on both sides to dimensioning the pieces. The section shows you how to use each machine safely and competently, as well as how to use the basic range of hand tools.

Beyond these key basic techniques are the more advanced ones of routing, mortising, milling, shaping, and laminating. All of these, once mastered, will enable you to produce accurate joints, shaped components and, for the very ambitious, curved laminated components.

LUMBER SELECTION

Lumber selection is worth very careful thought for two reasons. First you need to decide what final effect you wish to achieve, where it will fit into the home, the color and grain pattern that will be most suitable, and any other consideration that will affect lumber choice.

Second, see what is available at your supplier so that you can purchase boards that will allow you to cut your components economically and use wood of suitable stability.

The cutting list

The start of a project is always exciting. Always remember, however, that you can save a great deal of time and money by first planning what you are going to do before you buy your lumber. First, make up a list of all of the components you require for your project and put against each component its dimensions—length, width, and thickness. This list is called a cutting list and is used to help you in the purchase and selection of your lumber. Try, for example, to design your components so that they can easily be planed from 1 in. (25 mm) or 2 in. (51 mm) rough boards. It is common practice for lumber yards to saw wood to 1⅛ in. (29 mm) which dries down and shrinks to

slightly over 1 in. (25 mm). A board of this thickness will give you a planed component of roughly ¾ in. (19 mm) when planed on both sides. Two-in. (51 mm) boards are often surfaced to 1½ or 1⅝ in. net thickness.

Consider carefully whether you need particularly stable components such as drawer sides or the loose leaf on a drop-leaf table. In both these instances you would want to use quarter-sawn lumber, which is particularly stable and less likely to cup or warp. Consider also

whether you are buying kiln-dried or air-dried lumber. If it is the latter then you must allow a period of at least one to two weeks after your initial planing of the wood for the material to settle and acclimatize to your workshop's humidity. If you are using kiln-dried lumber you can expect the wood to warp or twist much more quickly but for much shorter periods. In this case the planing or machining of the lumber is releasing stresses within the wood that have been placed there in the drying process.

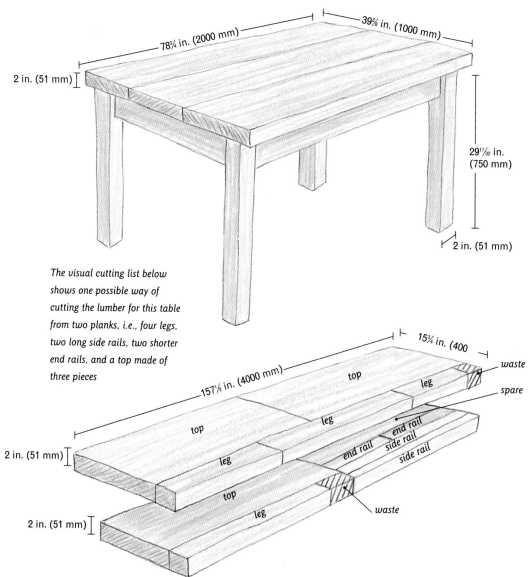

The visual cutting list below shows one possible way of cutting the lumber for this table from two planks, i.e., four legs, two long side rails, two shorter end rails, and a top made of three pieces

LEFT *The wastage in this log is clearly visible: the light-colored sapwood near the waney edge is the newer growth and is often discarded. Only the darker-colored heartwood from near the center of the tree, is of any use in this piece of walnut*

FAR LEFT *The face of this piece of softwood shows a figure which reflects its position in the sawn log*

Marking and cutting the lumber

Once you have selected your lumber and brought it back to the workshop, select which board will give you which component. It helps to stand the boards on end so that they are easier to turn over. The first crosscut is critical, for although it makes the boards much easier to handle, once they are 4 ft. (1219 mm) long instead of 8 ft. (2438 mm), for example, the options for using that board for long components have been reduced.

Use a chalk line to mark lines down the length of the board as illustrated below. At this stage do not attempt to come near to your finished sizes—just cut the components 3/16 in. (5 mm) or so oversize.

Having made chalk lines down the length of your rough-sawn board, it is time to saw down the lines. This process is best done on a bandsaw. Here the bandsaw would be used freehand without any fence or guides, and you simply need to guide the saw down the chalk line. A steady hand and good lighting around the bandsaw table help accomplish this task. Make sure that your bandsaw is fitted with a sharp blade and is properly tensioned. Also check that the movable blade guides are set so that no more than 3/8 in. (10 mm) of blade is exposed above the board. Keep your hands well back from the blade and do not let this machine lull you into a false sense of security. Although the bandsaw is a relatively gentle machine to use, it is still capable of inflicting a very painful and damaging cut to precious fingers.

Preparation
1 First brush the boards you have selected with a wire brush to remove all dirt, grit, and foreign material that may blunt your tools.

2 Use a chalk line to mark lines down the length of the board. This is a tool frequently used by builders and is available from the hardware store.

3 The line is drawn out of the container through the chalk and is snapped onto the job, leaving a straight, clean, colored line on the wood.

The jigsaw
4 If you do not have a bandsaw, the handpower jigsaw is a good tool for sawing both with and across the grain.

THE FIRST STEP IN PREPARING LUMBER

Once your boards have been sawn into smaller components, the next step is to plane them on one side. Although this could be done by hand, most woodworkers use a small jointer or sub-contract this work to a cabinet shop. The jointer is a relatively simple machine and, properly guarded, it can be very safe to use. The problem is that the main guard is easily removable and, once removed, this machine is potentially very dangerous. If you have not already done so (see previous page), brush down the surface of the board with a wire brush before using the jointer. This removes any grit that could easily damage the cutter head or scratch the table.

Using the jointer

Before starting, set the in-feed table ⁄ in. (1 mm) lower than the height of the blades. Now set the position of your guard. This is known as a crown guard and extends the full width of the cutter blades. If you want to be especially careful you can move the back vertical fence forward so that only the width of your components plus about ⅜ in. (10 mm) is showing in front of the vertical fence. Your crown guard will now cover any protruding blade right up to that rear fence.

To use the jointer, first start the motor, then lay your component on the in-feed table—usually the right-hand table. Now push the piece over the cutters; you should hear a change of tone as the

Using the jointer

1 Wearing safety goggles and ear protection, lay the component on the in-feed table.

2 Push the component over the cutters.

3 Lift your hand over the cutter guard.

4 Start to transfer pressure to the out-feed table.

5 Transfer your weight as the job progresses.

cutters engage the wood. As the piece appears on the out-feed table, transfer your weight so that the palm of your hand is pressing the front of the piece onto the out-feed table. As the piece passes further over the cutters, transfer your weight from the in-feed table to the out-feed table. As you do this, lift your hands over the guard, but do not at any time place your hands or fingers anywhere near the cutter guard. Always remember, when using any machine involving a revolving cutter head, that any loose clothing and long hair should be out of the way. Any jewelry should be removed and you should check the floor for any slippery surfaces, power cords, or debris.

Creating a reference surface

As you pass the board over the cutter, you will get a clearer idea of whether your board has cupped or is in any way twisted by seeing which areas have not touched the cutters.

It is essential to create a flat reference surface, or face side, using the jointer. From this reference surface all the other sides of your component will be made: the edges at 90° to the face side; the opposite side parallel to the face side; the ends at 90° to the face side. So this surface is worth planing carefully and is worth marking with a small "f." Traditionally, the "f" leans into the direction in which the grain runs and the stem of the "f" also points towards the face edge.

You may find that when you put your component across the jointer you get what are called tearouts, or small or rough patches,

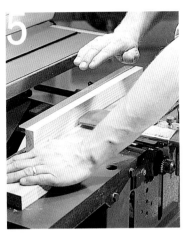
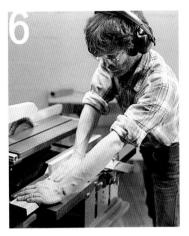

6 Ensure that pressure is now on the out-feed table only.

7 Finish the cut.

Subsequent stages

8 Inspect the first pass to determine if any subsequent operations are needed.

9 Feed the lumber through the planer.

where the grain has been torn out. If this occurs, turn the board around and try planing in the other direction. This is called planing with the grain.

Using the planer

Once the face side is planed, the opposite side can be done. Place face side down on the bed of your planer. This planer bed is moved up and down underneath the cutter head and positioned to plane a surface parallel to your face side and at a given distance from that side. You will need ear plugs or earmuffs when using the planer. Also, the planer is capable of producing a high volume of chips and dust, so it is essential to fit a dust extractor to the machine.

A planer drives the component under the cutters. Since you do not have to push the board there is a slight danger that your fingers can get trapped against the side of the planer or against the support rollers. Never bend down to see whether a planer is clogged and never put your hand on the bed to move a scrap of wood or pull out a jammed component.

Aim at this stage to thickness your components ¹⁄₁₆ in. (2 mm) oversize. You can then leave your components overnight "in stick"—that is, resting on small ⅜ in. (10 mm) square sticks that allow air to reach all four sides of the newly planed boards.

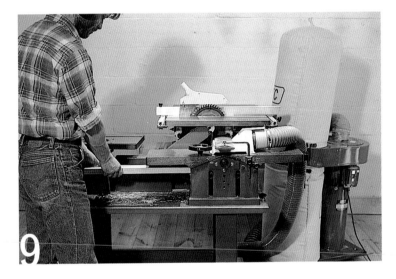

10 Check the thickness of the lumber with calipers.

FOUR **BASIC TECHNIQUES**

MACHINING EDGES AND CUTTING TO WIDTH

Planing a face edge is the process of creating a straight side at right angles to your face side or reference side. The "f" or face marks will point in the direction of the side you are going to use as a face edge, which will already have been ripped roughly straight using the bandsaw. Now you need to use your face side against the vertical fence on your jointer to create straight edges at right angles to your face side. To do this, move the vertical fence into position toward the front edge of the jointer tables. This reduces the amount of blade exposed to the minimum. Next check the vertical fence against the in-feed table for square, using a strong light source and a good engineer's square. Finally, set the guard in position, allowing just enough room between the vertical fence and the guard for your board to pass over the cutter head. When planing an edge, try to plane with the grain.

With one face edge planed, you can now use a table saw to cut a line parallel to the face edge at a predetermined distance from the face edge. If your finished components should be 4 in. (102 mm), you should be sawing your components to 4$\frac{3}{64}$ in. (103 mm), allowing a further $\frac{3}{64}$ in. (1 mm) to be planed off to final dimension. This enables you to get your components to the exact size for your project.

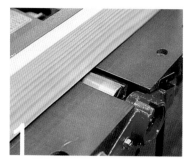

Using a planer
1 Set up the jointer ready for use.

2 Making the first pass on the jointer.

Ripping with a table saw

When ripping with a table saw, which is perhaps the most accurate way of creating a sawn straight edge, it is necessary to use the rip fence. This is a fence set parallel to the saw blade and movable to a preset distance from that saw blade: so whatever distance your rip fence is set from the saw blade, that will be the size of your component when it emerges. Several things are important to remember when ripping. First, there is the splitter and blade guard. A splitter is a steel plate at the rear of the table saw blade. Usually the blade guard is attached to the top of the splitter and from there covers the crown of the saw blade. Both the blade guard and the splitter perform essential functions and neither should ever be removed when you are sawing. The function of the splitter is to prevent boards, particularly kiln-dried boards, that are being ripped from closing up on the saw blade after they have been cut. This can occur when lumber has been dried very quickly and contains tensions that are released in the sawing process. If this happens and the splitter is not in position, there is a considerable risk that the board could be thrown back at you. Set your blade square, checking it with the small engineer's square against the surface of the table saw. If your blade guard is adjustable, set it to a height so that there is a gap between your job and the bottom of the guard of no more than ⅜ in. (10 mm). With the guard set up and the rip fence in place, rip your components to your chosen dimension. Keep your fingers away from the saw blade, press in towards the rip fence and forward to push the component through the saw. As your component is sawn, so your hands get nearer to the spinning blade. Do not go too near—use a preprepared push stick rather than put your fingers near the saw. Never pull a board through a table saw

from the rear. When ripping, you occasionally leave a very thin strip of waste scrap lumber to the left of the saw blade which can be thrown back at you. Always wear a face mask as well as ear protection when ripping.

Ripping with a bandsaw

The bandsaw can also be used for ripping. Set up the blade so that it is cutting at true right angles to the table. Set the blade guides so that they are approximately ⅜ in. (10 mm) above your component, with the blade guard above that, and set your rip fence to the required distance from the blade. A bandsaw will give a slightly coarser cut than a table saw, but, provided the blades are changed regularly, a bandsaw can produce very accurate work and is a useful machine in a small workshop.

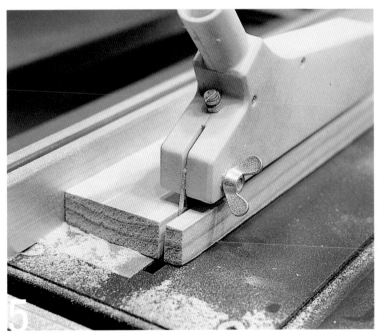

3 Press the component in toward the fence and forward.

4 Always use push sticks rather than your fingers for safety's sake.

5 Take care that the thin strip of waste lumber does not get thrown up at you.

Using a bandsaw
6 A bandsaw is a useful machine and can be used for ripping.

MARKING OUT FOR ACCURACY

"Marking out" is the process of marking on your components the exact dimensions—either of the component itself or of some aspects of the joinery on that particular component. If you have several components of identical size, simply use one test piece component to set up your machines to cut the entire batch to the same size.

Good marking out is vitally important for the accuracy of subsequent work. Take your time to get it absolutely right and then relax in the knowledge that you have set secure foundations for your project. Remember that if you mark out accurately and then cut to the line, it cannot help but fit.

Using striking knives

A striking knife is an essential tool. Very little marking out in a cabinetmaking workshop is done with a pencil, because a pencil line has a thickness, no matter how sharp the pencil may be. A striking knife, however, provides a mark of absolute accuracy. This is because a striking knife is sharpened with one bevel so that when it is used and a line is struck with the knife held at 90° to the wood, it provides a cut in the wood that denotes the exact end of your component. A line struck accurately with a striking knife will remain on the board after the joint is cut, after it is assembled and when the job is finished. The bevel side of your striking knife should always face the waste side of your component or joint.

When using a square with a striking knife, hold the square tight against the wood, with your fingers pulling the square into the job. Place your knife on the mark that denotes the dimension of your component and then slide the square up to your knife. Now grip the square tightly in position and strike a line by drawing the knife

down the outside of the blade of your square. Squares should be of extremely high-quality steel as striking knives can quickly wear down a blade of inferior quality.

Using rules and squares

There is a technique for using rules with absolute accuracy. Should you require, for example, a component of 23¼ in. (591 mm) length, place the rule with the 23¼ in. (591 mm) dimension mark in line with the end of your component. Sight this very carefully by looking down on the line. Avoid any errors of parallax by looking at the line from left or right and adjust the rule so that it is lying on your component and overhanging the end of it by exactly the right amount. Now strike a small line with your striking knife, using the end of your rule as a reference point. This is much more accurate

Accurate marking and measuring

1 Using a striking knife allows absolute precision.

2 Grip the square tightly so you can mark against it.

3 This is an accurate technique for measuring, using the end of your rule as the reference point.

than aligning the rule's zero with the end of the component and attempting to mark a line at the required measurement.

When using a square to check for squareness, place the stock of the square against the face of the board and slide it down so that the blade is just touching the edge. Slide along the edge of the board with a strong light source at the back of the blade. Without a strong light source, it is possible to make mistakes.

Using gauges

A marking gauge is a simple tool primarily used to scribe a line along the grain of the wood. The point of the marking gauge can be filed and adjusted so that it cuts a neat and clear line. It should be sharpened in a similar way to a striking knife, and used so that the beveled side of the blade is always on the waste side of your cut. Either draw a marking gauge towards you or push it away. When setting a gauge, set it by tapping the stop of the gauge against your bench. Once set, slightly tighten the adjusting screw.

A cutting gauge is set in exactly the same way and is a very similar tool, but it has a small knife rather than a steel point to make the mark on the job. Cutting gauges are most useful for marking across the grain of the wood, although a properly sharpened ordinary marking gauge will do just as good a job as a cutting gauge.

Using squares

4 Checking an edge for square.

5 A good light source is essential for checking the flatness of a piece.

Different types of gauge

6 Using a marking gauge along the grain.

7 A cutting gauge is useful for cutting across the grain.

8 A vernier gauge, or calipers, give a very precise measurement of thickness.

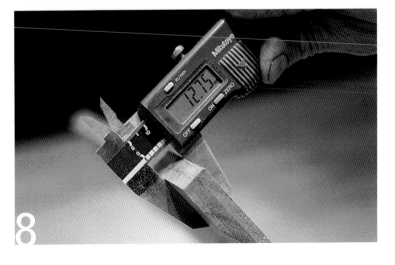

HAND PLANING SURFACES AND EDGES

Once the hand plane has been set up to work correctly it can be tested on a board. A correctly set-up plane will have a slightly curved plane iron. The purpose of this is to create a shaving of approximately ⅝ in. (16 mm) in width. This is a narrow ribbon-like shaving which emerges from the center of the throat of the plane and is easily controllable. A wider shaving than this can be created by a flatter, less curved plane iron, but it would require much more energy to work and would give the operator much less control. The curved iron also creates a shaving with a thickness in the center of approximately 1/100 in. (0.25 mm), but this tapers out to nothing at the edges of the shaving.

Quite often a hand plane is used to remove the machine marks left by a planer. In this process it is necessary to plane over a surface evenly and with great control. Three parallel chalk marks made across the board before starting enable you to see where the plane takes a shaving and what part of the board still needs to be planed. Once all the chalk marks are removed, all of the machine marks or planer marks will also have been removed. If further work is needed, the process can be repeated.

Planing with the grain
Try to plane the wood in the direction it wishes to be planed. You will often find grain direction affecting your choice of the way in which to work the plane along the board. You can get some idea of which way the grain is running by looking at the edge of the board.

Correct use of the hand plane
When using a plane, bear in mind that you are pressing down on the board as well as moving the plane forward, therefore the trunk of your body can exert considerable power downward if, and only if, the plane is kept close to your body. Move forward over the board by keeping your front foot forward and swaying over the work on your knees, rather than pushing the plane forward only using your forearms and shoulders. In this way a plane shaving can be started and stopped and continued down a long board because the plane is kept close to the body and kept under control. Such control would not be available to you if the plane has extended too far forward. In a similar way a long board can be easily planed in a series of short steps, each time starting and stopping the plane under control.

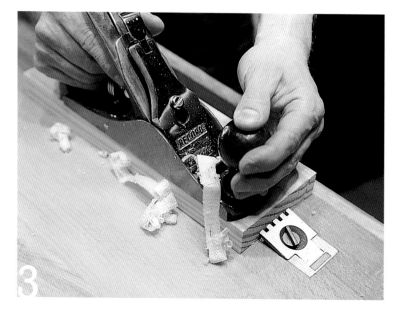

Using chalk as a guide
1 Chalking across the job before starting enables you to see where the plane takes a shaving.

2 As the plane progresses it becomes evident which part of the board still needs to be planed.

3 As you start the cut, the pressure is on the front of the plane, but as the cut progresses pressure should move so that it is on the rear handle in the final stage of the pass.

Determining the grain
4 You can tell which way the grain is running by looking at the edge of the board.

The correct stance for planing

5 Using a plane requires pressing down on the board as well as moving the plane forward. Begin to plane with one hand applying pressure on the front, or toe, of the plane.

6 Move forward over the job by keeping your front foot forward and using your knees. Transfer the pressure slightly as you move the plane forward.

7 Finish the planing movement with the other hand pressing down on the back, or heel, of the plane.

Planing edges

When planing the edge of a board, bear in mind that your plane iron is slightly curved. If the edge is already square at right angles to the face edge and all you wish to do is take off a single shaving, plane with the board in the center of the sole of your plane. If you wish to correct the angle, phase the plane off to one side or the other.

A shooting board is often used to plane the edges of a thin board (less than ⅜ in./10 mm thick) upon which it will be too difficult to balance a bench plane. A shooting board can be used for planing both with the grain and across the grain. When using it across the grain, be careful not to extend the board too far beyond the support piece; otherwise breakout, or "spelching," will occur if you plane through your work.

Hand planing edges

8 Removing a fine shaving to one side with a well-sharpened and adjusted plane.

9 Planing with the board in the center of the plane's sole.

10 Phasing the plane off to one side.

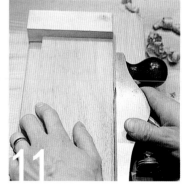

11 A shooting board is particularly useful for planing narrow edges.

FOUR **BASIC TECHNIQUES**

USING HANDSAWS ACCURATELY

To be able to use a hand saw with confidence and with accuracy is one of the great pleasures of woodworking. Many beginners find this such a frustrating mystery, however, that it drives them to pick up the nearest power tool or needlessly invest a great deal of money in machines that they feel will do the job more accurately than they ever could. These pages describe, first, how to choose a saw for a particular job; second, how to support the job so that you can concentrate on sawing rather than holding the work; and, finally, how to control a saw and adjust your stance during the sawing process. It should be stressed, however, that using a handsaw is not difficult.

Holding the piece for accurate sawing

The most satisfactory way to hold a board for sawing is to use a vise in a large, heavy bench to do the job for you. If you can use your bench in this way, you can set up your body to control the saw accurately and swing your arm in the correct manner. If, however, you also have to hold down a piece of wood that is jumping all over the place, the chances are that you will not be standing in the right place to swing the saw accurately.

It is possible to saw board material when it is supported horizontally on sawhorses. Because the board itself has sufficient weight to give it stability, you will have less of a problem holding it down while sawing.

Problems arise when you try to crosscut relatively small pieces of wood while also holding them down on a low sawhorse or workmate. In the example shown here, the craftsman is attempting to do two jobs at once—both saw the wood and hold it in position—and the chances of success are compromised.

A useful piece of equipment when sawing is a bench hook. This hooks over the edge of your bench and allows you to secure board in position without compromising the sawing stance. It is important that boards much longer than the width of the bench hook are supported at their far end so that the board sits squarely on the bench hook, parallel to the surface of the bench.

If, before sawing begins, the scribed line is reinforced and cut quite deeply into the wood, and a small v-groove is pared out on the waste side of the line, this small channel enables the saw to

FURTHER INFORMATION

Holding the work securely

1 Sawing down a line, with the work held vertically in the vise.

2 Sawing down the length of heavy board material supported on sawhorses. It is often helpful to extend your forefinger along the side of the saw handle as a guide, and to give you greater control as you saw.

3 It is hard to hold the piece firmly when crosscutting a small piece of wood on a trestle or workmate.

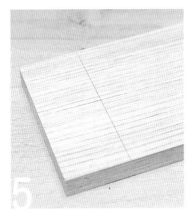

4 A hardwood bench hook is useful for holding the wood when crosscutting small pieces. You can buy one ready-made or make it yourself in the workshop.

5 Clearly scribe the cutting line before sawing.

6 Paring a "V" along this line with a chisel before starting creates a small channel in which to rest the saw for the first cut.

Lighting

7 A well-positioned bench light ensures precise and accurate sawing.

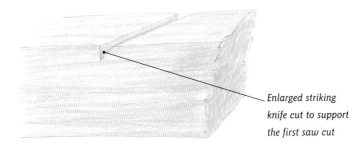

Enlarged striking knife cut to support the first saw cut

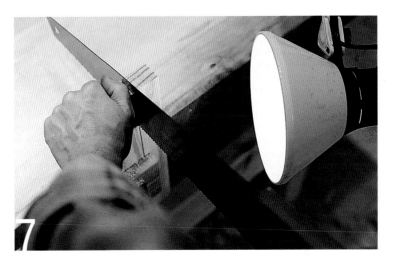

get a clean start. It also creates a clean scribed shoulder to the cut where the risk is that the saw would tear or fail to cut the fibers cleanly. This is especially useful in soft-grained or fibrous woods.

Lighting

Use a bench light wherever you can to illuminate the saw, remembering that if you cannot see where you are going, the chances of your cutting accurately to a line are infinitesimally small. A bench light can throw an invisible scribe line into high relief by catching it at the right angle. If you can see your scribe line, the chances are you can saw to it more accurately.

Using the kerf

The kerf of the saw is the width of the cut created by your saw. The kerf is created by the teeth being bent to left and right to make a cut that is wider than the thickness of the saw plate. It is necessary to have a kerf that is wider than the plate of your saw so that you can guide the saw slightly left or right as you progress

down a cut. However, if your saw cuts a very wide kerf, it is going to require a great deal more energy and a great deal more effort to make the cuts. Always try to reduce the kerf that saws make, since the less effort you put into the cut, the more control you will have over its direction.

The aim is to saw at "half mark"—that is, to saw with the kerf in the waste side of the job. A good sawyer will saw at half mark, taking out one half of the scribed line and leaving just a faint trace of the scribed line still present on the job.

Choosing your saw

Choose your saw with care. Most sawing can be accomplished by using either a small panel saw with a relatively short blade but with fine teeth, or a backsaw such as the tenon saw. Finer work should be done using a dovetail saw. Most cabinetmakers favor using a dovetail saw over a tenon saw and will set up a 10 in. (250 mm) dovetail saw with a relatively wide kerf to accomplish the jobs normally done by the slightly coarser and heavier tenon saw.

Learning how to saw

In order to understand how to use a saw, the process of ripsawing down a line has been broken down into easily managed steps.

The first step is to mark out the board and set it up in your bench vise. Here a dovetail saw is being used to ripsaw a piece of fine-grained mahogany, about ¹³⁄₁₆ in. (21 mm) thick, which is being sawn down to a scribed crosscut line, probably 1⅜ in. (35 mm) from the end of the board. This is the kind of cut made when sawing dovetails or ripping a board to width. Once the board is marked out, support it in the end vise of a cabinetmaker's bench with no more than about 2 in. (51 mm) of the board protruding above the surface of the bench. Set the board vertically, siting with the end of the bench to ensure that the piece is upright. If the board is held vertically, your chance of sawing down that line is greatly enhanced.

Positioning your body Next, take up position with your legs 2 ft. (600 mm) apart and your chest at right angles to the face of the board. Take the saw in your hand and imagine a line drawn straight from the tip of your saw, through your hand, up your arm, past your elbow to your shoulder—this should form a perfectly straight line.

The forward and backward action of the saw is a motion taken from the pivot of your shoulder, and that shoulder should be placed exactly in line with where you want to cut. Your chest should not be turned to face the board. Keep your body sideways as if you were about to serve a tennis ball. If you face the cut directly, the chances are that this straight body line will be compromised.

The sawing technique Now start your cut. Position a fingernail or your thumbnail in the gauge line to give your saw a starting location, then rest the saw against this finger/thumbnail. The start is critical. Rest the tip of the saw lightly on the board and, with confidence, simply give one clean push.

Having made a clean start you can now concentrate on the direction in which the saw is going. The first two strokes of the saw will determine which way the saw is going to go. After two or three strokes, there is no point attempting to correct the direction, so determine the saw's direction early on in its travel down the board. Concentrate on the gauge line and "think" the saw down this line.

At this stage it is essential that you slacken your grip on the handle of the saw. A backsaw has a brass strip running down the back of the saw blade that provides all the weight that is necessary to drive the saw into the board. If you grip the saw too hard you will increase the work that the teeth are being asked to do and drive the saw offline. So hold the saw like a child's hand. Increase your concentration. Do not attempt to control the direction of the saw by wiggling it left and right. Instead "think" the saw down the line. It is a little like riding a motorcycle down a winding country lane:

12 Check the direction of the saw and ensure that the first few cuts follow the gauge line, sawing at "half mark."

The sawing stance
8 It is important to develop the correct stance for sawing. Start with your legs 2 ft. (600 mm) apart and your chest at right angles to the face of the board.

9 The action of the saw forward and backward is a motion taken from the pivot of your shoulder, which should be placed exactly in line with the intended cut.

Sawing techniques
10 A piece of mahogany is supported vertically in the vise with the scribed line clearly visible ready for sawing.

11 The start is critical; use a fingernail in the gauge line to position the saw accurately.

you do not positively lean a bike over to take a fast corner, instead it is all to do with minute shifts of your body and concentration.

Move the bench light to enable you to see the line as you saw down it. Also make sure that you use the full length of the saw blade with fluid strokes of the saw. Next, concentrate on the stop—the specific point you are sawing down to—which can be achieved by stopping sawing exactly on the marked line.

With a little practice it is possible to learn how to saw accurately at half mark with very little effort. The technique is not difficult to acquire and is extremely satisfying.

13 Relax your grip slightly on the handle so as not to drive the saw offline.

14 Saw with an easy action, "thinking" the saw down the line.

15 Sawing to a specific point on a gauged line— you need to stop exactly on that line.

Using a coping saw

16 Use a coping saw to follow a curved line from the end of the work, starting with initial strokes.

17 Continue sawing along the line, taking care to maintain accuracy.

18 When using the coping saw on an internal shape, drill a small hole on the shape's edge, insert the blade through this hole, then tension in the saw frame and carefully cut to the line.

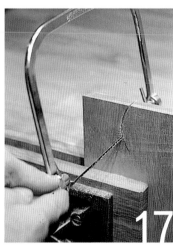

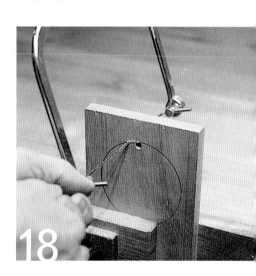

USING CHISELS

When using a chisel the sharpness of the edge of this tool is of paramount importance. Never let the edge of your chisel become blunt. As soon as you feel that you need to exert undue pressure to make a paring, hone the edge of your chisel. When using a chisel consistently it is not unusual to need to hone an edge once every half hour or so.

Paring vertically

Positioning your body The stance to adopt when paring vertically is to hold the chisel close to your body with your elbows tucked in so that you can exert the power of your shoulders and trunk rather than your hands and forearms. Your lower forearm will rest on the board you are paring. You will also grip the blade of the chisel and exert an upward pressure. Your upper hand will hold the handle of the chisel and exert a downward pressure. In this way the chisel is held in tension, rather like an isometric exercise. This gives great power and control to the user. You can drive it through end grain and yet control the cut, preventing the chisel from skating away from you and digging into the surface of the bench. (Note that it is best to use a cutting board to protect the surface of your bench.)

Chisel width With a narrow chisel of ¼ in. (6 mm) it is possible to make a paring in relatively soft wood, such as mahogany or walnut, that is the full width of your chisel. With a wider chisel than this it would be impossible to make a full-width paring and still retain control of the chisel. (In this instance you might want to use a mallet, but again control would be lost.) Instead, wider chisels are used only with the corners to extend and enlarge an existing land created by a narrow chisel taking a full width shaving. So a ¼ in. (6 mm) land carefully pared at right angles across the end of the board would be enlarged using a ⁵⁄₁₆ in. (8 mm) chisel, taking a ¹⁄₁₆ in. (2 mm) paring to the left and another to the right. The central ¼ in. (6 mm) land would be untouched. The principle is to extend a land using the widest chisel available because the width of the chisel will give you greater accuracy and flatness.

Paring back to gauge lines When paring back to a gauge line always pare away a shaving that is not too thick. This is because a chisel is in fact only a sharpened steel wedge; if the shaving you are attempting to remove is too thick, then instead of allowing the chisel to make a paring at right angles to your surface it will drive the chisel back, possibly past your gauge line.

As you pare away, approaching your gauge line, pare three-quarters of the way down the end grain, then turn the board over and pare three-quarters of the way down from the opposite side. In this way you will approach your gauge lines with the end grain of

Holding the chisel for vertical paring
1 The lower hand rests on the job, the fingers gripping the blade of the chisel. The upper hand grips the handle and pushes down.

2 Hold the chisel at right angles to the job in the correct stance, in order to achieve maximum control.

your board getting more and more like a flat surface at right angles to the face side. As you approach the gauge lines, you are left with the final shaving. Click the chisel into the gauge line—you should be able to feel the sharp edge of your chisel engage in the gauge line—and you can then make the final cut three-quarters of the way down. Turn the board over and do exactly the same on the opposite side; pare three-quarters of the way down and you will have a true surface, hand pared at 90° to your face side.

Paring end grain with chisels of different width

3 Start paring with a narrow chisel the full width of the chisel.

4 Switch to a slightly larger size chisel.

5 Enlarge the paring using the sides of the larger chisel.

Paring back to gauge lines

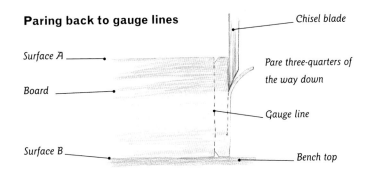

Chisel blade

Surface A

Board

Pare three-quarters of the way down

Gauge line

Surface B

Bench top

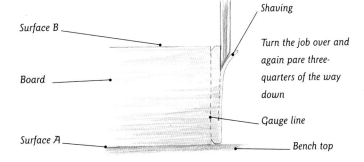

Surface B

Board

Surface A

Shaving

Turn the job over and again pare three-quarters of the way down

Gauge line

Bench top

10 The recess on the left has been pared correctly in stages, with thin shavings being removed, little by little. The right-hand recess is an example of paring attempted in one step. This produces a shaving which is too thick and uncontrollable and leads to inaccuracy.

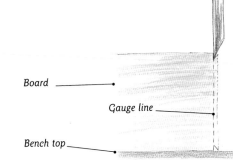

Board

Gauge line

Bench top

When the waste is pared back so far that it is not possible to take off another shaving, put the chisel in the gauge line and pare three-quarters of the way down. Turn the job over and repeat. The end is now pared square

Paring back to a gauge line

6 Remove a thin shaving, taking it three-quarters of the way down the piece.

7 Turn the piece over and repeat from the other side.

8 Turn the piece over once more, back to its original position.

9 Repeat the process to produce a surface pared exactly at right angles to the face of the piece.

FOUR **BASIC TECHNIQUES**

Tenting There is an alternative technique to paring down to your gauge line called "tenting." This involves paring back to the gauge line as described earlier but without attempting to be at right angles to the face side. Here you deliberately leave a tented surface between the two gauge lines. Then, having reached the gauge line on both sides of this ridged central area, you remove this ridged area or "tent" with a series of parallel shavings that gradually increase in length until they extend almost from one gauge line to the other.

Paring horizontally

There may be occasions when you want to pare horizontally. In this case, clamp the board in the end vise of your bench, so that it is 6–8 in. (152–203 mm) above the surface of the bench. At this height it is possible to keep the board from vibrating too much, and it will allow you to get into the correct stance.

Positioning your body The stance for horizontal paring is very similar to that adopted when using a dovetail saw. Stand with your

"Tented" surface pared away from both sides

Tenting
12 Pare at an angle from gauge lines, top and bottom.

13 This leaves a ridged or "tented" area in between the two gauge lines.

14 Now pare the "tent" away to give a flat surface from one gauge line to the other.

legs far apart and your chest and shoulders at right angles to the face of the board. A straight line should be formed from the blade of your chisel, through your wrist, up through your forearm, to your elbow. This should be as near to parallel with the surface of your bench as possible. In order to achieve this it may be necessary for you to spread your feet farther apart, so lowering your elbow and shoulder. In this stance, power is given to the cut by tucking your elbow tight into your chest and, once again, leaning on your knees and trunk rather than applying power with the arm and shoulder.

Paring chisels Greater control and flexibility can be given by using a paring chisel in this stance. Here a long-bladed or long-handled chisel is used. The length of the tool enables you to exert much finer control over the cuts. Never use a paring chisel with a mallet. This is a delicate tool and should be kept for paring alone.

A cranked or "dog-leg" paring chisel is useful in cabinet-making for cleaning out the inside of carcasses after assembly. Invariably there will be a small amount of "squeeze out" of glue on the inside of a joint. If a cabinet has been waxed inside before

Holding the chisel for horizontal paring

15 Take the correct stance ready to pare horizontally.

16 A paring chisel is best used in this way, its length allowing greater control.

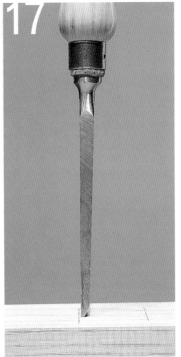

Using a mortise chisel

17 The mortise chisel must be held at the correct angle to the work.

18 The correct stance for holding the mortise chisel and the mallet, ensuring that the chisel is correctly positioned and angled.

19 Side view of this stance showing the work firmly secured to the bench.

Using a cranked paring chisel

20 Pare away surplus adhesive using a cranked paring chisel.

assembly, this glue will be easily removed by the careful application of the corner of the chisel. A cranked paring chisel enables you to pare across the depth of even a fairly wide carcass.

There may be times when you want to use a chisel with a mallet or a soft-faced hammer. Although this technique allows you to remove waste relatively quickly, you will pay for this with the inevitable loss of control, since it is difficult to ensure that the chisel is held at right angles to the surface of the wood.

Mortise chisels One example in which this is not necessary is when using a mortise chisel. Although mortises are almost always cut either on the machine or with a router, they can be cut by hand using a mortise chisel and a mallet. To do this, support the board above the bench leg, hold the mortise chisel with a straight arm, and use a flat-faced joiner's mallet, again with a straight arm. This stance, as you stand at the end of the bench and face down the length of the board, enables the chisel to be drawn back along the length of the mortise, levering out the waste and at the same time siting the chisel and ensuring it is kept at 90° to the board.

HAND PLANING ACROSS END GRAIN

Quite often a sawn surface needs to be planed back to exact dimension along the grain, using a bench plane as previously described, or across the grain, using either the bench plane or a small block plane. If you are using a bench plane, it is necessary to set the board up in the vise of your bench with the end grain facing up. Larger components such as carcass sides can be treated in this way because they give enough support to the larger and heavier bench plane. Bench planes have a certain amount of weight and mass and this weight is valuable in driving the plane through the cut. It may be necessary for you to plane in from both sides, but if that is not possible take a small 45° paring or backing cut to help prevent breakout.

Using a block plane

For smaller components it is possible to use a block plane. This is a small plane used with one hand and is especially designed for use on end grain lumber. The block plane is designed with a very low cutting angle of between 13 and 19°. Many planes of this type have an adjustable throad. This should be set very close to the blade, probably no more than 1/64 in. (0.4 mm) away from the end of the cutting iron. Unlike bench planes, block planes are honed and sharpened with the edge straight across rather than slightly rounded, and so a shaving made with a block plane is a shaving created using the full width of the blade. Set the block plane with a sharp, well-honed iron set to cut a fine shaving and you will find that planing end grain becomes straightforward and pleasant work.

LEFT *A small block plane used for cutting end grain*

TOP *Sawn end grain prior to being planed*

ABOVE *A 45° angled cut to prevent breakout on the end of a board*

Using a bench plane

1 Before using a bench plane to finish the end grain on a large board, first set up the component vertically in a vise.

2 The plane blade needs to be sharp and finely set.

3 Use a shooting board to cut and square end grain or long grain.

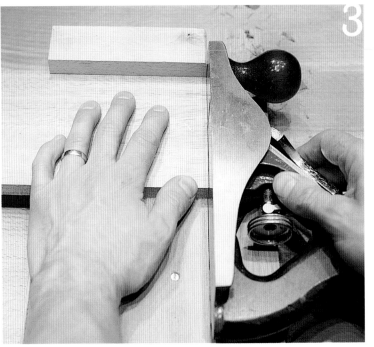

Using a shooting board

When planing small components it is possible to use a jig called a shooting board. This is a bench accessory that can be either workshop made or bought from a manufacturer. A shooting board is clamped to the bench top and a bench plane is run down the length of the shooting board on its side. The workpiece is supported at right angles to the plane and held against a stop at one end of the shooting board. In this way small components can be trimmed extremely accurately and with great control. Shooting boards can be used to trim either the end grain of a component or the long grain. Shooting boards are especially made for working on small components, probably less than 15¾ in. (400 mm) in length.

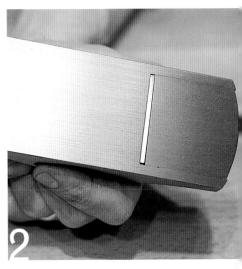

FOUR **BASIC TECHNIQUES**

CUTTING TO LENGTH

Much of the marking and cutting of joints is carried out with the material slightly longer than finished size, but there comes a time when the piece has to be accurately dimensioned in its length. This section explains the ways in which this can be carried out with various machine tools. However, it is possible to undertake this operation by hand, using the sawing and end planing techniques shown previously.

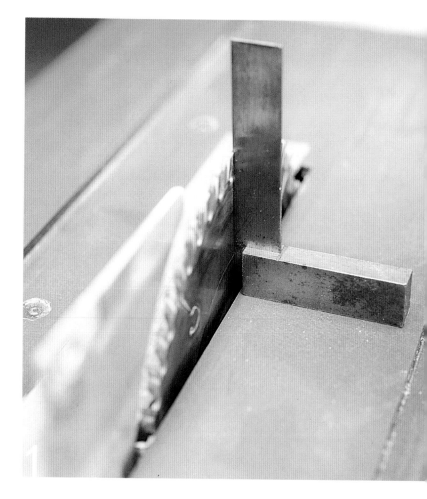

Crosscutting with saws

Table saw A table saw is the most commonly used machine for sawing a component to length. It is essential that a table saw is first set up square in both directions. A small engineer's square is used to check that the saw blade is exactly at right angles to the table of the machine, and that the crosscutting attachment is also running at a true 90° to the blade. Alternatively, you could check this against a perfectly planed square of plywood. When you use the crosscut attachment it is common practice first to attach a false fence. This is trimmed by the blade of the table saw and then provides a perfect reference surface for locating your board on the miter gauge (not illustrated here) or sliding table fence. It tells you exactly where the saw will cut and also provides back-up to the workpiece, helping prevent breakout at the back of the cut.

Bandsaw Crosscutting can also be done on the bandsaw. If set up correctly, this can be a very accurate machine, but the surface of the cut is slightly coarser than that of the table saw. Set up the miter gauge and the relationship of the blade to the machine table in exactly the same way as with a table saw. If the board is trimmed slowly and carefully, highly accurate and clean work can be achieved using a bandsaw.

Radial arm saw The radial arm saw is a common machine in commercial workshops but is less often found in the home workshop. It is included here because it is specifically designed as a crosscutting saw. With this machine the saw is drawn across the board and cuts through not only the rear fence but also very slightly into the table upon which the board is supported. Because the blades used on radial arm saws are specifically designed for crosscutting, you tend to get a very fine finish straight from the saw. Radial arm saws can also be used with a stop on the back fence to enable a number of components to be cut to a predetermined length.

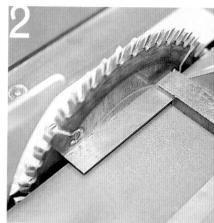

Using a table saw
1 Check that the blade is at 90° to the table surface of the saw.

2 Check, too, that the sliding fence is at 90° to the blade.

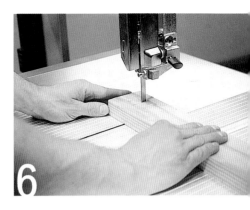

3 Fix a false fence to the miter gauge.

4 Trim it to make a good reference surface for your work.

5 The fence indicates where the saw will make its cut.

Using a bandsaw

6 You can also use a bandsaw to cut across the grain, ensuring before use that the bandsaw is set up accurately at 90° to the machining table.

7 Careful use ensures an accurate cut.

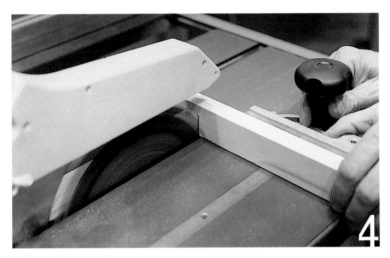

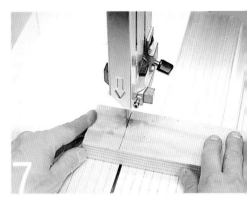

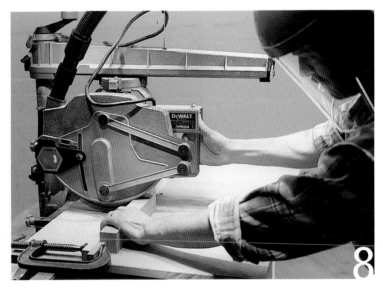

Using a radial arm saw

8 Crosscutting is also possible with a radial arm saw.

Using a router

9 Another option is to use an electric plunge router to groove across the grain.

Other crosscutting machines

It is not necessary to have large machines to trim components to length. A circular saw or a router can also be used for this task. It is necessary to clamp a straight scrap of wood at right angles across the board and to guide the saw or the router using that fence. This technique is especially useful when cutting dados across the insides of carcasses to accept shelving components.

THE ROUTER

A small ¼ in. (6 mm) router is one of the most versatile power tools a woodworker can possess these days. It can be used to dimension lumber, to cut joints, and to decorate and create moldings. The most important facility is the accuracy provided by using a router. Routed surfaces are dead square, dead flat, and perfectly accurate.

Routers can do the job of many of the tools or machines that you do not already possess. For example, a router can function as a saw, creating truly straight edges at perfect right angles to a face side. To do this, you need nothing more complicated than a long guide fence which can be placed on your project at equal distance from the edge that you wish to plane and cut dead straight and true. Another feature of a router is that it can create a curved surface, simply by being guided along a curved rather than a straight fence. (The curved template can be created using a bandsaw and finished using a compass plane or spokeshave.) This curved template or fence can then be used to create a number of curved components, each with exactly the same curve routed on them.

Once you have your face edge, you can create a parallel surface using the side fence provided with the router. This guides the cutter along a line you determine exactly parallel with your existing face edge. For work of this kind it is best to use a straight cutter of suitable size. Never plunge and cut more than the overall diameter of your cutter. If you are using a ⁵⁄₁₆ in. (8 mm) diameter straight bit you would cut ¹³⁄₁₆ in. (21 mm) lumber using three passes. If routing an edge as described above, it is best first to trim to within sight of your line using a handsaw or a bandsaw, and then to finish off the cut with the router, rather than attempting to

clear a lot of waste and create much dust and noise using your router.

Bear in mind that the router spins in one direction and that you should always have the router bit turning into the edge or moulding that you are cutting. In this way the fence of your router will be pulled up against the edge rather than being pushed away.

Rabbets, dados, and mortises

Rabbets can be cut away using a router cutter fitted with a guide bearing. This guide bearing runs against the portion of lumber underneath your rabbet and guides the cutter. It is not good practice to run a rabbet of this kind all in one cut; instead make two passes, the second pass being a fine, light, cleaning-up cut.

It is possible to create the same rabbet using a simple straight cutter and the side fence provided with the router. In this case the side fence would be running against the edge of your board.

Dados can be created relatively easily by setting up a router with a suitably sized straight bit, and setting up a long fence in a suitable position, parallel with the gauge marks of the dado, and then guiding the router against this fence.

RIGHT *View from above of a router in use. Ensure the router bit is turning into, rather than away from, the edge that is being cut*

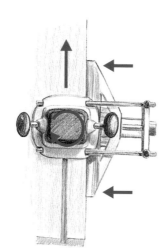

FURTHER INFORMATION

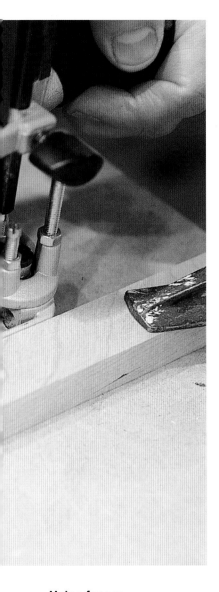

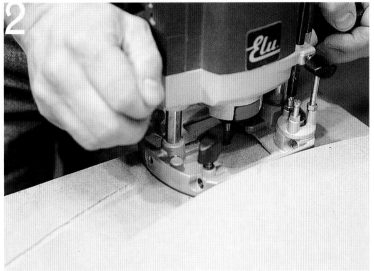

2 Using a router with a curved fence to make repeatable curved shapes.

3 Cutting a groove using the router's own side fence.

Router cutters
4 A router cutter with a guide bearing.

5 This guide bearing guides the cutter against the edge of the lumber to cut a rabbet.

6 A cutter used for producing shaped moldings.

7 The router cutting along the length of the lumber as before.

Using fences
1 Using a straight fence with a router to cut an accurate line, a given distance from the fence face.

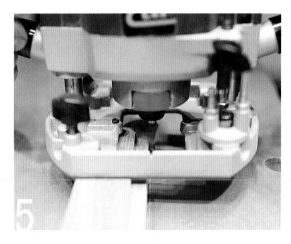

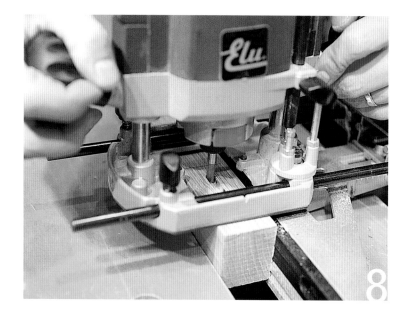

Mortising is usually done with a mortising machine, but failing that, a router can be used to cut small mortises. This is easily achieved on relatively wide stock, but on narrow stock it is often necessary to pad out the sides of a rail with a piece of scrap lumber on either side. This gives a suitable platform upon which a router can stand. The router is then guided off the side of components using the side fence provided with the router.

Moldings

One of the most common uses for a router is to create moldings. This can be done with a wide range of cutters creating decorative shapes and forms, from a simple rounding over cutter to a decorative and classic ogee. Cutters are guided either by the side fence or workshop-made template or jig, or by a bearing or pin situated on the cutter itself. Occasionally, a decorative cutter will have two sizes of bearing. This effectively enables the cutter to cut two moldings from one cutter. Large scribe and stick molding cutters are sold in pairs, most commonly for molding the frame of frame-and-panel kitchen doors. These create a molding around the door and also create the joint between the stile and rails. As these are relatively large cutters, a large router is recommended for use with them, preferably one with a ½ in. (13 mm) collet and that is table mounted.

Routing mortises

8 Cutting a mortise on a reasonably wide component.

9 If the component is narrow, use some extra material on both sides to give a suitable platform.

Routing rabbets

10 Making a rabbet using the side fence.

The router table

Routers can be used in various ways upside down in a router table. This enables the work to be taken to the router rather than the other way around. Bear in mind when using a router table that the direction of the rotation of the cutter is reversed and work should be fed into the cutter, usually from the right-hand side. Router tables are especially useful when molding or machining small components. It is not necessary to buy a commercially made router table as you can easily make one in the workshop that will probably function far better than those commercially available.

Using the router table

11 A router inverted under a router table, showing the projecting cutter and the safety guards.

12 Feeding the component over the router cutter against the side fence, with the shore guard giving downward pressure.

Template rings

Template rings are another means of guiding the router. These are rings that fit around the cutter and rub against your chosen template or fence. This system effectively enables you to control exactly where a router will cut, with great variety and considerable accuracy. For example, the technique allows you to cut a template from a scrap piece of particle board—this can be of any size or shape, it could even be a hole or negative shape. The template is placed upon the job and a template ring fitted to the router. The ring rubs against the edge of your template and the cutter routes out the shape in your job proportionately. The degree to which the job is larger than the template is a result of the relationship between the cutter and the template ring. Either of these can be changed to achieve the result you require.

Template rings

13 The template ring and the router base—the ring is fixed by the machine screws to the base.

14 Use the template ring against the edges of the aperture cut in the template to give the required profile.

DRILLING, MILLING, AND MORTISING

A frequent operation in woodworking is to make various sizes and types of holes in the components in order to make joints, fix various fittings, and so on. Simple hand tools are frequently used to attach items such as hinges or catches, as well as to make repetitive joints such as mortise and tenons.

Drilling

Many of the light processes can be carried out using hand tools and one of the most useful is the hand drill or wheelbrace. A twist drill bit is inserted into the chuck, which is tightened by hand. You need to mark accurately where the holes are needed, ideally marking the center of the proposed hole with an awl or a punch, since twist drills need this location when the hole is started. If you have many small holes to drill, a light electric drill is useful, preferably battery type, so that you have flexibility in the way you approach the work.

If you have many holes to drill a most useful machine tool is a drill press, either bench or floor mounted. They usually have a range of speeds to suit various materials and drill bits and accept adapter kits, including a mortise attachment and sanding drums.

Most operations can now be carried out with the above tools, but larger holes were originally cut using a hand brace with a series of bits. These are still useful in the workshop, especially if your range of machine tools is limited.

Mortising

A mortise machine is the most common tool for making square holes or mortises. A mortise bit is effectively an auger surrounded by a square, hollow chisel. The auger cuts slightly ahead of the chisel, and the four corners of the chisel pare out the square corners after the center circle has been removed. In order to use this machine, a considerable amount of downward support has to be exerted to pare out the four corners. This is why mortise machines have very long handles to give added leverage to the downward pull. However, it is possible to pull too hard and force the mortise bit into cutting too quickly; this causes waste to clog up inside the cutter, driving the center point offline and causing overheating and burning. Mortises therefore need to be cut steadily but firmly.

FURTHER INFORMATION

**Drills and mortising
machines**   44

The router   72

Drilling by hand
1 With the work held in the vise, ensure that the wheelbrace and twist drill are at the correct angle before drilling.
Position yourself so that you are looking directly down over the work in a straight line.

2 Turn the handle, ensuring that when starting to cut, the center of the drill remains in the correct position on the work.

3 A simple depth stop can easily be made by wrapping some masking tape around the drill bit.

Mortise bits need to be sharpened with great care. A reamer especially designed for the brand of cutter is set up with a metal plug that fits onto the end of the reamer and also fits the size of chisel being used. The reamer sharpens the inside of the chisel and is used in a hand-operated drill. It should not need too much pressure. The outside of the chisel needs to be honed and the cutting surfaces of the auger should be filed and stoned.

Mortiser adapter kits can be purchased for drill presses; these function relatively well but can be slow and tedious to use. A drill press or a conventional electric drill fitted into a drill stand is a very useful piece of equipment that allows a drill to be presented to the work at 90° and a cut to be taken to a pre-determined depth. Always make sure that a guard is present on a drill press and always be careful to take the chuck key out of the chuck when a bit is removed.

Milling

Although care must be taken, it is also possible to use a cross vise with a drill press to create a woodworker's milling machine. In this case a router bit would be set up in the drill press and the drill press set to run at its fastest speed. Although router bits are designed to work at much higher speeds than a drill press can provide, they can function, although rather clumsily, in this way. Be careful to take cuts very slowly and gently, taking away only as much as the cutter will allow. In this way the side cheeks of tenons can be milled flat, rabbets can be cut, and even small moldings can be worked on small components.

Drill press
4 Drill press in use with the guard in place.

Mortising machine
5 A mortising machine in action showing the chisel making a cut in work which is securely held by waste stock and a clamp.

6 The square hole produced by the mortise bit.

7 Detail showing the auger within the square hollow chisel of the mortise bit.

Milling
8 Another way of cutting a mortise is to use a horizontal mortiser.

9 A slot mortiser effectively cuts mortises.

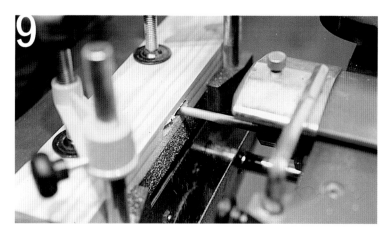

SHAPING, BENDING, AND LAMINATING

Curved shapes and components can be created in a variety of ways. It has been described in an earlier section how a router is used to make these, but there are other power tools that can help put the curves into your woodworking.

Shaping with saws

Unless you buy a particularly powerful jigsaw you will find yourself limited to working with thin board material or lumber of a thickness of 1 in. (25 mm) or less. Although technically a jigsaw will cut a thickness of more than 1 in. (25 mm), it will not do so very accurately. The jigsaw is mostly used to rough out a shape, probably cutting just slightly shy of your guideline.

Scroll saws are much more involved pieces of equipment. An intricate design can be worked using a scroll saw and, because of the fineness of the blade, the surface created is of a polished and burnished nature. Quite often, scroll saws slightly burn and blacken the wood as they cut, but it is usual not to attempt to clean up the surface left by this saw.

Bandsaws are extremely versatile for curved work. You are limited only by the throat of your bandsaw and by the size of your bandsaw blade. Quite often a relatively large bandsaw will take a very small ¼ in. (6 mm) band which will enable you to cut quite tight curves. The table of the bandsaw can also be tilted should you wish to cut a curve at a 45° angle or less. In this case, compound curves within intricate shapes can be created.

A bandsaw or a jigsaw will usually saw a shape shy of a marked line. To finish to the line, your options are either to use hand tools such as spokeshaves or compass planes, or to use a spindle sander fitted in a drill press. The spindle sander will provide you with a clean, curved surface at 90° to your face side.

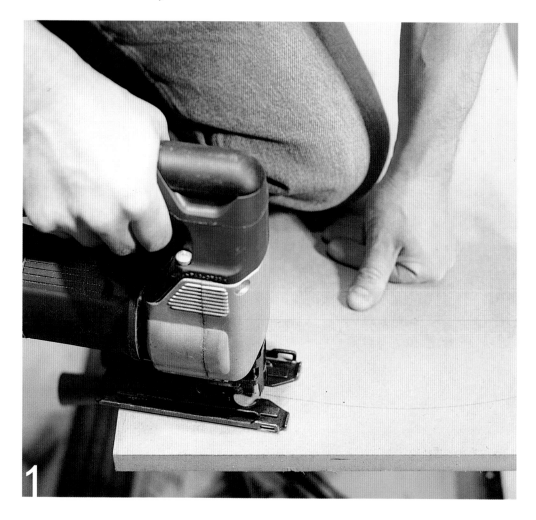

Hand tools like spokeshaves and compass planes require considerably more skill to operate as they will be cutting into and out of the grain of the timber and so demand great awareness of the material by the craftsperson.

The Arbortech

The Arbortech is a comparatively recent invention that employs the same kind of cutting edge found on a chain saw but in the form of a small circular cutting wheel. The Arbortech is used in conjunction with a small portable grinder and enables large amounts of waste material to be removed in a relatively controlled manner. Arbortechs are, however, potentially very dangerous pieces of equipment if used without the proper guard. Even when set up properly they should always be used with some caution.

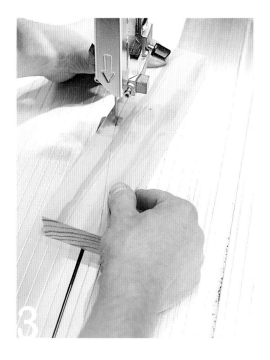

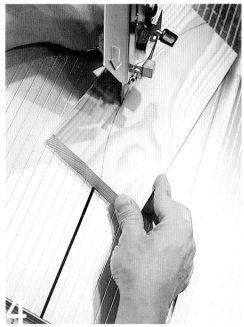

Shaping components using saws

1 The jigsaw is a useful tool for cutting curves prior to cleaning up the cut edges.

2 Cutting very fine curves on a scroll saw.

3 Similarly, the bandsaw can be used for cutting curves.

4 The angle of the bandsaw table can be tilted to provide more shaping options.

5 Spindle sanders are available in several different diameters. The one shown here is used in a drill press to finish bandsawn components.

Shaping with a sander

6 A bench-mounted belt-and-disc combination sander can be used to shape components once the bulk of the waste has been removed with a saw. Here a convex curve is being shaped and sanded.

7 Sanding a concave face against the end roller.

8 Using a disc sander with table and protractor to trim to the precise angles necessary for miter joints.

FURTHER INFORMATION

FOUR **BASIC TECHNIQUES**

Shaping, bending, and laminating 79

Bending and laminating

One of the limitations of working with wood is that curved components may create areas of weak, short grain that could very easily split or crack. Two of the ways that have been developed to overcome this inherent weakness in wood are steam bending (a wet method) and laminating (a dry method).

Steam bending Steam bending is used very widely in the Windsor chair-making industry. Here a 1¹¹⁄₆₄ x 1¹¹⁄₆₄ x 78⁴⁷⁄₆₄ in. (30 x 30 x 2000 mm) component is heated in a steam chamber for 1–1½ hours. During this process the wood absorbs the hot steam and acquires a flexible, bendable nature. While still hot and flexible, the component is taken out of the steamer and very quickly bent around the required shape—or "former"—similar in this instance to that of the back of the Windsor chair. It is held on the former and allowed to dry and cure overnight, then cooled; this completes the first stage of drying. The component is removed from the former and kept under tension so that it does not spring back. It is then hung to dry out completely. This second stage of drying may take some weeks. Steam bending equipment is not commercially available. However, workshop-made equipment is widely used and consists very largely of a steam chamber made from 4 in. (102 mm) PVC pipe, which may need to be insulated to retain heat, a source of steam in the form of a kettle or boiler, two bungs, and two sections of tubing.

Laminating A dry and more controllable method of bending, although one that involves considerably more work, is laminating. This is achieved by taking a shaped former—not unlike that used in steam bending—and wrapping thin flexible strips called laminates around the former. The laminates can be made using ¹⁄₁₆ in. (2 mm) thick constructional veneers, available from a specialty veneer supplier, or they can be cut on the table saw using a ripsawing blade. The laminates are coated with glue on both

sides, then bent around the former and secured in place using a forest of clamps. The clamps are necessary to hold the laminates in close contact with both the former and one another. If you do not use enough clamps you will have gaps between the laminates that will cause unsightly glue lines. Once the glue has

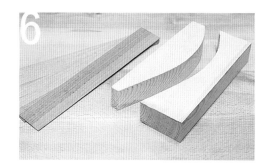

cured, which takes at least one day, the clamps can be removed; the laminated component will now hold the shape of the curved former. The squeezed out glue can then be removed with a sharp plane, leaving the finished laminated piece with little or no visible evidence of how it has been curved.

Laminating

6 Constructional veneers or thinly ripsawn material is used for the laminates. The male and female molds are cut from solid wood.

7 Apply the adhesive to both sides of the laminates. The excess glue squeezes out as the mold is closed with bar clamps.

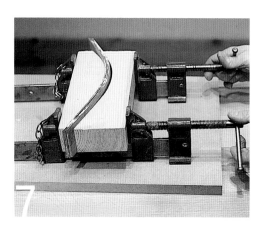

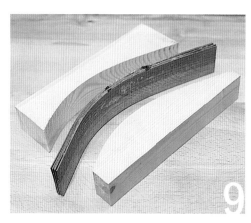

8 In order to achieve consistent pressure throughout the stock, use clamps on the top side when finally tightening the mold.

9 When the adhesive has cured, remove the cramps. The laminate will stay in its formed shape.

10 The final result is a curved component in which the laminates are barely visible once the edges have been cleaned up.

Fittings such as handles, knobs, catches, latches, and hinges used to be available from any hardware store. Nowadays you need to plan ahead and almost invariably order your hardware through a specialty catalog. This could offer, for example, several types of hinge, each available in different sizes and probably one or two metal finishes. There are plenty of options, too, when it comes to handles, and these can radically affect the style and look of your project.

    This section is therefore not comprehensive but offers an introduction to some of the types of fittings available and guides you through the process of fitting both brass butt hinges to a conventional door and self-closing hinges, most commonly used in kitchen cabinets.

HANDLES AND PULLS

Knobs and pulls, cabinet handles, and drawer handles can be a furniture designer's nightmare. They are the means by which the designer lends style and distinction to the piece of furniture, yet the temptation is always to leave them until last. By doing this the designer limits him or herself to increasingly narrow choices and options.

There is a vast range of styles of knobs, handles, and drawer pulls, available from shops or catalogs or which can be made—carved or routed—in your own workshop. The choices fall generally into two categories: first, knobs or handles which are applied and second, drawer pulls or handles which are incorporated into the design of the piece.

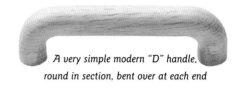

A very simple modern "D" handle, round in section, bent over at each end

A more traditional arch-type handle

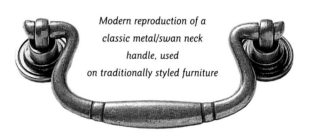

Similar in style to the top one, but with a more complex section giving interesting detail

Modern reproduction of a classic metal/swan neck handle, used on traditionally styled furniture

ABOVE *A series of applied long handles showing a range of styles*

Applied knobs or handles

These are surface mounted, usually with a dowel or mortise or quite simply with a screw fitted from the back of the door or drawer. There are infinite styles of these knobs or "D" handles. Aesthetically, they always run the risk of looking like an afterthought and quite frequently they are exactly that—an afterthought which has been applied to a cabinet without due care and consideration. Had the choice been made a little earlier you would have had the option of using drawer pulls or handles which are incorporated into the design and structure of the piece of furniture.

Incorporated pulls or handles

Handles that are incorporated into the furniture are not necessarily complex but certainly effective. In the Linenfold Cabinet by David Savage, illustrated below, one door overlaps the other and a small finger hold has been routed into the edge of the outer door near the top to allow a grip on the door to open it. This is the simplest of handles but nevertheless extremely elegant and very effective. Similar finger holds may be routed in the bottom edges of drawers, creating visual interest as well as having a practical purpose.

Some designers make use of finger plates. These are invariably workshop-made and lend style and a point of visual focus as well as being useful in preventing finger marks on frequently used door stiles.

LEFT *Here a small finger hold has been routed into the edge of the outer door near the top (Linenfold Cabinet—David Savage)*

Handles made using a router

Router cutters are available for cutting recesses into drawer fronts, door stiles, and rails. They are almost invariably used with a template and a profile ring to guide them to form the shape of the finger hold required.

Another type of routed workshop handle is that produced by using a router to create a curved molding at the back of an applied handle. This is evident in David Savage's Cherry and Sycamore Cabinet, below. Here, quite simple applied handles were cut out and shaped with a router in a soft "finger friendly" curve. The handles are made in a contrasting wood to that of the drawer fronts both to accentuate the design, and to tie in with the wood used for the carcass sides and for the cock beading around the edges of the drawers.

LEFT *Four different types of knobs, the shapes and materials varying from very simple to quite complex*

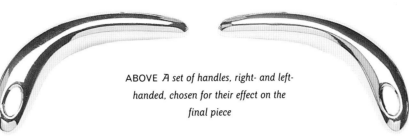

ABOVE *A set of handles, right- and left-handed, chosen for their effect on the final piece*

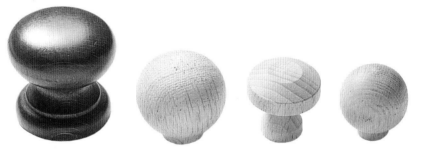

LEFT *An interesting and unusual modern handle*

ABOVE *A traditional drop handle that will add elegance to a period piece of furniture*

LEFT *Another range of simple wooden knobs which could be made in your workshop if you have turning facilities*

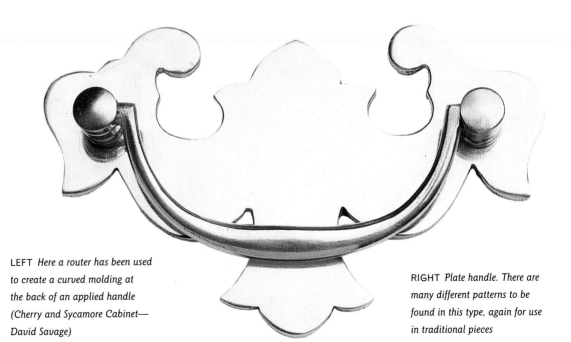

LEFT *Here a router has been used to create a curved molding at the back of an applied handle (Cherry and Sycamore Cabinet— David Savage)*

RIGHT *Plate handle. There are many different patterns to be found in this type, again for use in traditional pieces*

DOOR STOPS, CATCHES, LATCHES, AND HINGES

Often the furniture-maker will not wish to emphasize these fittings, but will be concerned that they serve their function effectively and discreetly; in a few cases, however, they may be chosen to enhance a particular period or style. Spend some time choosing the most appropriate type of fitting for your work from the huge range available.

Types of door catch

Some form of latch or catch is required to hold a door closed. One of the earliest types of latch was a wooden Sussex or Suffolk latch. These are wooden sneck catches operated either by lifting a small wooden bar which goes through the door and raises the latch or similarly by putting a finger through a hole in the door to lift the latch. Frequently seen in Britain on old wooden pub doors, this type of latch is very simple and could be applied to any type of door.

Bolts may be used where the closing stiles of two doors meet; almost invariably one door is held shut and the second door closes against it. Brass surface-mounted bolts are very popular. These will fit neatly on to the edge or the back of a door and catch in a fitting attached to the carcass.

Magnetic catches are another way of holding a door closed and come in many forms. The most widely available are, sadly, the most ugly—small magnetic discs set in relatively large blocks of white or brown plastic. A neater and simpler solution is a small magnetic barrel which fits into a hole drilled in the front surface of a carcass divider or on the edge of the carcass itself, leaving only a small black disc visible. An equally small metal plate is fitted to the inside of the door and is attracted to the magnetic surface of the catch. The pull of the catch can be controlled, if necessary, by fitting the striking plate slightly off-center.

Ball catches are another option and comprise two opposing balls which are each fitted against spring resistance. The balls capture a brass fitting which is attached to the

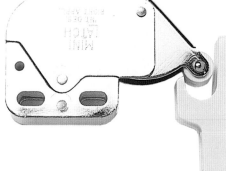

LEFT *A magnetic catch—a very simple and unobtrusive type of catch. The magnet fits firmly into a hole, while the plate is held by a pin*

RIGHT *A push latch, also called a touch latch or pressure-to-open latch, is used when you do not want anything showing on the outside*

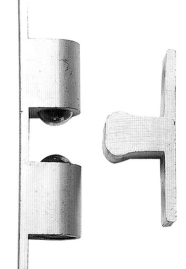

LEFT *A brass ball catch that can be adjusted to ensure it fits well*

RIGHT *A turn latch – an example of a fitting made to be seen for effect*

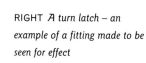

RIGHT *A surface-mounted bolt— one of the simplest types of bolt, available in several sizes, different metals, and various types of finish*

door. Making this fitting work smoothly requires some patience. You may find the fitting on the door requires filing and the springs which hold the balls against the door catch may need adjusting for tension.

Push latches are popular where you don't want an exterior handle, for example, on a cabinet door. A small plastic fitting is attached to the back of the door. When the door is pushed firmly inward the catch allows the door to move inside the cabinet by ³⁄₁₆–³⁄₈ in. (5–10 mm). The door is then thrown forward by a spring mechanism within the catch which enables you to get a hold on the corner of the door and open it.

Hinges

The simplest hinges to fit are called drill hinges. These simply require two holes to be drilled—one in the carcass and one in the edge of the door. The most commonly used hinge is the butt hinge, the fitting of which is described in the following section.

Soss hinges are far more complex and sophisticated types of hinge. They require special routed recesses to accommodate the completely concealed hinging mechanism.

Finally, one of the most common hinges used today is the surface-mounted, self-closing hinge used by many cabinetmakers. This hinge has the benefit of being relatively straightforward to fit and, once fitted, allows the position of the door to be adjusted in all directions.

BELOW *Surface-mounted self-closing hinges are very useful for doors in fitted and larger cabinets*

Drill hinges are very simple to fit and the style can vary from simple to ornate

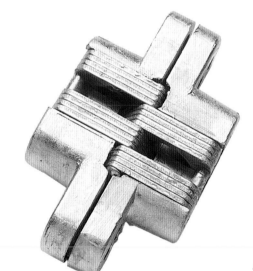

BELOW AND LEFT *Soss hinges are available in sizes ranging from the fairly large ones shown here to small neat ones that fit into drilled holes. Their main feature is that they are invisible when closed*

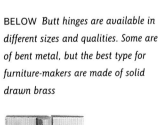

BELOW *Butt hinges are available in different sizes and qualities. Some are of bent metal, but the best type for furniture-makers are made of solid drawn brass*

Door stops, catches, latches, and hinges

FITTING BUTT HINGES

It is essential to use good-quality solid drawn brass butt hinges. Some work may be required on the hinges before they are fitted to the cabinet. They will certainly need polishing, first with 180 and then 320 grit silicon carbide paper, and then with steel wool. Before using, check that the edges of the hinge are square and also check the action of the pivot. Stiff hinges should loosen up very quickly but loose hinges should be discarded.

Normally doors are fitted inside a carcass opening so they will first need to be shot in order to fit the opening exactly. The hinges can then be positioned on the edges of the door. Check that the position of the pivot is going to allow the door to swing open far enough. This positioning is a critical part of the process and you may find it is best achieved by drawing an enlarged cross-section of the position of your hinge and working out how the door will open and how far back it will go. You should certainly spend a little time on this before you actually start chopping out the hinge recess.

Awls and screws

Marking the position of the screws is critical for successful hinging. This is best done on small carcass hinges with a bradawl or a birdcage awl. The latter is a square-bladed bradawl, having four faces which come to a very sharp point. The point locates the position of the screw in the center of the hinge screw hole. Once

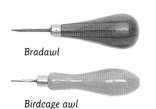

Bradawl

Birdcage awl

LEFT *Awls are used to mark the position of a screw and, then with smaller screws, to make a pilot hole*

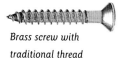

Brass screw with traditional thread

Steel screw with double thread

marked, the bradawl is driven in to create a pilot hole for the screw. Having four cutting faces, it can very quickly create a hole or be used to modify an existing one which is slightly out of place, simply by leaning over with the tool. In this way a misplaced screw can be repositioned slightly as necessary.

When fitting hinges with brass screws, never attempt to do the job without a duplicate set of steel screws of the same size. These are used during the fitting process because brass screws are softer and would invariably break off or become damaged. Instead, position the hinge and fit the steel screws. If all is well and the door is fitting nicely then, and only then, fit the more expensive and more attractive brass screws.

Positioning and marking

1 On a frame-and-panel door position the top of the upper hinge level with the bottom of the upper door rail. Similarly, the bottom of the lower hinge is traditionally positioned in line with the top of the lower rail. Use a pencil and square to begin.

2 Position the hinge on the door edge, and mark precisely with a knife.

3 Set a marking gauge to the dimension from the center of the pivot of the hinge to the back of the flap.

4 Gauge a line on the edge of the door between the cut lines.

5 Use another marking gauge if possible or, if not, readjust your gauge to the distance between the hinge face and center of pivot and gauge a line on the face of the door.

Making the recess

6 Cut out the recess by first sawing a start cut where the edge of the hinge will sit, then pare up to this. This prevents your chisel from overshooting the recess and damaging your door.

7 Carefully chisel out the waste so that the

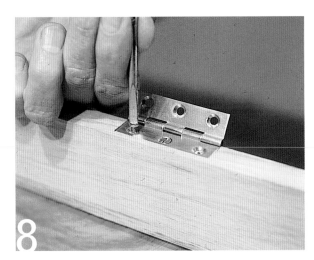

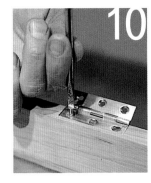

hinge will fit exactly into the recess.

Fitting the hinge

8 Fit the hinge first using a set of steel screws.

9 It is best to lubricate brass screws before use, using wax, candle wax, or petroleum jelly.

10 Fit the brass screws.

11 Once the hinges are fitted offer them up to the carcass and mark the corresponding positions. Mark the position of the screw for the center hole of the hinge flap. Insert a steel screw.

You might find it helpful while working with your lower hinge to secure the upper hinge temporarily by driving an awl into one of the holes for the screws.

12 Make a knife line around the hinge and cut out the recess as before. Make any adjustments necessary and use the steel screws first. Once the door has been hinged it may be necessary to take a few more shavings from around the edge of

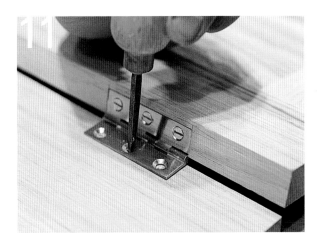

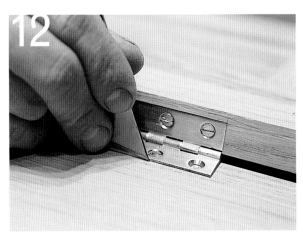

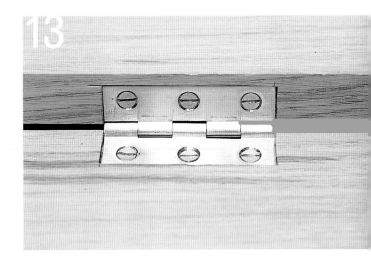

the door in order to get an even clearance all around. This is best done after fitting the hinges. You will find the hinges will need to be on and off a few times before the fitting is completed.

13 Only when the hinge is fitted to your satisfaction should you use the set of brass screws.

Fitting butt hinges

FITTING SELF-CLOSING SURFACE HINGES

The great advantage of surface-mounted doors, as used in kitchen cabinets, is that they are much easier to fit than doors fitted inside a carcass opening. One of the most convenient, if not the most elegant, solutions to hinging a surface-mounted door is to use the self-closing surface hinge, also known as the concealed cup hinge.

Choosing your hinge

When choosing the type of cup hinge to use you must first determine whether the door is going to be a full overlay—overlapping the carcass, as in the case of a single cabinet door, half overlay—where two doors meet at the center of a frame member, or inset—where the door fits inside the carcass. All three positions are possible but each requires a different version of the same hinge, so be careful when ordering your hinges.

Fitting the hinge

1 Using a special drill bit drill a shallow hole on the inside of the door.

2 Once the recess has been cut it is remarkably straightforward to fit and screw the hinge in place.

Attaching the door

3 With the rear part of the hinge now in place offer up the door to the carcass. Mark the position of the screw holes using an awl.

4 Remove the rear part of the hinge and screw in position. Then remount the door and adjust. The hinges generally have the advantage of a three-way adjustment, which makes it

possible to locate the door position precisely. This is especially useful when hanging a series of doors where it is important to line them all up exactly and make sure there is an even gap between the two closing stiles.

SIX **FINISHING**

The purpose of finishing is to enhance and protect wood. Finishes vary in their performance; some are hard wearing, some very durable, and others easy to use. No finish will suit all criteria in every circumstance and inevitably the final selection will be a compromise. Probably about 30% of the total length of time required for the project will be spent on finishing. You may find that local cabinetmakers and salesmen in paint and finishing departments will be helpful in advising you on a particular finish.

PREPARATION

The time spent on preparation should never be skimped, since thorough work will ensure that the beauty of the wood is shown to the full when the final finish is applied. Experiment on scrap before finishing the actual piece to check whether the color and luster are as intended.

Paper type		Hardness	Cost	Application
	Garnet	Poor	Low	Unfinished lumber
	Aluminum oxide	Fair	Medium	General
	Silicon carbide	Good	High	Hard lacquers, etc.

Abrasive materials

Abrasive paper The coarseness of paper is denoted by a number—various grading systems are used for different types of paper. For aluminum oxide and silicon carbide papers the grades most used by cabinetmakers are 80, 100, 120, 150, 180, 240, and 320 grit. The three main types of paper that cabinetmakers use are garnet, aluminum oxide and silicon carbide (see table).

Steel wool Steel wool is available in nine different grades from "5" at the coarse end, for stripping, to "0000" at the fine end for cutting back and final finishing. It is very resistant to clogging and will follow the contours of even the most complex molding.

Sanding

Hand sanding For sanding by hand, a cork sanding block will ease the task and increase the life of the paper. Always sand with the grain. It is best to work up through the grits, sanding with finer and finer grades: start at about 100 and go on to 150 and 240 grit.

As a final touch use a piece of worn, fine grit paper to take the edge off any corners. This is known as "arising" or removing the arises.

Mechanical sanding Mechanical sanders can be used but they do have drawbacks. Belt sanders are aggressive and can quickly sand through veneers, or gouge work; orbital sanders, by their design, sand across the grain for most of their cycle. The

advantage of mechanical sanders, however, is speed, which may be worth a small sacrifice to quality.

Final preparation

Work-piece and workshop The working area should be warm (59°F/15°C), well lit and ventilated. The piece and the workshop should be thoroughly cleaned and vacuumed. Get as much dust out of the grain and pores as possible, particularly where dark and pale woods are side by side. All traces of wax and silicon used to lubricate tools during construction must also be removed.

Clear an area for your finishes, making sure that you have plenty of rags, mixing sticks, and containers at hand—disposable graduated cups are ideal.

Handling Apply the finish in sequence: start with corners and undersides, and finish up with the primary surfaces. Check if any areas require masking first.

On complex pieces it may be easier to finish the components before final assembly. Mask off glue surfaces first. Lightly wax the components before assembly and remove any excess glue once dry.

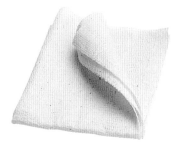

LEFT *Wire brush for texturing work*

BELOW *Tack cloth for removing sanding dust prior to applying a finish*

ABOVE *Two different grades of steel wool and a special proprietary flexible sanding block*

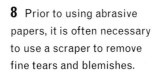

8 Prior to using abrasive papers, it is often necessary to use a scraper to remove fine tears and blemishes.

9 When using an orbital sander move it up and down the work-piece in overlapping parallel strokes.

Applying grain filler
1 Applying a grain filler with the grain.

2 Grain filler must also be applied across the grain to ensure an even application.

Three ways to sand a molding
3 Using a piece of abrasive paper, press into the shape with your fingers.

4 Use a flexible sanding block that will adjust to the molding shape.

5 Wrap some abrasive paper around a piece of dowel to follow the curve.

Other sanding methods
6 Wrap a strip of abrasive paper around a cork sanding block and use it to sand with the grain, working through the grits of paper.

7 Sand edges with abrasive paper, again ensuring you sand with the grain. Take care not to round over sharp corners or edges unintentionally.

Using a sanding machine
10 Sanding an edge, with the work safely held against a fence on a horizontally mounted belt sander.

11 Here the belt has been set vertically and is being used with a table and a miter gauge to sand end grain.

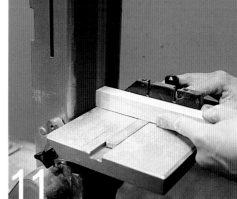

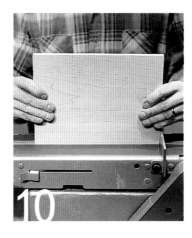

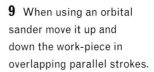

MATERIALS AND METHODS OF FINISHING

Having prepared your surfaces carefully, it is now time to select and apply the finish most appropriate for your project.

Lacquers, oils, and waxes

Lacquers Lacquer and varnish and are collective names for clear finishes. There is a huge range of products and, unfortunately, not enough room to describe them all.

The lacquers mentioned can be subdivided into two: solvent based and water based. Solvent-based lacquers are more traditional and perform marginally better. Water-based lacquers are more pleasant to use and generally safer. All the finishes here will give a high-quality finish and are available in gloss, semi-gloss, and satin lusters.

Wetting out Water-based lacquers sometimes raise the grain—to overcome this problem try "wetting out." To do this, damp down the piece with water to intentionally raise the grain. Leave it to dry and sand down the risen grain. Repeat the sequence once or twice: on each subsequent occasion less grain should rise.

Brushes and rubbers To apply the lacquer either use a soft brush or make up a disposable rubber from folded cotton. Spraying is an alternative technique, but more equipment is necessary and set-up times are longer.

Application of pre-catalyzed cellulose lacquer This is a good general-purpose subtle finish. It is a forgiving method and mistakes can be easily rectified by cutting back and reapplying the lacquer.

First thin down the lacquer: one part base coat to one part thinner. This helps to distribute the solids evenly and to stop the tell-tale ridge marks left by brushes.

Next apply two coats with a soft brush: once the first coat has dried (only a few minutes), cut back with 320 grit silicon carbide paper. After the final coat cut back with 0000 grade steel wool. Last, apply a thin coat of wax and buff with a soft cloth.

Lacquer	Protection	Durability	Ease of use	Repairability
Solvent based				
Pre-catalyzed cellulose	3	3	5	5
Acid-catalyzed melamine	4	4	3	1
Polyurethane	5	5	5	4
Water based				
Acrylic	4	4	4	1
Polyurethane	4	4	4	1

On a scale of 1 to 5, 5 = best; 1 = worst

French polish This is a traditional finish with a highly polished appearance. French polishing is a laborious and skilled technique which has evolved into a specialized trade. The main types of French polish are all based on shellac, a resin derived from an insect secretion. Nowadays a more common use for shellac is as a sanding sealer and as the base for a wax finish.

Oils Oils are very quick and easy to use; they offer only moderate protection from heat and moisture but are exceptionally easy to repair. The level of protection is in direct proportion to the number

These examples of a range of different finishes show the wood (oak and pine) before and after treatment.

Clear teak oil

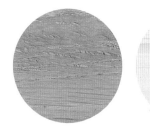

The natural wood: oak (left) and pine (right)

Teak oil—a blend of oils that dries with a slight sheen

of coats; at least six coats are required for maximum moisture resistance. A disadvantage of oils is that they tend to attract dirt.

Application of boiled linseed oil To aid penetration into the wood thin down to 1:2 mineral spirits to boiled linseed oil. Apply liberally with a rag or brush. Leave for 15 minutes and with a new rag clean off the excess oil and burnish. A light application of wax can be put on top of the oil to improve the sheen.

Waxes A beautiful finish but, used alone, wax gives almost no protection from heat or moisture and will also give a fairly dull finish. More protection and a richer effect can be achieved if it is used over a base of lacquer or oil. Traditionally, furniture wax has been a blend of beeswax and turpentine, sometimes with extra ingredients such as carnauba wax to improve its performance.

Applying lacquer

1 Applying a first coat of lacquer with a brush.

Applying polish

2 Make a disposable pad wrapping a wad of cotton in a piece of cotton sheet.

3 Use the completed pad to apply a finish, normally a shellac-based polish (used in French polishing) or an oil.

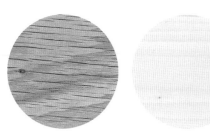
Danish oil— a blend of oils and resins that offers good protection and dries hard

Boiled linseed oil—this is faster drying than raw linseed oil

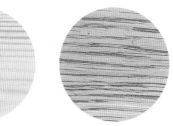
Medium oak wax

Tung oil—a hard-wearing oil, used in other blends to improve resilience

Clear wax

Dark beeswax

Lime wax Lime wax is used to emphasize the grain and give a lighter overall effect. It is only really effective on open grain woods such as oak and elm. Apply the lime wax as shown here. If the first attempt is unsuccessful, go over the work lightly with a wire brush to open up the grain, which allows more wax to be left behind. On close grain woods such as maple, the wax will not penetrate the pores and the effect is limited to crevices and corners.

Color

Dyes and stains There is a long history of staining furniture with bright colors. Colored furniture will fade over the years, which is part of its charm. Dyes are available in powder, alcohol, and water-based forms and can be mixed with others in the same range. The colors do not penetrate deeply so care must be taken not to sand through the stain when finishing.

Fuming Some timbers will darken when exposed to ammonia fumes—the effectiveness of the process varies from species to species. The color will depend on how long the wood is exposed to ammonia fumes: for a very dark brown the ammonia will have to be changed several times.

To fume a piece of furniture, either make a temporary fuming tent from clear plastic or modify a cupboard by blocking up all the ventilation. Place the piece inside with a shallow dish of ammonia and check the color periodically.

Bleaching Bleaching makes wood paler. The two-pack bleach commonly available consists of a solution of caustic soda and hydrogen peroxide, and is effective to varying degrees on a wide variety of woods. The extent of the color change depends on the wood and the number of applications. Oxalic acid is a milder alternative. It is also a good reviver of wood and will remove many stains, including iron, ink, and water.

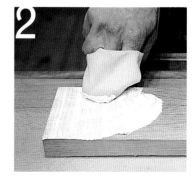

Applying lime wax

1 Before applying lime wax, first rub the wood with a coarse grade steel wool or wire brush to open up the grain.

2 Apply the lime wax with a cloth, rubbing it well into the grain and crevices.

3 After 5–10 minutes remove the excess wax with a hard cloth.

4 Finally, polish with 0000 grade steel wool.

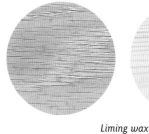

Liming wax　　　　*Verdigris wax*　　　　*Gloss acrylic water-based lacquer*

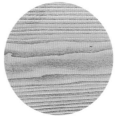

Black patinating wax　　　　*Dark tan shoe polish*　　　　*Satin acrylic water-based lacquer*

Texture

Textures are an alternative way of emphasizing the nature of wood. Instead of giving it depth by fine finishing, the intention is to bring it into relief by picking out the grain pattern. By their nature such surfaces are more difficult to clean so they are generally restricted to pieces that are not constantly handled.

Sandblasting Sandblasting wood quickly wears away the softer fibers to create an effect similar to driftwood. The surface quality will depend on the grit type and the power of the machine. Interesting effects can be made by masking off areas.

Scrubbing Scrubbing some woods with caustic soda will pick out the grain like sandblasting but without leaving hard edges. Again, the effectiveness of the process varies between species. The scrubbing solution is very caustic so take adequate safety precautions.

Scorching Lightly scorching wood leaves a very smooth and soft texture on even the roughest of woods. It is very quick to achieve, and can be used on any wood, even when unseasoned. It is particularly applicable to rough carving and more sculptural work

Color washing

5 Apply a colored stain with a brush.

6 Then cut back with 0000 grade steel wool to allow more of the natural wood color to show through and soften the effect. A coat of clear wax or varnish can then be applied.

Scorching

7 Scorch a piece of softly grained wood with a blow torch.

8 Remove the charred wood and carbon deposits with a wire brush prior to polishing and burnishing.

as the grain is lost and the form emphasized.

Scorch the wood with a gas blow torch, preferably one where the heat of the flame is concentrated in a small area. Use a plant water sprayer to extinguish any areas that begin to smolder. When the piece is thoroughly blackened, apply black boot polish and burnish with a hard cloth.

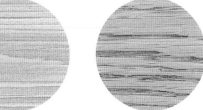

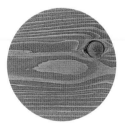

Blue alcohol-based wood stain   *Blue acrylic wood dye*   *Walnut acrylic wood dye*

Two-part bleach   *Clear wax applied to scorched oak (left) and pine (right)*   *Oak that has been fumed*

Materials and methods of finishing   95

SAFETY

The materials used in finishing need to be treated with respect. Most manufacturers will supply on request an information sheet on each of their products. This will give you health and safety advice, as well as useful information on other aspects of the material such as coverage and curing times.

LEFT It is advisable when using most finishes, especially those that may be toxic, to use a barrier cream to protect your hands

Principal hazards and personal protection

The principal hazards are: first, toxic finishes—in vapor, raw, or cured form; second, caustic finishes—in vapor or raw form; and third, flammable finishes—in vapor, raw, or cured form.

Personal protection is of paramount importance and includes the following considerations.

Eyes A face visor or goggles gives basic protection from splashes into the eyes.

Lungs Respirators, ranging from single- and double-cartridge to full-face battery-powered ones, offer protection from air-borne contamination, which is often unseen.

Skin Rubber gloves are an obvious protection. These can vary from thin surgical gloves to industrial rubber gauntlets. Another invaluable protection is barrier cream, since many finishing materials can cause dermatitis. In addition, wearing a rubber apron and boots provides further protection from caustic material.

FURTHER INFORMATION

Workshop precautions

Ventilation The main precaution to take in the workshop is to have good ventilation. As long as toxic and flammable fumes are removed from the work area hand finishing does not require a sophisticated extraction system.

Storage Many finishes are flammable or toxic and should be stored accordingly. If finishes have been decanted from their original containers make sure that they are clearly labeled with warnings.

Disposal Keep a drum for waste chemicals and do not throw unwanted material down the drain. Contact the local authorities to find out what chemical disposal provisions have been made in your area.

LEFT Suitably dressed for using some of the synthetic resins, with a face visor and respirator, a rubber apron, and heavy industrial gauntlets

BELOW For some jobs thin surgical gloves are sufficient

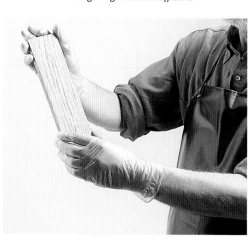

Learning to make joints by hand is a rewarding process. It instills a sensitivity and understanding that will not be lost even if machinery is later introduced into the workshop.

A series of basic joints is described here, and each is then followed by a project that makes use of the technique.

It would be advisable to practice the joint concerned before moving on to the project. Hard-woods are easier to work with than softwoods for quality joinery and are recommended for practice and projects alike.

LAP JOINTS

The lap joint is a basic joint which has little structural integrity. It is dependent on glue for strength and may be reinforced with screws or nails. The shoulders of the joint do, however, impart rigidity to frame work.

In high-quality work, the mortise-and-tenon joint would normally be employed except for intersecting frame members where the lap joint is the only option.

The most common use of the lap joint is in softwood joinery and construction work where it is used with nails or screws. The joint works best in straight-grained wood, which allows the waste to be chopped out quickly and accurately. Straight grain is also important for strength. The joint removes half the thickness of the stock, so the remaining wood must be free of defects or short grain if the strength of the frame is not to be compromised.

For making any joint it is important to follow through the sequence on both parts of the joint at the same time; that is, mark out both parts of the joint, cut all the shoulders, and so on. This way, if you are making several joints, the work proceeds in a consistent way. You will get into the rhythm of each operation, and the job will be both quicker and more accurate.

Possible variations of the basic joint

Corner ("L") and cross- ("X") lap joints are both developments of the T-lap joint. In the case of the L-laps, both parts of the joint are identical.

The process for the X-lap uses the same marking technique as for the first part of the T-lap shown opposite, but this time on both pieces of wood.

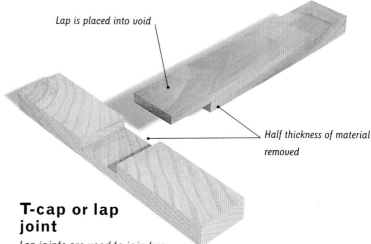

Lap is placed into void

Half thickness of material removed

T-cap or lap joint

Lap joints are used to join two members of the same thickness by removing half of the thickness of each, and placing the material left in position to fill the void that has been cut away.

Useful tools & equipment

One of the advantages of the lap joint is its application in site work, where it can be easily made using just a few tools. A hand miter saw with depth stop is useful for cutting the shoulders accurately.

In the workshop the bandsaw, bench saw or radial arm saw may all be used to cut laps. The bandsaw can be quickly set up to cut effective joints, and the radial arm saw, fitted with a dado head, is appropriate for production situations. As always, however, for "short runs" the time spent setting up a machine must be balanced against the time it will save over an alternative method.

Pencil

Try square

Marking gauge

C-clamp

Tenon saw

Striking knife

Chisel

Glue and brush

Smoothing plane

Constructing a T-lap joint

Marking out

1 Using a sharp pencil and a try square, mark two lines across the first component the width of the wood which is to be let into it.

2 Mark a line around the end of the second piece. The distance from the end of the wood is the same as the width of the first piece.

Ensure that the handle of the square is held firmly against the wood so that the blade is perpendicular to the work. Remembering to work from the face side and face edge, use the square to mark the line on the two edges.

3 Set the cutting gauge to half the thickness of the wood. Check this on a piece of scrap wood of the same thickness by marking from each side.

4 Mark the sides of the joint on both parts. Shade the parts to be removed. (Note: some woodworkers may wish to use a marking gauge in these operations.)

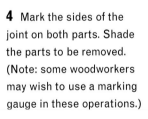

SEVEN **JOINTS AND JOINTMAKING**

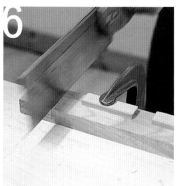

8 Start from one side and begin cutting about ¹⁄₁₆ in. (2 mm) from the top of the wood, with the chisel pointing up slightly.

Return to the first component and repeat this process until, in small increments, you reach the gauged line. This line acts as a guide for the chisel on the final cut. Turn the work around and repeat the process.

Cutting the shoulders

5 To cut the joint, the work must be securely held by C-clamping to the worktop. On the first component the shoulders of the joint are cut using a tenon saw. A start for this cut may be made by scoring a line with a striking knife and carefully chiselling a "V." However, with a bit of practice this may become unnecessary.

6 Repeat this process with the other piece of the joint. On the second component saw the shoulder on the end.

Removing the waste

7 After making this crosscut, use a sharp chisel to remove the waste, using a series of shallow cuts. Waste from a lap on the end of a rail may be removed either with or across the grain.

9 When complete, there will be a slight hump in the cheek of the joint which may now be pared off level using the chisel. (Alternatively, the waste may be removed by sawing or using a router.)

Assembly

10 Fit the two parts of the joint together. Some fine planing may be required to ensure a snug fit.

Before gluing, prepare two small squares of scrap to protect the work from the C-clamp: hardboard is good, or anything similar.

Apply glue evenly to all of the meeting faces using a small brush (it can be helpful to clamp one piece of wood to the bench, the joint overhanging), and gently clamp.

When the clamp is on and some pressure has been applied, check that the shoulders are fully together, and finally tighten the clamp.

When the glue is almost dry, pare off the surplus with a chisel. This is a lot neater than wiping it off while it is still wet.

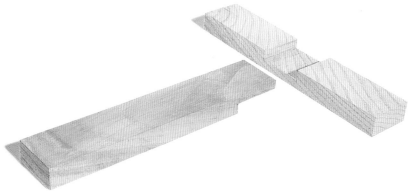

GLASS-TOPPED TABLE *see plan page 210*

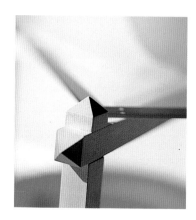

ABOVE *This shows the interesting effect achieved by the pyramid detail on the ends of the rails*

This small and decorative table is a relatively straightforward project which uses lap joints. Because the components are so small—1 in. (25 mm) square—it is important to use a relatively hard wood. The table shown here is made in North American maple, which is remarkably stable and very strong, but it could just as easily have been made in oak, cherry, or ash. Softwood and lighter, more springy wood such as walnut is less suitable, as the components would be more inclined to flex and give a slightly unstable structure.

The ends of the rails and the tops of the legs may be left square or planed into pyramid shapes as illustrated here. Once the glass is put in place in the wooden structure, triangular shapes are created throughout the design, and this pyramid detailing echoes and enhances the design theme.

The glass tops are ¼ in. (6 mm) thick, have ground and polished beveled edges, and fit squarely on the table frame. If preferred, larger pieces of glass can be used, positioned diagonally. The glass rests either directly on the finished wood or upon domed rubber stops, available from hardware stores.

FURTHER INFORMATION

CUTTING LIST AND MATERIALS

Component	Quantity	Finished dimensions
A Legs	4	18⅛ x 1 x 1 in. (460 x 25 x 25 mm)
B Rails	4	28¾ x 1 x 1 in. (730 x 25 x 25 mm)
Glass tops*	2	¼ in. (6 mm) thick
Suggested lumber		A and B—North American maple
Suggested finish		Wax, shellac or Danish oil
Alternative lumber		A hardwood such as oak, cherry, or ash
Notes		
*10 domed rubber stops (optional) on which to rest the glass may be used		

Tool list

Smoothing plane

Pencil

Try square

Marking gauge

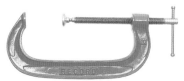

C-clamps and clamping blocks

Backsaw

Striking knife

Chisel

Mallet

Electric plunge router

Block plane

Abrasive paper and cork sanding block

Glue and brush

Bar clamps

TOP RIGHT *Detail showing the glass sitting on the rails, supported by rubber stops. Note the interesting contrast between this corner and the pyramid ends*

BELOW *A further detail of a lap joint used to join the cross rails*

BOTTOM *Another detail showing the subtle intersections between glass and frame*

Construction

Preparing the lumber

1 Having machined the components to dimension, remove all the machine marks made by the planer by skimming all of the surfaces with a smoothing plane. This is done at this stage because the lap joints need to be snug and tight, and if this cleaning up were done at a later stage there would be a risk of opening up an otherwise tight joint.

Marking and cutting the joints

2 Assemble the components on the bench and mark up the shoulders using a striking knife or pencil and a try square. Because there are two sets of four identical components, it is efficient and more accurate to mark up each set of four at the same time.

3 Having marked the positions of the shoulders, gauge the depth of each lap joint using a marking gauge. Your objective is to mark up, and then cut to your line, a joint that is slightly tight across its width so that with one or two shaves of the plane that tightness can be relieved.

4 You need to make sure that the backsaw (a large dovetail or a small tenon) cuts inside the waste but at "half mark."

If you are unsure of yourself, take the sensible precaution of first deepening the gauge line across your component by enlarging it with a striking

knife and then taking a small V-shaped paring with a chisel on the waste side of your gauge line. This gives an exaggerated "V" with one vertical shoulder and provides an accurate start to the sawing by enabling your saw to sit inside the "V" snug up against the vertical shoulder.

Removing the waste

5 Once you have sawn down each of the shoulders in turn, use a chisel to remove the waste material in between them down to the gauge line. Work from either side of the lap, paring slightly upward to eliminate the danger of going below the gauge line on the far side. You can, if you wish, do one or two saw cuts in the center of the waste of the lap to give you a "depth stop," or a sense of how near you are to the gauge line on either side.

6 When you have completed the paring of the bottom of the joint, you are ready to begin to fit it.

Alternative methods

7 Although the sawing and chiseling of a lap joint of this type can be a good exercise, you may wish to cut some of these components in one step using an electric plunge router. This will greatly reduce the time taken to make the project. Assemble your four identical components and clamp a board across them to create a guide for the router. In this way one shoulder is routed and the base of the lap joint

can be cut on four components with one machine setting. You may need to make two or three passes of the router to achieve the full depth of the joint.

To cut the opposite shoulder you could set up a second fence, or a less accurate option would be to move the first fence to a second position.

Ensuring a good fit

8 Now go for a trial fit. Because you have sawn or cut the shoulders slightly tight, your first attempt at fitting one component into the other may be unsuccessful. Do not force the fit; instead, using a bench plane, take a stopped

shaving off one or both sides of the right component.

9 By planing each side you will gradually open up the joint so do this carefully, one shave at a time, until you have a perfect fit.

Shaping the ends

10 Next, mark out the details for the pyramid-shaped ends which will be on all components except the floor feet. Take a pencil and draw a line ⅜ in. (10 mm) from the end or at your chosen depth, all the way around the base of each pyramid. Then mark a cross on the end of each component.

11 Remove the waste with a small backsaw and then plane the end grain down to the fine pencil lines using a smoothing plane or a small block plane.

Prefinishing

12 Since all the components will have been lightly planed before jointing, it should be necessary only to sand each component lightly prior to finishing. Start by using either a 120 or 150 grit backed by a cork sanding block. Then you could move through the finer grits to 180 grit. Maple is a very dense hardwood and will take an exceptionally fine finish, so if you have the time and the patience, sand right through to 320 grit. For all wood that has been skimmed with a hand plane, however, 180 grit—or possibly 150—is all that is necessary when cleaning up. Certainly for purposes of adhesion do not use finer than 240 grit if you intend to finish with coats of lacquer.

13 The light, contemporary look given by using maple can be retained when finishing this project by using a transparent rather than a yellowing finish. Wax is the easiest finish to apply and has the advantage of changing the color of the wood very little. Although it gives very little protection to the wood from finger marks or hot liquids, wax

could be used to finish this particular project since the glass surface will protect the wood to a degree. An alternative is to give the table frame a light sealing coat of transparent shellac or two or three coats of thin Danish oil.

Apply the finish with a cloth, taking care first to mask off all the areas of your joints that will be receiving glue.

Assembly stages

14 Plan your assembly as follows: the first stage of assembly will be the two cross frames, each of which has two rails. There is a lap joint at the center, plus another four, one on each end to accept the legs. Remember that these are in a different plane to the one that you cut at the center. Make the four legs, which will have two laps on each, one for the top frame and one for the center frame. Now work all pyramid ends. Try a dry assembly and if all joints look good, plan to assemble first the cross frames and then, when they are dry, the legs. The structure will then be complete.

For each joint apply a little glue to each component, covering all the meeting faces, then bring each joint together.

15 Apply a clamp to each joint as you form it, squeezing the clamp down until glue just comes out of the joint. Do not wipe it away but let it dry.

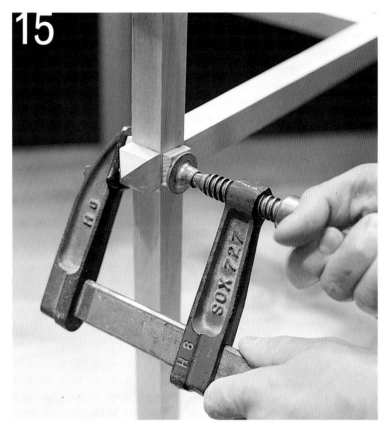

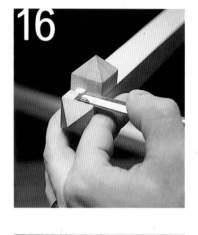

16 Because the exterior surfaces have been waxed or oiled, the glue will not stick very well and can be gently eased away with a small paring chisel.

17 Finally, fit the self-adhesive rubber stops—five on each shelf.

18 Place the glass on top to complete your table.

DOWEL JOINTS AND BISCUIT JOINTS

The dowel joint is a simple extension of the butt joint. In the butt joint, two flat edges or faces are simply glued together with no integral structure. In the dowel joint, dowels—short round pegs, normally made of beech but can also be metal or plastic—are fitted in the joint and contribute both structural strength and additional gluing area.

The dowel may be used in any frame or carcass joint that is not likely to be subjected to heavy stress. In such situations, the speed and simplicity of the dowel make it an attractive alternative to stronger, more complex joints.

Biscuit joints are a development of dowel joints. Instead of dowels, flat oval-shaped pieces of compressed beech are set in a slot, and the moisture of the glue causes the "biscuit" to expand, forming a strong joint. Slots are made with a biscuit jointer, a purpose-made portable machine, and are cut with a 4 in. (100 mm) diameter circular saw set in the machine. The jointer has a plunging mechanism, depth stop, and fence.

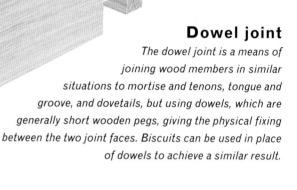

The faces to be joined

Holes drilled to accept dowels on both joint faces

Dowels positioned in holes in one face ready for assembly

Dowel joint

The dowel joint is a means of joining wood members in similar situations to mortise and tenons, tongue and groove, and dovetails, but using dowels, which are generally short wooden pegs, giving the physical fixing between the two joint faces. Biscuits can be used in place of dowels to achieve a similar result.

Possible variations of the basic joint

Both dowel joints and biscuit joints are highly adaptable and can be used easily in situations where other joints may be awkward, for example where angles other than 90° are involved. They also provide a viable alternative to the housing joint.

Useful tools & equipment

Doweling jigs can be bought, although they are easy to make in the workshop.

A drill stand or bench drill are valuable for making either the joints themselves or jigs. In production work, horizontal boring machines are used: a simple borer based on a horizontal drill stand could be constructed if a lot of doweling is anticipated. For dowel boring a spur drill bit produces clean results. The spur (center point) of the bit is easy to position accurately. The bit sizes match standard dowel diameters and are often sold with an adjustable rubber depth stop (although masking tape wrapped around a drill bit is an equally effective marker and makes a quick and economical alternative).

Center finders are marking aids comprising a shank the same diameter as the drill bit, a flange, and a center point. One part of the dowel joint is bored and center finders placed in the holes. The corresponding part of the joint is offered up and tapped with a mallet onto the center finders that mark the second set of hole positions.

Marking gauge

Try square

Pencil

Bench drill or electric drill on stand

Spur bit (with depth stop or masking tape)

Piece of plywood, approximately 3–4 in. (76–102 mm) wide x ¼ in. (6 mm) thick

C-clamps

Panel pins and hammer

Glue and brush

Countersink (drill) bit

Masking/parcel tape

Mallet

Constructing a dowel joint

Marking out

1 The goal in marking out dowels is to produce rows of corresponding center marks on two different pieces of wood. The face and edge of the joint are marked in the same way.

Set a cutting gauge to half the thickness of the stock; then run it along the end of the face part of the joint to make a center line.

2 Mark the intervals of the dowels across the center line using a small try square. The space between the dowels varies according to the size of dowel and type of work. For a 5⁄16 in. (8 mm) dowel the spacing may be 1 in. (25 mm) in frame work and 3–4 in. (76–102 mm) in edge joints.

Measure and mark the intervals on the face part of the joint only. Extend the

pencil mark right to the end of the workpiece.

3 Scribe the intervals on the corresponding part of the marked piece. The cutting gauge is then run along the face of the end grain part of the joint to produce a center line.

5 The scribed marks are continued across the end grain of the piece using the small try square.

This marking method is applicable when the holes are to be bored freehand. However, if more than one or two joints are to be made,

it is quicker and more accurate to make a jig (see overleaf). Instead of using the gauge and pencil for marking dowel centers, you could use an awl or a center punch to make a precise hole at the cross point of the lines to ensure that the center lip of the drill locates in the correct position.

6 If you are not using a jig, now drill the sets of holes in each joint face. First drill the holes marked on the joint face on the face side of the wood, securing it on the bench with a C-clamp.

7 Insert the other piece in the vise and drill the holes in the end grain, positioning the drill accurately.

Making a jig for boring

8 This has two functions: it removes the need for a lot of time-consuming marking out and it guides the drill bit, thus increasing accuracy.

The jig is made from a length of wood the same thickness as the stock being joined. It is rectangular in section and the same overall length as the joint.

The narrow edge of the rectangle is marked out in the same way as a dowel joint with a center line and perpendicular marks

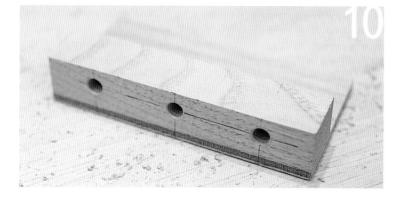

indicating the hole centers. Any inaccuracies in the jig will be transferred to the whole job, so it is essential to take care at this stage.

The boring is best done with a bench drill or electric drill on a stand. This will produce a clean, straight hole and, in turn, better

joints. The holes for the jig are bored with the same bit to be used for the dowels.

9 Metal stops are available for spur bits. These are rings that slide up to the required position on the bit and indicate when the correct depth has been

reached. This is equal to the depth of the jig plus half the length of the dowel plus 1/16 in. (2 mm) clearance. (Tape wrapped around the bit is an alternative depth marker.)

10 A piece of plywood the same length as the jig, 3–4 in. (76–102 mm) wide

and ¼ in. (6 mm) thick, is pinned and glued to the side of the jig. The plywood forms a clamping bracket to fix the template to the work.

Using the jig
11 Lay the face side part of the joint on the bench with the joint projecting over the edge of the bench and clamp it, leaving the joint area free of obstruction. Align the ends of the jig with the ends of the work. Fix the jig to the work with panel pins through the plywood or small C-clamps across the jig itself.

Double-check the depth stop against the work (see Figure 9). Hold the drill steady during boring: to prevent damage to the jig, do not start the drill until the bit is located in the guide hole.

Transfer the jig to the end grain part of the joint. The set-up is the same except that the jig is mounted at the end of the work-piece. The annual rings in the wood cause the

density to vary across the width of the board and a firm grip on the drill is required to prevent the drill bit from wandering.

12 Once drilled, either from the marking out or the jig, slightly countersink the holes—this aids alignment and accommodates any dust or excess glue.

Sticking tape up to the edge of each joint makes applying glue easier and aids cleaning up later. Apply glue to both parts of the joint, the holes, and dowels. Tap the joint together and clamp until dry.

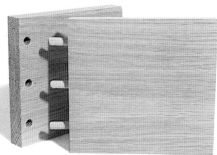

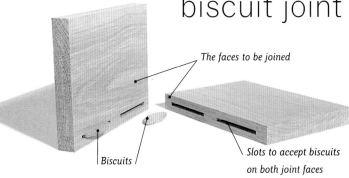

The faces to be joined

Biscuits

Slots to accept biscuits on both joint faces

1 The marking out of biscuit joints is simpler than dowels as the base plate of the biscuit jointer has preset center and end alignment marks. The joints need only be every 6 in. (152 mm). These are marked with a short perpendicular line.

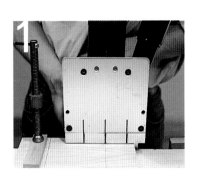

2 Hold the fence of the jointer against the face of the work and align the center of the base with the marked line. Plunge to the preset depth. For butt jointing repeat the process on the edge of the corresponding piece. For right-angle jointing, position the fence against the edge of the corresponding piece

and plunge the jointer to a preset depth into the face of the work.

Gluing and assembly is as for the dowel joint. The biscuit is made of compressed wood and much of its strength is derived from the grain direction being diagonal and the way it swells with the moisture of applied glue in the slot.

CD STORAGE BOX *see plan page 212*

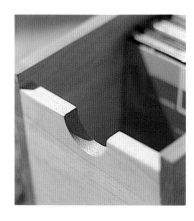

ABOVE *A detail of the front of the box, with the lid open, showing the finger hole*

This small hardwood box, designed to hold **CDs**, is a simple carcass construction with stopped (blind) doweled joints, although the dowels could be replaced by biscuits or pins. The rear sides of the box are cut at a slight angle so as to put more wood around the pivot point of the lid, which greatly strengthens the box at this point.

First select your lumber so that the grain of the wood runs horizontally all around the vertical surfaces of the box. Then accurately dimension the components according to the cutting list. Note for the front piece, however, that it will be easier to make the finger hole if this component is initially left slightly over depth. In addition, measure the width of the lid marginally narrower than the width of the base. This gives the lid some freedom of movement and enables it to open and close without marring the finish on the sides of the box.

Tool list

Square

Pencil

Rule

Drill with spur bit (with depth stop or masking tape)

Coping saw or drill press with Forstner or sawtooth bit

Block plane

Bar clamps

Glue and brush

Paring chisel

FURTHER INFORMATION

CUTTING LIST AND MATERIALS

Component	Quantity	Finished dimensions
A Sides*	2	$9^{21}/_{32}$ x $6^{7}/_{8}$ x $^{15}/_{32}$ in. (245 x 175 x 12 mm)
B Front	1	$5^{1}/_{8}$ x $6^{11}/_{64}$ x $^{15}/_{32}$ in. (130 x 157 x 12 mm)
C Back	1	$5^{1}/_{8}$ x $5^{25}/_{32}$ x $^{15}/_{32}$ in. (130 x 147 x 12 mm)
D Base	1	$8^{15}/_{32}$ x $5^{1}/_{8}$ x $^{15}/_{32}$ in. (215 x 130 x 12 mm)
E Lid	1	$9^{7}/_{8}$ x $5^{1}/_{8}$ x $^{15}/_{32}$ in. (251 x 130 x 12 mm)
Suggested lumber		A, B, C, D, and E—Maple

Additional material
Fluted dowel rod: $15^{3}/_{4}$ (400 mm) x $^{3}/_{16}$ or $^{1}/_{4}$ in. (5 or 6 mm)
diameter, cut into $^{19}/_{32}$ in. (15 mm) lengths

Suggested finish	Oil polish
Alternative lumber	Any mild hard-working hardwood such as cherry or walnut

Notes
*Whole dimensions given here—sides are in fact angled.

ABOVE *Detail of the top back corner, the rounded rear of the lid, and the slight angle on the rear of the two sides which provides extra strength around the pivot*

BELOW *Detail of a front corner of the box, showing the slight projection of the rounded front of the pivoted lid*

BOTTOM *Detail showing the angled sides which slope upward slightly from front to back*

Construction

1 The box will need to be assembled in two stages; first, the front and back will be doweled to the base, after which the sides will be doweled in position.

Marking the position of the dowels

2 Because the sides of the box are angled, at the places where they meet the back and the top of the box, note that you will be placing dowels in positions that are not parallel with the edge of the component. The square is therefore used to mark the position of the back on the side components.

3 Very carefully mark out the position of the dowels using a square and rule.

Drilling the holes

4 Drill the holes using a spur bit which will locate

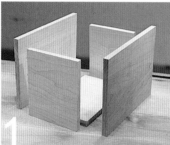

exactly on the intersections marking the positions of your dowels. It helps to use a drill with a depth stop that indicates the depth to which the drill should work, but be aware that this band can be pushed up the drill in use, giving an artificial reading. An alternative option is to use masking tape wrapped tightly around the drill bit.

Once the dowel holes have been drilled, check that they are in exactly the right position by doing a dry assembly. This can be done most effectively by using a spare set of the correct size dowels that have been slightly reduced in size by rolling them under a heavy weight. This enables you to put the job together, check that the holes are in the right position, and then take the job apart again relatively easily.

Cutting the finger hole

5 Next make the finger hole in the front of the box, using a coping saw. Alternatively, the hole can be easily cut with a ¾ in. (20 mm) radius Forstner or sawtooth bit used in a pillar drill. If this component has been left slightly over depth it gives a center point on which to locate the drill.

Once the hole has been drilled, cut the front component back to the required depth.

6 The finger hole can now be sanded to a finger-friendly shape, or the edge could be further shaped by a router fitted with a rounding over bit, working over those areas that a finger might touch.

Rounding over the edges

7 The round overs to the rear and front of the box lid are achieved by drawing suitable curves on the sides of the lid in pencil and then, using a small block plane, working a series of flats that approach each line step by step. When you cannot get any nearer to each line with a plane, use 120 grit abrasive paper backed by a cork sanding block.

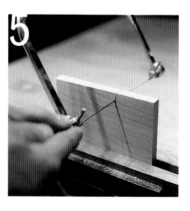

grit. Take great care at each stage to remove all of the sanding marks left by the preceding grit, especially the coarse 120 grit.

Use a finish that complements the wood—in this case an oil polish was built up in two or three coats. Take care to mask out those areas where glue will be applied.

Assembly

9 Now prepare to assemble the front and back to the base. This is best carried out with bar clamps as shown; the "rail" at the top is a waste piece, cut exactly to the inside dimension to ensure that the back and

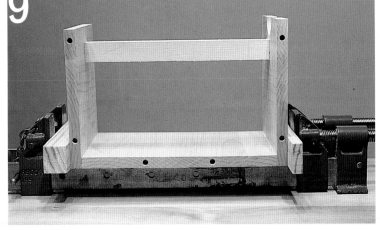

Prefinishing and finishing

8 Having checked that the project will go together, you can now begin the process of finishing the areas that cannot be easily finished after assembly: the inside of the box and the box lid and the back of the box. All these surfaces should be sanded down to at least 180 grit, going carefully through the grits from 120, through 150 and then finally to 180

can be positioned on assembly.

As you assemble the job make sure that your components are the right way around. It is easy in a moment of panic, when you are trying to work very quickly, to turn a component upside down and make a simple assembly procedure very complicated. To avoid this, it is useful to mark your components with small self-adhesive colored stickers so that each joint is color coded. Alternatively, you could label all your components A-A, B-B, and so on.

front stay parallel. It is not fixed and is simply removed when the glue has cured.

Do not worry about getting clamp marks on the outside of your components because you will be cleaning up the outside after assembly.

10 Now prepare to glue the two sides to the first assembly. Remember to fix the pivot dowels into the ends of the top so that it

11 Using small artists' brushes, put a small amount of glue on each of the gluing surfaces: a dab of glue in the dowel holes and a carefully painted smear of glue on the surfaces that butt up together. You do not want a lot of glue squeezing out or you will have to spend ages cleaning it up. PVA is recommended for this project, but it gives you less than 5 minutes of "open" time to do this job so it is quite critical that the glue is painted on very quickly and accurately.

Use bar clamps as shown.

12 Once the glue has set, you can carefully pare off those areas where glue has squeezed out of the joint.

Now clean up and finish the outside of the box: the two sides, the bottom, and the front. These should be hand planed and sanded to a fine finish and then polished in a similar way to the inside of your box.

Finally, if you like, you could line the bottom of the box with felt, leather, or suede so that the CDs may be placed in the box quietly.

MORTISE-AND-TENON JOINTS

The mortise and tenon is a strong joint used primarily in frame construction, though it can also be applied to carcass work. The mortise is the female part of the joint, the tenon is the rectangular part that fits inside it.

Since it is so strong the mortise and tenon provides the ideal solution when making frames that are liable to be used under stress. In table frames, for example, the main alternative is doweling, which is unlikely to stand the test of time. Good-quality door frames are usually mortise and tenoned and the joint is used extensively in production joinery.

The form of the joint described in the steps here is not the simplest but in a general sense is probably the most useful.

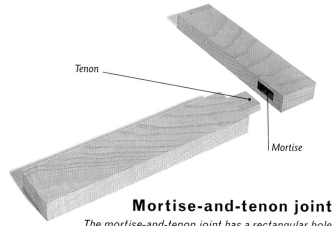

Tenon

Mortise

Mortise-and-tenon joint

The mortise-and-tenon joint has a rectangular hole in the edge of one component, called a mortise. On the end of the component that joins it a tenon is cut by removing material so that the remaining projection fits the mortise precisely.

Possible variations of the basic joint

There are different types of mortise-and-tenon joints, each appropriate in different situations. The through-wedged and pegged version, for example, is entirely structural and particularly appropriate for exterior joinery.

In carcass work a number of mortise and tenons may be used in a line, connected by a narrow housing the same thickness as the tenon. The interpre-tations of the mortise and tenon are virtually limitless and by applying the joint to new situations it continues to evolve.

Useful tools & equipment

The mortise-and-tenon joint lends itself well to mechanical production and a number of general-purpose machines can be used to speed up the work.

A drill stand will enable an electric drill to remove most of the waste from the mortise, leaving only the cleaning up to be done by hand.

Over recent years small bench-top mortisers have been developed. These are derived from the design of larger industrial models. A combination bit comprising an auger and a square-section hollow chisel are pulled into the work with a lever, producing a square hole. A series of holes are cut to make a mortise. A portable router fitted with an appropriate bit will also produce mortises very effectively.

A miter saw can be set up with length and depth stops to cut tenon shoulders. Radial arm, bench, and bandsaws can all be used, too.

Try square

Metal rule

Pencil

Mortise gauge

Mortise chisel

Marking gauge

Mallet

Bench dogs or C-clamps

Masking tape

Tenon saw

Bevel-edged chisel

Smoothing plane

Glue and brush

Bar clamp

Constructing a mortise-and-tenon joint

2 Mark the shoulders around the tenon with the try square. The length of the tenon is generally about two-thirds of the width of the rail. Start work on the face side or face edge and work round the piece, holding the square tight against the work for each side. If the last line meets up precisely with the first, the wood is accurately prepared and the tenon shoulders will be in line.

3 The width of the mortise is a little over one-third of the thickness of the rail. In practice this is rounded up to the next chisel size. The mortise gauge is set to the exact width of the chisel. This setting will also be used to mark out the tenons and the tool must be used carefully to avoid disturbing this adjustment.

Marking out

1 The mortise is marked first and its length must be determined. This will not normally be less than half the width of the rail. It is important that the mortise does not go too close to the end of the frame since it will be in danger of breaking out. For this reason a short extra length is often left on the piece, which is known as a horn, and is removed after assembly.

The mortise is often offset away from the outside, again to prevent it being too close to the end of the piece. In wider rails or T-joints it will be central.

Mark the length of the mortise across the wood with the try square. Mortise-and-tenon joints are usually cut in sets and the joints marked out in groups to ensure that all the mortises are in the same place.

Technique: Mortise-and-tenon joints

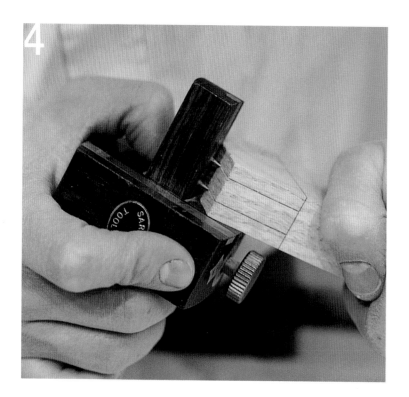

6 On the work itself, the gauge is used from the face side only. The grooves made need to be clear and stop at the pencil marks. If a number of mortises are being made, they are all gauged at this stage.

The width of the tenon is marked with the marking gauge in a similar way to the cheeks, but working off the face edge rather than the face side.

Cutting the mortise

7 The mortise is always cut first so that the tenon can be fitted to it later. Firmly secure the work in a vice or use bench dogs or C-clamps to hold the job.

Before beginning to cut the mortise, mark a line ⅛ in. (3 mm) in from the ends. This is an initial working

4 The mortise gauge is used to mark the position and thickness of both the mortise and the tenon.

On the piece that will have the tenon the mark is started on the edge of the rail, toward the end, along the end grain and along the opposite edge to the shoulder line. The gauge is held against the face side of the work.

5 When marking the mortise set the gauge to the center of the rail. This is best done on an offcut of stock of the same dimensions as the work. Set the mortise gauge approximately with a metal rule. Working from both sides of the offcut, adjust the gauge until the marks it makes are the same from either side.

line; once the mortise is to depth, the ends are trimmed to give a neat finish.

The first work with the chisel is a row of shallow cuts at intervals of about ³⁄₁₆ in. (5 mm). These must be at right angles to the sides of the mortise and act as a guide for the later stages of chopping out.

8 Work along the joint again with deeper and more positive cuts, and begin to lever out the chips as they become loose. The aim is to develop an action with the chisel that is firm but controlled, neither reticent nor likely to damage the work.

In the final stage it is helpful to stick a piece of masking tape around the chisel to mark the depth of the mortise. Continue chopping down until the required depth is reached, levering out the chips. The bottom of the joint can be scraped with the chisel.

9 Carefully pare back the ends of the joint with a freshly sharpened chisel. The lines marking the length of the mortise may be continued down the sides of the rail to provide a visual guide for the chisel and ensure that the ends of the mortise are vertical.

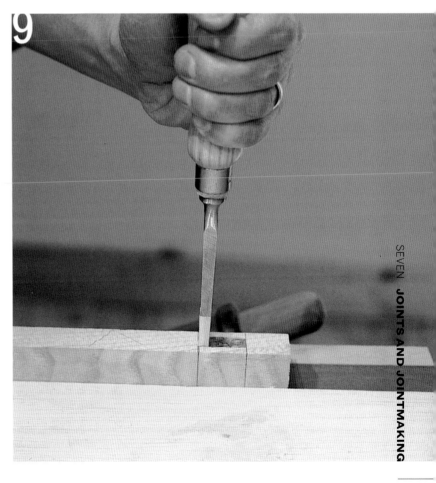

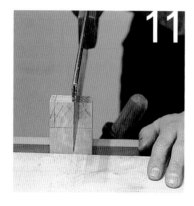

Cutting the tenon

10 The tenon cheeks are cut with the tenon saw. Set the work in the vise facing away from you at an angle of 45°. Cut down from the top corner along the end and face lines. Mark the area of waste to make sure that the saw cut is on the correct side of the line.

When the first two saw cuts have been made, turn the work around and repeat the process. As with all joints, efficient and accurate work is achieved through taking the time to get the job right the first time rather than having to make adjustments later.

11 Set the work vertically in the vise to finish the saw cuts. The diagonal cuts already made will guide the saw which is held horizontally. A few steady strokes will complete this part of the job.

Finally, saw the sides of the tenon.

12 The shoulders are also cut with the tenon saw. The work is mounted horizontally on the bench; bench dogs or C-clamps are best as they provide a positive hold. A bench hook is adequate but holds the piece of work less securely.

The saw cut is started at a slight downward angle and, once established, is leveled off. The process is then repeated on the reverse side.

To cut the shoulders in the edges of the rail, clamp the work in the vise. Start the cut by rubbing the saw blade against the long shoulders that have already been cut.

Assembly

13 Clean up any waste or slight unevenness in the shoulders with a chisel. Work from the edges into the middle of the joint to prevent breakout at the corners.

14 The end of the tenon may be chamfered all round at this stage to aid entry into the mortise.

15 Check that the joint fits on all four sides and that there is a small tolerance for trapped glue at the bottom of the tenon. Rails have been known to split when such an allowance has not been made.

The inside edges of the rails are planed to a finished surface as they will be inaccessible after assembly. This removes any pencil marks. Glue is applied to each surface with a brush and the joint clamped up with a bar clamp and allowed to dry under pressure.

The complete joint is then faced off with a smoothing plane used at an angle of 45° to the grain to prevent damaging the surface, and finished with either abrasive paper or a cabinet scraper.

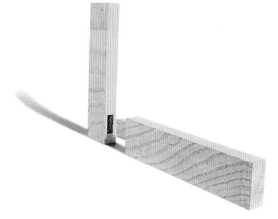

Technique: Mortise-and-tenon joints

WORKBENCH *see plan page 214*

ABOVE *Detail of a rail showing how the tenon protrudes through the leg and is held in place by a wedge*

The workbench is at the center of any woodworker's workshop. Even those who use machinery for much of the work will need a bench for making joints and finishing by hand. All too often, even in professional shops, the bench will be barely adequate and in poor condition. A bench that is well designed, however, will contribute to both the speed and quality of the work produced on it.

CUTTING LIST AND MATERIALS

Component	Quantity	Finished dimensions
A Legs	4	33 x 3¾ x 3¾ in. (838 x 95 x 95 mm)
B Rails	4	21 x 3¾ x 1¾ in. (533 x 95 x 44 mm)
C Stretcher rails	2	39 x 5¾ x 1¾ in. (991 x 146 x 44 mm)
D Top*	1	40 x 23½ x 1¼ in. (1016 x 597 x 32 mm)
E Apron	1	40 x 3¾ x ⅝ in. (1016 x 95 x 16 mm)
F Vise jaw	1	10 x 3¾ x ⅝ in. (254 x 95 x 16 mm)
G Vise packing	1	10 x 5 x 1 in. (254 x 127 x 25 mm)
H Wedges	1	14 x 1¼ x ⅝ in. (356 x 32 x 16 mm)
Suggested lumber		A, B, C, and H—Pine; D—Beech; E and F—Oak; G—Plywood

Additional material		
Cast-iron woodworking vise	1	7 in. (178 mm)
Coach screws and washers	4	2 x ¼ in. (51 x 6 mm)
Wood screws	4	2 x 3⁄16 in. (51 x 5 mm) (No. 10)
Wood screws	6	1½ x 3⁄16 in. (38 x 5 mm) (No. 10)
Wood screws	2	1 x 3⁄16 in. (25 x 5 mm) (No. 10)
Expansion plates	6	
Bench stop	1	
Wood screws	2	1 x 5⁄32 in. (25 x 4 mm) (No. 8)

Suggested finish	Finishing wax; polyurethane, if liked
Alternative lumber	Any tough, close grain hardwood

Notes
*The solid wood top is glued up from narrow boards, 4–6 in. (102–152 mm) wide. Allow extra thickness of ⅛ in. (3 mm) for final finishing after assembly.

Tool list

Try square

Metal rule

Pencil

Marking/mortise gauge

Brace or electric drill—twist bits/countersink: ⅝ in. (16 mm) auger

Masking tape

Mortise chisel

Tenon saw

Striking knife

Bevel-edged chisel

Smoothing plane

Jointer plane

Panel saw

Glue and brush

Bar clamps and clamping battens

Hammer

Screwdriver

Cabinet scraper

Fine abrasive paper

Mallet

Wrench

RIGHT *The benchstop, designed to raise from the bench surface and lie flat when not needed*

BELOW *Planks have been glued together for the bench top, the grain chosen to make it as stable as possible and prevent warping*

BELOW LEFT *A substantial metal vice with wooden jaws*

Construction

This project provides a sturdy, basic bench at the smaller end of the scale. The vise and bench stop, combined with a couple of C-clamps, provide a very wide range of clamping options. If space allows, the same design could be used to build a bigger bench between 5 ft. 6 in. (1676 mm) and 8 ft. (2438 mm) in length.

The construction is of solid wood. The pine base, with large mortise-and-tenon joints, provides a rigid structure, and the top is of beech, a tough and relatively inexpensive hardwood. An alternative for the top would be two pieces of 1 in. (25 mm) thick plywood screwed together. The front jaw of the vise is made of oak, as is the front apron, which forms the rear jaw of the vise and, with a C-clamp, enables long pieces of work to be secured.

A strong, medium-sized vise has been fitted with no metal exposed in the bench top, keeping it away from valuable tool cutting edges.

Incorporating a tail vise and a row of bench dogs would improve the scope of the bench, and specially designed hardware could be fitted to this design later. A shelf between the stretcher rails could provide storage.

A piece of hardboard or plywood the same size as the top is useful to protect the top when gluing or finishing. The woodworking vise may be protected for metalworking operations by removable aluminum jaws.

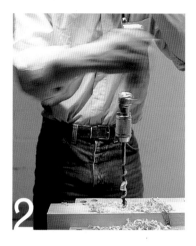

The base frame

1 Mark out the end frame mortise-and-tenon joints following the procedure described earlier. These tenons are simpler than those shown previously as the edges of the rail form part of the joint.

2 Removing waste from large mortises is best achieved with a hand drill. The slow action of the brace and bit makes depth control easy and a piece of masking tape can be used as a depth guide. An electric drill may be used, however, preferably on a drill stand.

3 Clean up the mortises with a chisel to true up the sides and square off the ends. Leave the mortises slightly shorter than the

tenon widths as final fitting is achieved by planing the edges of the rails to fit.

4 Cut the tenon cheeks with a tenon saw, holding the work securely to help produce a clean cut.

5 To cut clean shoulders, first cut a V-shaped groove using a striking knife and chisel. This provides a channel for the tenon saw and ensures accuracy when cutting the wide joints.

6 A final fit is made by planing the edges of the rails with a smoothing plane; check the fit at regular intervals. The tenons need to be a tight fit. Check the depth of the mortise against the length: there should be a gap at the

bottom of about ⅛ in. (3 mm). Do not glue up the end frames at this stage.

7 Mark out the stretcher rail mortise and tenons. These are through wedged joints so the tenons are much longer than normal.

The other main difference is that the mortise goes right through the rail rather than being stopped. Mark out the mortise in the normal way, then mark its length around to the opposite side of the rail using a try square.

Mark the width of the mortise with the mortise gauge, taking great care to run the gauge against the face of the work at all times. Shade the areas that are to be removed.

Mark the tenons—this time the shoulders run around all four sides of the joint. The small mortises that will take the wedges are marked out after the tenon is cut.

8 The through mortise is a simple development of the stopped mortise. The first stage of the joint is normally cut to about two-thirds of the thickness of the rail, then the rail is reversed to cut open the mortise. To true up the sides of the joint,

hold the work vertically in the vise and pare the waste back to the gauged line. Work from one face of the work, and then the other. Do not push the chisel all the way through as this could damage the joint.

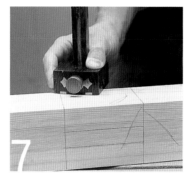

9 The length of the tenon is such that it cannot be cut with a tenon saw. A panel saw is needed to cut the cheeks and sides of the tenon. The technique is the same as that for the tenon saw. The size of the tenon and the flexibility of the saw mean that the accuracy of the cut must be constantly checked. If in doubt, cut to the waste side of the line and pare back with a wide chisel later. (An alternative method is to cut the tenons using a bandsaw.)

10 As with the end rail tenons, making a V-shaped groove to guide the tenon saw is advisable for cutting the shoulders. The action of the wedges pulling the shoulders against the face of the leg is what will keep the bench rigid, so they need to be accurate.

Cut the edge shoulders next and pare all the shoulders flat with a chisel. The through tenons need to

fit smoothly with very little play. Mark the position of the outside of the leg on the protruding part of the tenon.

11 Mark and cut the small mortises for the wedges in much the same way as the large leg mortises. They are 1 in. (25 mm) long and ⅝ in. (16 mm) wide. Position the mortises to extend ⅛ in. (3 mm) over the line that marks the outside edge of the leg so that when the stretcher rail and leg are assembled the mortise will be partially inside the leg.

To cut the mortises, clamp the work to the bench with a piece of waste wood

underneath the tenon. In this position the mortise can be cut from one side without the need to reverse the work. Remove the bulk of the waste with an auger or drill, then square it out with a chisel.

12 Plane the chamfer, with either a smoothing or jointer plane, holding the work horizontally in the vise. Chamfer all other long edges of the frame with normal straight chamfers of about ⅛ in. (3 mm). Chamfers remove sharp edges and splinters, as well as making the frame less susceptible to damage.

Assembly

13 Apply glue to the mortises and tenons and assemble the end frames.

14 Clamp the assembled frames with bar clamps. Clean off the excess glue when it has "gone off" but has not completely set.

Wedges

15 The wedges come from a strip of the same stock as used for the base and are made in pairs. This is easier than trying to work very small pieces of wood. Mark the tapered wedges on the outside edges of the legs using a straight edge. Mark a

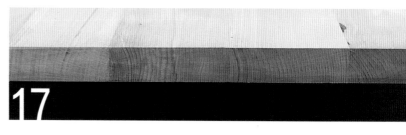

line from the bottom corner up to a point ⅝ in. (16 mm) in from the top corner. Draw a corresponding line on the adjacent face of the leg. Cut the wedges with a tenon saw then plane smooth.

16 Slide the stretcher rails into position and insert the wedges. Tap the wedges finally home with a hammer.

The bench top

17 Lay out the parts of the bench top so that the annual rings, visible on the ends of the boards, face in alternate directions. If possible, the grain in the individual pieces should run in the same direction to make facing off easier. In addition, try to arrange the boards to create visual balance and harmony. In practice it is difficult to accomplish all of this, and a

degree of compromise is usually required. Remember that in a bench top, stability is the main priority.

18 Prepare the individual butt joints on the edges of the planks chosen for the top; it is essential that they are planed to a perfect fit in order to give the glued joint its strength. If you decide not to use biscuits, tongues, or dowels, apply adhesive to the faces to be joined and clamp up.

22 Fit the top to the base using metal expansion plates. These are slotted to allow for wood movement, the slotted part being screwed to the top, across the width.

23 The bench is now substantially complete and the top is held flat and secure. In this position it can be planed. Facing off big panels by hand can be very rewarding. Prepare the jointer plane with a sharp iron and lubricate the sole of the plane with wax. Working at an angle of 45° across the top, remove thin shavings. Systematically cover the whole area and repeat until the top is completely flat.

24 Finish the top finally with a cabinet scraper and lightly sand by hand, using a fine grit paper.

19 If a biscuit jointer is available, biscuits may be fitted. These add strength to the joint and aid alignment, but the joint will be quite adequate without them. When prepared, set up the parts together with the clamping battens to check that everything fits and then glue up.

20 Wipe the excess glue off while it is wet: if a joint is to be planed after assembly, it is easier to remove any excess glue at this stage.

21 Provided the underside of the top is fairly flat, it need not be finely finished. The ends and edges, however, will need truing up with the jointer plane. Alternatively, the ends could be trimmed with a portable circular saw run along a batten clamped to the top. The top of the bench itself is planed flat later.

Fitting the vise

25 The bench top is insufficiently thick to take the vise, so a doubler needs to be fitted. This is made of plywood to avoid splitting when it is bored to take the various screws. Position it as close to the left-hand leg at the front of the bench as possible (or right-hand leg if you are left handed) and ½ in. (13 mm) back from the front edge of the top. Bore and screw it to the underside of the bench top using four 2 x ³⁄₁₆ in. (51 x 5 mm) (No. 10) wood screws, first checking that the screws will not obstruct the carriage bolts that hold the vise in place.

26 Before proceeding, it may be easier to remove the base of the bench to give better access to the vise. Offer up the vise and mark a line around the rear jaw to indicate the area to be removed to allow it to fit.

27 The bulk of the waste for the recess can be removed with an electric drill and the job finished with chisel and mallet. Offer up the vise again to check the fit.

28 The position of the carriage bolts can now be marked and their pilot holes bored. The pilot hole should be approximately two-thirds of the overall diameter of the bolt and seven-eighths of its length. Use washers to spread the load of the bolt head and protect the vise casting. Fit the bolts and tighten with a wrench.

29 Refit the frame and turn the bench upright. Check the apron for length and mark the 45° angled corners. Leave 2 in. (51 mm) of vertical stock to cover the bench top. Saw the angles with the tenon saw and plane smooth.

30 Offer up the apron to mark the position of the recess needed for the vise mechanism. Remove waste with a tenon saw and chisel.

31 Fit the apron with screws at intervals of 8–10 in. (203–254 mm). Bore and countersink the holes, holding the apron in position with the vise while you drill pilot holes and fit the screws.

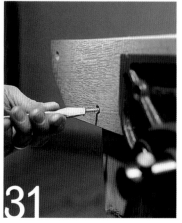

32 Plane the top of the apron flush with the bench top and chamfer all round.

33 Fit the front vise jaw following the same method used to fit the apron.

Fitting the bench stop

34 Position the bench stop about 4 in. (102 mm) from the end of the bench and 2–3 in. (51–76 mm) from the edge. Use a square to ensure the stop is at 90° to the edge of the bench, and mark around the edge first with a sharp pencil, then with a knife.

35 The recess for the stop is cut in the same way as a mortise joint.

36 Once the flange depth is reached, you will need to cut further smaller recesses to take the barrel of the fitting and the hinge. These may be cut using both a drill and a chisel.

37 Drill pilot holes to take the 1 x 5⁄32 in. (25 x 4 mm) (No. 8) screws that hold the fitting in place.

Finishing

38 A full finish on a bench is undesirable as it will tend to look scratched and worn after even moderate use. Once the top is sanded, two coats of finishing wax or linseed oil will provide moisture resistance and protection from dirt, and prevent any excess glue which lands on the bench top from adhering. Occasional light cabinet scraping and waxing will keep the bench in nearly new condition.

The base frame does not really need any finish, though a sealing coat of polyurethane can be applied if desired.

MITER JOINTS

A miter joint is formed when two pieces of wood are beveled at the ends and joined to form a corner. The bevels are usually 45° and make a right-angled joint. As a simple glued joint the miter is not particularly strong, but it is appropriate for decorative applications such as picture frames.

Each end is cut to 45° when making a square or rectangular frame

Miters are common in carpentry in the fitting of moldings, skirtings, and so on. When the work is fixed to a wall the strength of the joint is not important. Miters are useful when making lippings for veneered work. In cabinetmaking the miter is often used for its visual effect as the joint exposes no visible end grain and allows the figure in the wood to continue around the frame without a visual break.

Miters are often used in factory-produced carcass work. In the small workshop the technique can be useful, although it is difficult to do well without a mechanical saw.

Possible variations of the basic joint

The basic miter can be structurally improved by fitting dowels or biscuits. This not only strengthens the joint but also has the useful by-product of making it easier to assemble.

A useful feature of the miter joint is that moldings, rabbets, and grooves continue around the frame uninterrupted. This removes the need for complicated scribing.

Miter joint

The miter joint is used where two pieces join at a 90° corner, each end being cut to an angle of 45°.

Constructing a miter joint

Marking out

1 Whether a miter box, saw, or guillotine is used, it is advisable to mark out the miter. This is essential if a jig is not used, but even if it is, laying out the work and marking the direction of the miter is important.

If a frame is being made, the parts are laid out in pairs. Top and bottom are laid together and the sides likewise.

The outside dimensions of the frame are marked using a try square and pencil. It is easier to cut the miter if the stock used is slightly longer than its finished dimension.

2 The miter is marked using a sliding bevel set to 45° or a 45° try square. The parts of the frame are again marked in pairs. The 45° line is marked from the outside extremity of the frame towards the centre, forming a "V" at each end pointing

Useful tools & equipment

The miter box is a simple jig used to guide a tenon saw through a rail at 45°. The box comprises three pieces of wood 9–12 in. (229–305 mm) long by about 4 in. (102 mm) by ¾ in. (19 mm) joined in a "U" shape. A slot is made across the jig the same width as the kerf of the tenon saw. The work is held at the bottom of the "U" for sawing.

Purpose-made miter saws are now widely available. These include a fine blade saw with a guide mechanism, end and depth stops and an adjustable cutting angle that can be adjusted from 45 to 90°.

The guillotine is a specialized machine for cutting miters. A knife is pulled through the work with a lever leaving a perfectly smooth surface. Larger guillotines are pneumatically operated.

Most types of fixed circular saw will cut accurate miters. Most radial arm saws and bench saws with a tilting arbor will also cut miters across a board for carcass work.

Try square

Pencil

Sliding bevel
or 45° try square

Tenon saw

Masking tape

Piece of board, approximately 10 x 4 x ¾ in.
(254 x 102 x 19 mm)

Smoothing plane

Clamping blocks and four C-clamps, or Spanish windlass

Glue and brush

(An adjustable set-square or combination set is useful for marking angles other than 45°)

toward each other. They are marked this way around to check that the inside of the miters correspond with one another.

3 Once both pairs of rails are marked in this way, a jig can be used. For freehand cutting, however, additional marking is necessary. Using a 90° try square, mark lines across the edges of the rails from the ends of the miter.

The marking is completed with the 45° square on the reverse side of the rail. Working from the face edge of the stock, hold the square or bevel against the work and carefully mark a line from the outer tip of the miter.

Sawing
4 Sawing freehand, hold the work in the vise so that the miter is vertical. With a tenon saw positioned so that the blade is pointing up at about 45° and on the

waste side of the marked line, begin the cut with a few short downward strokes. When the action is established, longer forward strokes are used.

As the saw cut progresses, keep working to the waste side of the line and check that the reverse side of the joint is also

being cut evenly. As the saw cut nears completion, revert to short cuts to prevent breakout on the inside edge of the miter. A piece of masking tape wrapped around the base of the joint up to the edge mark is an added precaution.

Technique: Miter joints 131

Truing up

5 To true the miter, set the piece of work in the vise at 45° with the miter horizontal. A flat piece of board clamped to the bench immediately behind the vise can form a simple plane guide. The work-piece is set so that the marked line of the miter is exactly in line with the top of the board.

6 Resting the sole of the plane on the board, plane along the miter with the blade at a skew angle. This action reduces the risk of the plane damaging the tip of the miter while the guide board ensures a flat joint.

7 Set out the work on the bench to check that each joint fits. *Remember:* if adjustments have to be made, remember that altering one joint will affect all the others. When removing stock from one joint, the one diagonally opposite will require evening up.

Assembly

8 Gluing the mitered frame together may be done in one of two ways. The first is to glue small triangular blocks to the outside edge of each joint. These should be about half the size of the miter. The blocks form a flat surface across which a C-clamp can be applied.

The advantage of this system is that each joint is

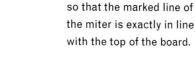

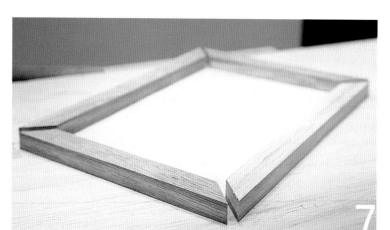

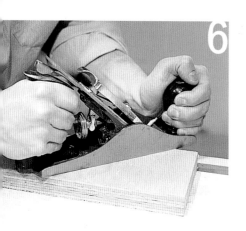

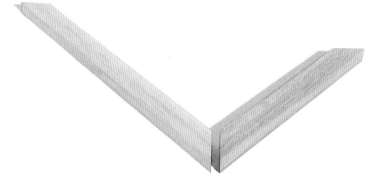

10 The frame is laid out and a block placed at each corner. Strong string is led around the blocks and tied off. A short stick is twisted into the string and the twisting action pulls the blocks together, bringing the joints under pressure.

In either case, a dry run is advisable before glue is applied to the joint. The glue blocks are knocked or sawn off after assembly and the joint cleaned up with a smoothing plane.

assembled separately under consistent pressure. Having set up the clamping blocks and C-clamps (one for each corner), work around the frame applying glue and clamping each joint in turn.

9 The second method is to use a Spanish windlass. This is more appropriate for light-duty applications such as picture frames. Four L-shaped blocks are required: for strength these should be of plywood, and with a groove running around the outside edge of each block.

MIRROR FRAME *see plan page 217*

ABOVE *Detail of the corner of the frame, showing well-fitted miter, the veneer keys used to reinforce the joint, and the decorative veneer line*

Miter joints are most often seen in decorative frames where visual effect is important. The miter is structurally quite adequate for this type of work, although some form of reinforcement is usually incorporated. This project features keys in the joints to strengthen them. The contrasting strip of decorative veneer, although technically a laminate, gives the impression of an inlay.

Little wood is required for this project, and any hardwood may be used. Small projects of this kind provide an ideal opportunity to use rare or exotic woods, difficult to justify in larger jobs. The frame shown here is in American cherry with black walnut veneer. It would serve just as well as a picture frame, or could be scaled up for a much bigger mirror.

Tool list

Glue and brush

4 x C-clamps

Smoothing plane

Pencil

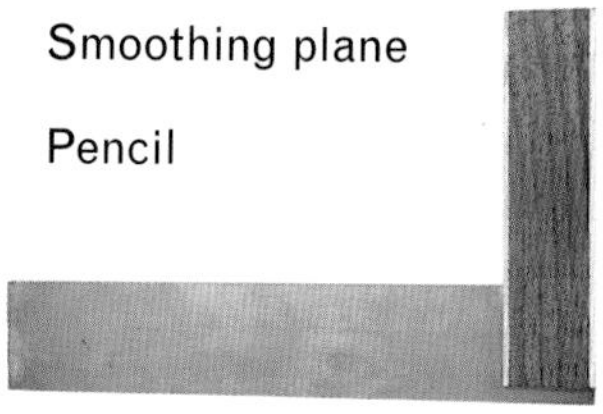

Try square

Sliding bevel

Tenon or miter saw

Chisel

Frame clamp

Marking gauge

Fine abrasive paper

Cabinet scraper

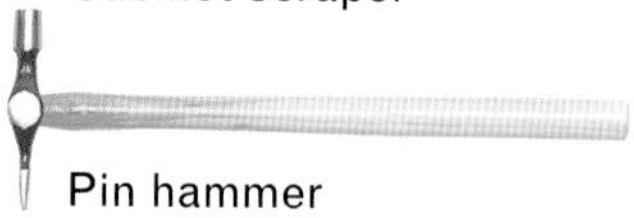

Pin hammer

Molding pins and nail punch

CUTTING LIST AND MATERIALS

Component	Quantity	Finished dimensions
A Frame sides	2	13 x 1 x ¾ in. (330 x 25 x 19 mm)
B Side rabbets	2	13 x ⅜ x ⅜ in. (330 x 10 x 10 mm)
C Frame ends	2	9 x 1 x ¾ in. (229 x 25 x 19 mm)
D End rabbets	2	9 x ⅜ x ⅜ in. (229 x 10 x 10 mm)
E Frame laminates and corner keys		
	5	14 x ⅞ in. (356 x 22 mm)
F Clamping blocks	2	14 x ¾ x ¾ in. (356 x 19 x 19 mm)
	1	14 x ⅜ x ⅜ in. (356 x 10 x 10 mm)
G Backing panel	1	13 x 9 x 1⁄16 in. (330 x 229 x 2 mm)
Suggested lumber		A, B, C, and D—American cherry E—Black walnut veneer F—Scrap stock G—Plywood
Suggested finish		Danish oil, polyurethane varnish, or wax
Alternative lumber		Hardwood such as rosewood and sycamore veneer, or ash and brown oak veneer

Notes
It is advisable not to order the glass until the frame has been assembled. Eyes and hanging wire required to complete project.

SEVEN **JOINTS AND JOINTMAKING**

ABOVE *Corner detail showing the decorative veneer line and the internal chamfer*

BELOW *Similar to above, the detail shows the effect of light on the chamfer and the contrast of the veneer line*

BOTTOM *A detail from behind, showing the pin that fixes in the plywood back, and the fitting of eyes and hanging wire*

Construction

Preparing the sections

1 The frame section is formed by gluing together the veneer, rabbets, and rails. (The rails are the frame components and the "rabbets" are the narrow strips of wood that create a rabbet.) Apply glue to both the veneer and the rails. Lay the clamping blocks on either side of the assembly and apply the clamps. Repeat the process for the other three strips. Carefully trim the edges of the veneer flush with the rail using the smoothing plane.

2 The process for gluing the rabbets is the same, but there is little margin for error. The top of the assembled section must be flush and carefully clamped. Wipe the excess glue off while it is still wet.

3 Plane all around the four assembled sections to clean up glue marks and any unevenness, being careful to remove a minimum of stock.

4 Mark the chamfers in pencil, then chamfer the inside edge of the frame with the smoothing plane at a consistent 45° angle. Set the plane to a fine cut and remove the same number of shavings from each piece.

Making the joints

5 Following the technique described earlier, mark out the miters. Accuracy is particularly important if the laminated strips are to line up properly in the finished job. Ensure that the rabbets are on the inside of the work.

6 Cut the miters using one of the methods previously described. The miter saw shown has a fine tooth blade which, when the work is held firmly in place, gives a clean and accurate cut and avoids the potential breakout from a tenon saw. Although the joint may be glued from a miter saw cut, trimming the miter with a smoothing plane gives a neater result and makes the most of the fine details where the veneers meet.

Remove any excess glue from the inside of the rabbet with a chisel.

Assembly

7 Clamp the frame dry first to check the fits of the miters and to rehearse the clamping procedure for the gluing stage. The frame clamp shown here speeds up and simplifies the clamping process but is not essential. The C-clamp method is particularly appropriate to this situation where perfect alignment is required. Assembling the joints individually makes the procedure easier.

Apply glue to the joints following the procedure described earlier. When the glue is thoroughly dry, clean the faces of the frame with the smoothing plane, first clamping the work securely to the bench so that the action of the plane does not distort the frame and risk fracturing one of the joints. Finish the edges similarly—this time with the frame held in the vise. Work from the corners toward the center to avoid damaging the fine corners of the joints. Remove glue on the inside corners with a chisel.

Fitting the corner keys

8 The keys are fitted into slots cut with the tenon saw. Mark the positions for these by drawing lines across the outside edges of the frame 1 in. (25 mm) from the corner. Set the marking gauge to half the thickness of the frame and scribe a line around the corner between the two pencil lines.

9 Clamp the work in the vise with one miter pointing upward. The saw cut must be straight and the bottom of the slot cut flat. All the dust needs to be removed from the slot.

Cut a piece of veneer about 2 in. (51 mm) long and check for fit. It should fit

fairly easily without being forced. If it is too tight, sand by rubbing it on a piece of abrasive paper laid flat on the bench. Keep checking until a good fit is obtained.

10 Glue both sides of the key and push it into place, making sure that it rests on the bottom of the slot. Trim the veneer back with the tenon saw, then plane it

flush to the frame. Repeat for the other three miters.

Finishing

11 The finish on fine work is very important and the first stage is surface preparation. On fine grain woods it is best to use a cabinet scraper, but fine abrasive paper and a sanding block may be used. Take care not to round over

the corners, other than to take off their sharpness.

The chosen finish should enhance the natural contrast of color in the wood. Danish oil is used here and quickly builds up a low to medium luster.

12 Use a piece of thin plywood as a backing panel for the mirror, holding it in place with brads. These are easier to fit if a nail punch is used. Leave about ¼ in. (6 mm) protruding.

Fit eyes on either side of the frame to take a hanging wire. These are located approximately one-third of the way down the frame.

HOUSING JOINTS

Housing joints are normally used in carcass work for fitting shelves and dividers. The housing is a trench precisely cut to take another piece of wood, usually across the width of the work. The structural integrity of the housing joint is limited and it is dependent on a tight fit for its strength.

The basic joint runs right across the board, but it is common to stop the housing short of the face side of the job. The corresponding shelf or divider is notched to fit. This arrangement allows the interior work to be set back slightly from the carcass and generally produces a neater job.

Housing cut on inside face

Shelf or divider fits into housing groove

Housing joint

A housing is a groove cut in the face of a component which will accommodate another member that fits in at right angles to it.

Possible variations of the basic joint

A through, or stopped, housing joint can be modified by cutting a rabbet on one or both sides of the shelf or divider. This requires a narrower housing.

A dovetail housing, as its name suggests, is a groove of dovetail section. The corresponding part of the joint has a dovetail tongue. This joint has great structural strength. To make a dovetail housing by hand would be a challenge compared to using a portable router with a dovetail cutter.

Useful tools & equipment

A portable router makes light work of cutting housings. The base of the router is run against a batten clamped to the workpiece.

A radial arm saw can be used for cutting housings. This may be done with either a number of passes of a standard saw blade or a special dado block. (Dado is another word for housing.)

Try square

Pencil

Marking gauge

Metal rule

Marking knife

C-clamps

Bevel-edged chisel

Tenon saw

Masking tape

Mallet

Manual router

Smoothing plane

Glue and brush

Constructing a housing joint

Marking out

1 First establish the position of the housing and mark a line across the work using a try square and pencil. The width of the housing must be carefully measured. In a basic housing it will be marginally less than the board that is to be let in.

Use a marking gauge to check the thickness of the shelf or divider and to see if the thickness is consistent across its width. The width of the housing will be slightly less than the setting of the marking gauge.

Sawing

4 Secure the work to the bench with C-clamps before beginning the sawing.

To provide a key for the saw, the scribed lines marking the width of the housing are opened up to a "V" with a chisel. Working by hand rather than with a mallet, and on the inside of the housing, hold the chisel at an angle of 45° to the face of the work. The edge of the chisel is held parallel to the scribed line and ¹⁄₁₆ in. (2 mm) in from it. Push the chisel down into the incision.

Working along the line in steps the width of the chisel, open up the "V." When one side is complete, turn the work around to repeat the operation on the other side of the joint. The set of the tenon saw should just rest against the side of the incised line.

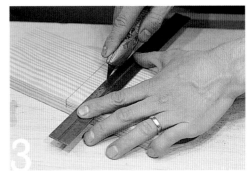

2 The depth of the housing should be about one-quarter to one-third of the thickness of the board; i.e., deep enough to make a strong joint but not deep enough to weaken the area around the housing. The depth is set on the cutting gauge and scribed on to the edges of the housing joint.

3 With a metal rule measure the width of the housing from the first line and scribe both lines with a marking knife. Use a number of shallow strokes against the metal rule until the line is cut into the wood. A depth of ¹⁄₁₆ in. (2 mm) is about right.

Using the try square, mark lines from these incised lines on the face of the board down both edges. They are drawn in pencil since they will be removed later.

5 Begin the saw cut with the blade located in the "V" groove with the handle raised up. When the sawing action is established, gradually bring the saw into a horizontal position without interrupting the cutting motion.

Continue the cut until the saw blade reaches the gauged lines at the bottom of the housing. It is helpful to mark the depth of the housing on the side of the saw blade with a strip of masking tape. During the sawing operation, check the lines on the side of the joint to ensure that the cut is vertical.

Removing waste

6 The bulk of the waste is removed using a chisel with a mallet. Work first from one edge with the chisel pointing up slightly and make a series of shallow cuts until the gauged depth mark is reached.

Turn the work around and repeat the operation. At this stage both ends of the housing are at the correct depth and there is a shallow inverted "V" of material left

Technique: Housing joints

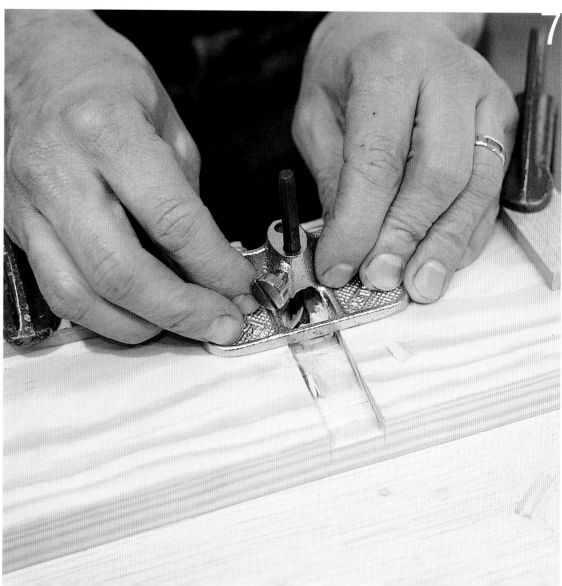

Assembly

9 The key to a good fit is constant checking until the joint is a firm push fit.

Using the marking gauge set to the depth of the housing, lightly mark a line around the end of the piece that enters the housing. This indicates the extent of the glue line. Stick masking tape up to the edge of each part of the joint.

Apply glue to both parts of the joint. A softwood batten, slightly curved on one side, is a useful gluing aid. The curved side is placed in contact with the work directly behind the housing. When the ends of the batten are clamped up tight, it exerts pressure along the whole length of the joint.

When the glue is dry, remove the clamps and tape and clean up the edges of the joint with a smoothing plane.

in the middle of the housing.

In a short joint, i.e., less than 8 in. (203 mm), this can be removed with a long chisel. The chisel is held horizontally and the waste pared down in shallow increments until the bottom of the joint is flat.

7 On a wider board a manual router, also known as a router plane, is more accurate. This is a simple tool consisting of a metal base with thumb plates cast into it. Through the base projects a blade, which is held in place with a screw that allows adjustment. The blade is L-shaped and ground to a sharp edge. The blade is set to the depth of

the housing. The base rests on the wood either side of the housing and, as it is pushed along, the blade cleans up the joint to the preset depth.

8 The fitting of the joint and final trimming is done on the corresponding part. Careful planing with a finely set smoothing plane both finishes the surface of the wood and trims the joint to fit snugly.

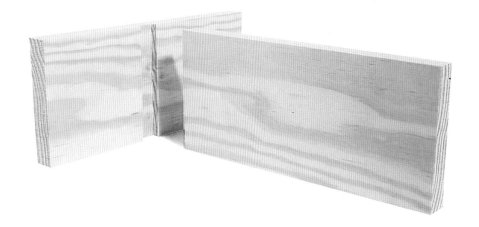

BOOKCASE *see plan page 217*

see plan page 217

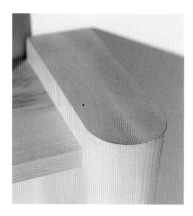

ABOVE *Detail of the bold curve on the front of the thick sides*

FURTHER INFORMATION

This bookcase is relatively straightforward to make, and an attractive and useful piece of furniture. It is made here in English ash. Many different woods could be used, however—hardwood or softwood—although cutting clean shoulders on the shelves and housings is more difficult in softwood. You could also consider making the bookcase with light-colored carcass sides and stained dark shelves.

The design of the bookcase features large, heavy 3½ in. (88 mm) thick side components. These are made by laminating together two 1¾ in. (44 mm) thick pieces, obtained from sawn stock, 2 in. (51 mm) thick.

Begin the project by preparing these thick vertical sides. Plane a face side on each and glue the face sides together. Apply glue to both surfaces and apply even pressure all around. Unless you have a press you will need to use about 20 C- or bar clamps and position them around each laminated component, roughly 4 in. (100 mm) apart. When the glue has cured, work a new face side and face edge. Then set a marking gauge to the required thickness (3½ in. or 88 mm), mark all around and plane to thickness. Mark the width (9¹¹⁄₁₆ in. or 245 mm) and plane. Then use a square and rule to mark the length (37¹³⁄₃₂ in. or 950 mm), saw and plane the end grain.

CUTTING LIST AND MATERIALS

Component	Quantity	Finished dimensions
A Sides	2	37¹³⁄₃₂ x 9²¹⁄₃₂ x 3½ in. (950 x 245 x 88 mm)
B Shelves	4	29⅛ x 7⅞ x ⅞ in. (740 x 200 x 22 mm)
C Plinth	1	29⅛ x 2²⁹⁄₃₂ x ⅞ in. (740 x 74 x 22 mm)
D Back—V-jointed tongue-and-groove panels (TGV)	8	32½ x 3¾ x ⅜ in. (826 x 95 x 10 mm)
Suggested lumber		A, B, and C—Ash; D*
Suggested finish		Danish oil
Alternative lumber		A hardwood such as cherry or maple, or a softwood such as parana pine

Notes
*Choose a hardwood with a strong figure such as oak or chestnut, or use a softwood such as Russian pine. If you do not have the equipment to make your own tongue-and-groove boards, purchase them ready-made from your lumber supplier.

Tool list

Glue and brush

20 C- or bar clamps

Marking gauge

Square

Steel rule

Bench saw

Pencil

Table saw or bandsaw

Jack or smoothing plane

Gooseneck scraper

Abrasive paper and curved sanding block

Panel gauge

Striking knife

Chisel

Tenon saw

Masking tape

Electric plunge router

Paring chisel

Shoulder plane

8 bar clamps, at least 40 in. (1016 mm) long, and clamping blocks

Electric sander or smoothing plane

Cork sanding block

Molding plane

Screws and screwdriver

BELOW LEFT *Detail at the base of the bookcase, showing the bottom shelf and plinth*

BELOW MIDDLE *Tongue-and-groove board with molding detail on the edges gives an interesting effect to the back of the bookcase*

BELOW RIGHT *The boards are fixed with screws from the rear and sit in a rabbet*

Construction

Molding the front of the sides

1 Having prepared the side components, shape the molding on the front of them. First mark out the shape in pencil on the end grain. Then remove the waste, either by passing it across the table saw with the saw blade canted over to 45°, or by using a bandsaw with the table tilted to 45°.

Once most of the waste has been removed, approach the marked line by planing a series of parallel flats that gradually approach the line as more and more facets are planed onto the end.

Finally, smooth around the molding using a curved scraper known as a goose-neck, and then finish with abrasive paper backed by a curved sanding block.

Cutting out the housings

2 Carefully mark the position of the housings, or dados, on the sides of the uprights. Mark out both uprights at the same time, using the rear of each as your reference surface.

3 Use a square to mark lines at right angles to your reference surface, and a large marking gauge, called a panel gauge, to mark the stopped front of the housings for the shelves.

4 Clamp a steel rule on the position of the shoulder, then scribe across using a striking knife, with the beveled side facing the waste side of your cut. Make deep cuts so that the saw cuts the shoulders in the right place. Remove the rule and pare a "V" groove on the waste side of the line,

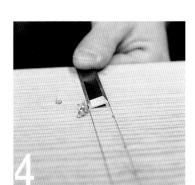

using a chisel. This allows the saw to sit snugly against the vertical shoulder.

5 Mark a small tenon saw with masking tape to indicate the depth of your housing, then saw down to

this depth to form the housings on both uprights.

6 Alternatively, an easier and more accurate way to cut a housing is to use an electric plunge router which cuts both the shoulders and the base of the housing in one operation. Guided by a fence clamped across the job, a router can cut the housing relatively quickly with two or three passes, increasing the depth with each cut.

Securely clamp your job to the bench, then, working from back to front, pare the

waste material of your housing with a paring chisel angled slightly upward.

The front, or stopped, end of the housing is the most difficult to finish off. Here you have to chisel vertical shoulders and pare into them as best you can.

Originally, the manual router was used to work the bottoms of housings like this. This has now been very largely replaced by the far superior electric plunge router.

Fitting the shelves
7 Cut the shoulders on the ends of the plinth and the shelves ⅜ in. (10 mm) from the end of each component. These, too, are most successfully cut with a router, using either a rabbet cutter or a straight cutter guided by a fence clamped across the job, or by guiding the router off the end grain of each shelf.

Since the strength of a housing joint is gained from having a very snug fit, the

shoulders are routed slightly tight and then planed with a shoulder plane to fit snugly.

8 Test the fit of the plinth ends and shelf ends in their housings. They should not be so tight that they require hammering home, nor should they rattle around in their housings.

You will now need to cut the rabbets into which the back panels will fit. A simple rabbet is needed on the rear edge of the top and bottom shelves, while there is a stopped rabbet on the inside rear edges of the sides. You will also need to cut the mortises that will accept the ends of the plinth.

9 Now that you know that each individual joint fits, you need to check that they all fit at the same time in the same way. If they do not, take a step back and examine whether the lengths of your shelves are

all exactly the same and the positions of your housings are all in good relation to one another.

At the same time, do a dry assembly to work out how you are going to assemble the carcass and where you are going to require clamping pressure. A carcass of this size will require eight bar camps of at least 40 in. (1016 mm) in length.

with a smoothing plane to plane out all of the machine marks and then going over all of the surfaces with abrasive paper.

If you are sanding by hand, start with 120 grit backed by a cork sanding block and sand carefully in line with the grain of the wood. When you are convinced that the finish is as good as you can get with 120 grit, move on to 150 grit and then to 180 grit. You will spend less and less time with each grade of abrasive paper, but it is important that you remove all of the marks and scratches of the preceding grade before moving on to the next one.

12 Apply two or three thin coats of Danish oil with a cloth, but bear in mind that the sheen is due not to the oil but to previous careful preparation of the surface. All you are doing with the Danish oil is enhancing the original scratch-free surface that you prepared with the abrasive paper.

Assembly

13 Once the components have been finished and polished, perform a dry assembly with the top and bottom shelves in place, using clamps and clamping blocks to protect the finished surface of the wood. Check that the

Prefinishing

10 First, mask with tape all the areas which will be receiving glue. Apply the tape and trim carefully with a knife—this is essential since it protects the gluing areas from the finishing oil which would prevent the glue from adhering well.

11 Next, remove all of the existing machine marks and any surface defects. If your components have come straight from the planer, you need to remove the slight ripple marks left by the planer. Do this either by using a sanding machine or by first passing over the job

14 When the adhesive has partly cured, use a chisel to remove excess glue. It should come away easily since it will not have stuck very well to the pre-finished, oiled surface.

15 Now prepare the materials for the back, which when fitted will hold the bookcase square. If you have the correct tools the tongues can be made as shown with a molding plane. A router with a suitable cutter could also be used, or if you wish, purchase ready-made tongue and grooving. Sand and finish these back panels.

carcass is square by measuring the diagonals, and adjust if necessary.

Carefully paint glue on the surfaces and then bring them together. If using PVA glue, make sure you apply this in a cool room and work relatively quickly. You have about 5 minutes of "open" time before the glue starts to gel and becomes less workable. If you want a longer "open" time, use a resin glue such as Cascamite, which will allow you about 10 minutes' working time.

Once assembled, apply pressure evenly, again being careful to protect the prefinished surfaces. Just squeeze so that each joint snugs up. Check again that the carcass is square. When it is all done, do not try to wipe off any glue that has squeezed out; just walk away and let the glue harden.

16 To finish the job, fix the tongue-and-groove back panels in the rabbets on the back of the top and bottom shelves and on the uprights, using screws in the center of each board. Note that you will have to reduce the width of the end boards for a symmetrical pattern.

Use Danish oil to finish inside the tongues and grooves of the panels. This is necessary because each panel will expand and contract slightly around the fixing point, exposing wood inside the tongue-and-groove joint.

Finally, clean down and check the oil finish, re-oiling as necessary.

DOVETAIL JOINTS

The dovetail is an ancient joint going back to Egyptian times. It has a configuration that makes it impossible to pull apart in one direction and, because of the large surface area of contact between the pieces, is very strong all around.

The applications of the dovetail are diverse and it is used by musical instrument-makers and boat builders, as well as joiners and cabinetmakers. In furniture, its most visible application is in drawer making. It is also widely used in traditional cabinet construction. The fundamental advantage of the dovetail is its strength, but the nature of the joint also gives it a strong visual appeal.

A number of jigs are available for making dovetails. These are usually for use with a portable router, the better jigs being rather expensive. Good as these may be, cabinetmakers take great pride in the quality of their hand-cut dovetails and regard them as an indication of their level of skill. Machine-cut dovetails are strong and efficient but just do not feel the same.

Possible variations of the basic joint

As with the mortise and tenon, the dovetail has almost endless possible permutations. The through dovetail described here is the simplest, but nonetheless it offers considerable scope for variation. Altering the number, size, and spacing of the dovetails in a given width will change the whole appearance of the job. Experimenting with contrasting woods for dovetails and pins and different sizes of dovetail in the same joint is likely to generate some exciting effects.

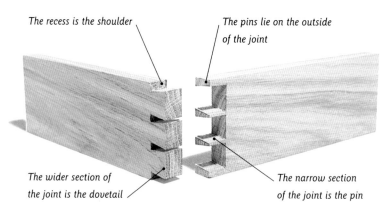

The recess is the shoulder

The pins lie on the outside of the joint

The wider section of the joint is the dovetail

The narrow section of the joint is the pin

Dovetails and pins

The dovetail joint comprises two parts: the dovetails, named for their fan shape, and the pins, which fit between them and form the top and bottom of the joint. The dovetails are usually—except in some machine cut types—bigger than the pins. The ratio of the bevel on the dovetails is generally 6:1 in softwoods and 8:1 in hardwoods.

Useful tools & equipment

Dovetail templates made of metal or plastic are more convenient to use than a sliding bevel. These are effectively a miniature try square with an angled edge for marking. They are sold in ratios of 6:1 and 8:1.

A jeweler's saw may be used instead of a coping saw for removing the waste on fine dovetails.

Dovetail jigs are used in conjunction with a portable router. The jig consists of adjustable templates which guide a bush and dovetail bit fitted in the router. The more economical jigs produce dovetails and pins of equal size, but more complex ones allow far greater flexibility in the size and layout of the joint.

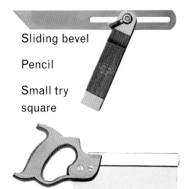

Cutting gauge

Sliding bevel

Pencil

Small try square

Dovetail saw

Coping saw

C-clamps

Plywood panel, approximately 12 x 6 in. (305 x 152 mm) to protect the bench

Short offcuts, 1 in. (25 mm) square and slightly longer than the width of the joint

Bevel-edged chisel

Mallet

Small striking knife

Hammer

Masking tape

Glue and brush

Smoothing plane

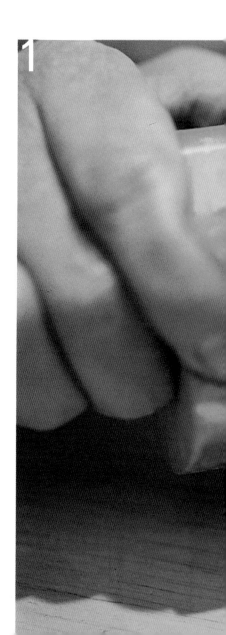

Constructing a through dovetail joint

Marking out the dovetails

1 Set the cutting gauge to slightly more than the thickness of the stock and scribe a line around each end of the joint. The cutting gauge is used in preference to the marking gauge because it has a small knife rather than a point. This produces a clean-cut line on cross grain work.

2 The spacing of the joints is largely a question of structural and aesthetic balance. The outer pins should not be too small or they could break off. In order to ensure equal spacing when the width of the work is not readily divisible by the number of dovetails required, draw a line of a length that is easily divided across the work at an angle. Account must be made of the pin spacings as well as the dovetail spacing.

Use a sliding bevel to mark the dovetails. Set it to the appropriate angle and hold it against the end of

the work, penciling in the lines. Shade the waste spaces between the dovetails to indicate the part to be removed and to ensure that the saw cuts are made on the correct side of the line. (Use a small metal try square to mark the line across the end of the joint.)

Cutting the dovetails

3 Clamp the work at a height comfortable for sawing. To keep the work firm in the vise, a piece of scrap wood may be held behind it as packing. A good posture is essential for accurate sawing, and ideally the top of the workpiece should be at elbow height. Begin sawing the dovetails with the saw pointing upward for two or three strokes. Once the sawing rhythm is established level out the saw, maintaining a steady action and cutting down to the scribed line. It

is easier to cut all the right-hand sides first, followed by the left-hand sides.

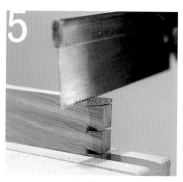

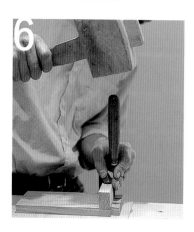

4 Remove the bulk of the waste with a coping saw. Start the cut in line with the dovetail bevel and after a few strokes work around to the horizontal. The aim is to remove as much waste as possible without touching the scribed line.

5 To remove the outside waste, clamp the work horizontally in the vise and saw to the scribed line with the dovetail saw.

6 To trim the joint, clamp the work on to the bench with a piece of plywood underneath the job to both protect the bench and prevent breakout on the reverse side of the joint. A square section offcut is clamped to the workpiece in line with the scribed line at the base of the joint.

7 Holding the chisel firmly against the guide block, tap the handle with a mallet.

Marking out the pins

8 To mark out the pins, hold the work in the vise vertically and about 1 in. (25 mm) above the vise top. A batten is placed behind the work so that the dovetails can rest level. Hold the dovetails firmly in position and scribe off the pins using a small knife. Fill the scribed lines in with a sharp pencil right away as they can be difficult to see.

Mark the lines on the face of the work with the try square held against the end of the work and again shade the waste areas. Both sides of the work may be marked in this way, though it is not strictly necessary.

Cutting the pins

9 Saw the pins in the same manner as the dovetails. Great accuracy is called for as there is no margin for error. Care and a steady hand will produce a good result. It is easier to cut the pins to the line to start with than leave waste to be trimmed back later.

The removal of the waste again calls for the coping saw. Keep checking the position of the coping saw blade at the back of the joint to make sure that it is not wandering too close to the scribed line. Allowance has to be made at the beginning and end of each cut for the beveled shape of the pins.

Set up the work to trim back the waste to the base of the joint as before. The wider area to be cleaned up requires more care than the small spaces between the dovetails. Cutting back to the guide block in one operation may damage the end grain, affecting both the efficiency and the neatness of the joint. To prevent this, pare the joint back gradually, pushing down on the chisel by hand, leaving about 1/16 in. (2 mm) above the guide block. Make the final cut by holding the chisel against the block and tapping the handle of the chisel with the mallet.

Technique: Dovetail joints   151

Assembly

10 Clamp the pin section of the joint vertically in the vise. Make sure that the dovetail part of the joint is in the correct relative position and check for fit. Do this by tapping with a hammer onto a block of wood resting on the

dovetails. This applies firm even pressure across the joint without causing damage. If the joint starts to go together evenly, it will require no further attention. Do not fully assemble the joint at this stage.

If the joint does not fit evenly, note where the tight

spots are and gradually ease them back with a chisel, checking frequently for fit. Dovetails should be tight but clearly not so tight that they split.

Mask the joint up to the glue lines using masking tape. Apply glue evenly over all parts of the joint that will be in contact, using a small brush. Ensuring that the surfaces of the joint are "wetted," i.e., the glue is soaking in. This helps to create a good bond.

11 The joint is finally assembled using the block and hammer to drive it home. Most modern glues work best when allowed to dry under pressure and clamping is advisable.

12 Once the glue is dry, remove the tape. The work needs to be held firmly for cleaning up. Using a finely tuned smoothing plane, work at an angle of 45° from the outside to the inside of the joint. This cutting angle overcomes the problem of differing grain directions and the job should require only a light sanding.

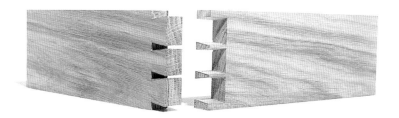

13 Hand-cut dovetails are a true delight. The accurate marking of the pins is one of the secrets of a neat dovetail joint. This is accomplished by scribing the pins directly off the corresponding dovetail part of the joint. Alternatively, the pins may be cut first and used to scribe off the tails. Only by practice will you find your preferred method of working.

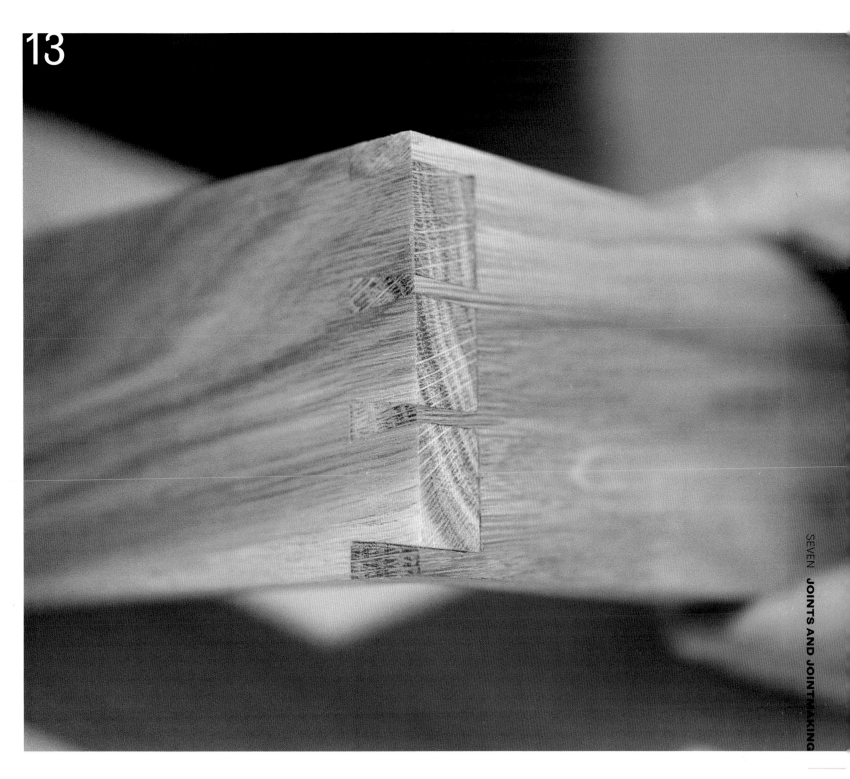

BREAKFAST TRAY *see plan page 218*

ABOVE *Tray handle. The dovetail detail on the handle echoes the joint at each corner of the tray*

This project makes full use of the single dovetail joint, the dovetail construction serving as both the structure and the decoration of the piece. The construction is of four strips of wood for the ends and sides, two blocks for the handles, and one piece of veneered plywood for the base.

The size of the tray can be varied to suit individual requirements. The type of wood chosen is a matter of personal preference, but a hardwood is more satisfactory than a softwood for cutting the joints. A contrasting wood for the handles accentuates the dovetail feature. The base should match either the frame or the handles.

As the parts are small, the offcut bin of a lumber supplier may provide you with some interesting and low-cost stock.

Tool list

Cutting gauge

Sliding bevel

Pencil

Small try square

Dovetail saw

Small marking knife

C-clamps

Bevel-edged chisel:
½ in. (13 mm)

Smoothing plane

Sanding block

Glue and brush

2 bar clamps or Spanish windlass

FURTHER INFORMATION

CUTTING LIST AND MATERIALS

Component	Quantity	Finished dimensions
A Sides	2	18 x 1¼ x ⅜ in. (457 x 32 x 10 mm)
B Ends	2	12 x 1¼ x ⅜ in. (305 x 32 x 10 mm)
C Handles*	1	12 x 1¼ x ⅝ in. (305 x 32 x 16 mm)
D Base	1	18 x 12 x ³⁄₁₆ in. (457 x 305 x 5 mm)
Suggested lumber		A and B—Ash C—Elm D—Ash-faced plywood
Suggested finish		Danish oil, clear polyurethane varnish, wax, or black- or white-colored satin lacquer
Alternative lumber		A hardwood such as oak or beech
Notes *Both handles are cut from the same piece of lumber.		

ABOVE *Corner dovetail joint. The finish darkens the grain, accentuating the visual effect*

BELOW *The handles are tapered from top to bottom, providing a positive grip and subtle visual detail*

BOTTOM *The bottom is beveled and set back slightly from the edges of the sides*

Construction

Marking and cutting the dovetails

1 Mark out and cut the four dovetails at the ends of the side pieces, following the sequence described earlier. (The corner joints in the tray are simpler than those made previously but the process is identical except that only one joint is required instead of three.)

To remove the outside waste, clamp the work horizontally in the vise and saw to the scribed line with the dovetail saw. Begin this cut with the saw pointing away from the corner, before bringing it level to finish off.

Marking and cutting the pins

2 The accurate marking of the pins, which in this case fall only at either side of the dovetail, is one of the secrets of a neat dovetail joint. This is done by scribing the pins directly off the corresponding dovetail part of the joint. As the space is confined, a small knife is easier to use than the usual striking knife. Fill in the scribed lines with a sharp pencil immediately as they can be difficult to see.

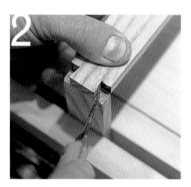

3 Clamp the work onto the bench before cutting the pins. Make some initial strokes with the saw held vertically before changing the angle to follow the scribed lines. This reduces the tendency of the saw to follow the grain of the wood rather than the cut line.

4 Check the fit by marrying the dovetails with the pins. Mark the adjacent corners AA, BB, CC, DD. This is important because the pins for each joint have been individually scribed and fitted.

The handles

5 Begin by marking the lengths of both handles, then mark center lines along the length and width. The handle dovetails can then be marked out. The handle stock is left in one piece for the time being; the longer piece of wood is easier to work on than two small blocks.

6 Now saw the two handle dovetails following the instructions in Step 1 above.

7 Finally, chisel out the waste around the handles. Push down gently on the chisel by hand, holding it perpendicular to the joint to ensure a clean finish.

8 The sides of the dovetails are paired flat and clean with a bevel-edged chisel. Accurate cleaning of these surfaces will make fitting easier later on.

9 To taper each side of the handles slightly, hold each handle in the vise and smooth it with a plane.

10 Mark the apertures in the ends of the tray in a similar way to the pins in the corner joints (see Step 2). The waste is removed following the procedure for the corner pins. If anything, the waste should be cut to just short of the central line, then pared back with the chisel until a tight push fit is achieved.

11 Round the tops of the handles with either a plane or a sanding block for a neat finish and a smooth feel.

The base

12 Trim the plywood for the base to ⅛ in. (3 mm) less than the size of the frame all the way around. Using a plane, bevel the edge of the base to 45° so that it is not visible when the tray is sitting on a table.

Assembly

13 As the tray will come into contact with water, it is essential to use a waterproof wood glue.

Fit the handles first. Apply glue to the parts of both end strips that will be in contact with the handles, then push each handle into position. Allow this to dry and clean up the excess glue with a sharp chisel.

Next apply glue to all the mating surfaces of the corner joints. The joints should be clamped either with bar clamps or a Spanish windlass. Clean up the inside of each joint with a chisel and the outside with the smoothing plane. Carefully sand the frame with a sanding block before fitting the bottom.

With the tray positioned upside down, apply glue to the mating surfaces of the frame and base. Put the base in place and weight it down until the glue has set. Scrape off any excess glue with a sharp chisel.

14

Finishing

14 The finish serves both to protect the wood from inevitable spills and the need to be wiped over after use, and to bring out the color in the wood. This will highlight the contrast between the two types of wood used for the frame and the handles.

The finish should be a water-resistant one (such as polyurethane), built up in two to three thinned coats. This may then be burnished with steel wool and polished with finishing wax.

Project: Breakfast tray

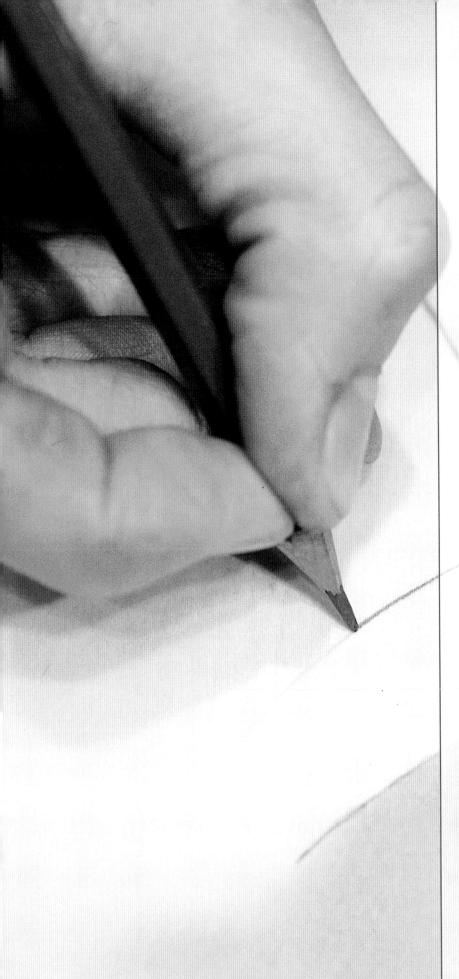

EIGHT DESIGN AND DRAWING

Design in woodworking can be extremely simple or incredibly complex, and may be defined by elements such as purpose, time-scale, materials, and budget, among others. This section outlines the basic principles which apply to design and illustrates the importance of the design brief. Design ideas are communicated through sketching and drawing, skills which can be acquired fairly easily as shown here, and mastered with practice. These techniques enable you to produce working drawings for your projects.

AN INTRODUCTION TO DESIGN

This section deals with the concept of "design." It asks "What is "design?" and takes you through a simple step-by-step breakdown of a "design method." It aims to give you an overview of the whole process and leave you with enough information to start designing for yourself.

What is design?

Design is essentially about solving problems, meeting requirements, and proposing solutions. Design can range from the extremely simple to the incredibly complex, depending on the nature and scale of the problem to be resolved. Design involves a whole range of intellectual and practical skills, including structural, aesthetic, and conceptual thinking, in addition to economic, environmental, production, and cultural considerations. In practical terms, all of this information

FURTHER INFORMATION

has to be communicated through concept sketches, working drawings, graphics, models, and prototypes.

A good designer is an informed person who takes account of all these factors and uses his or her creative ability to give an end result that reflects the needs of the producer and user. Designers therefore need to be acutely aware of their market and to use an appropriate mix of skills for each problem.

These pages serve only as a starter for a whole new area called "design." The basic principles described here apply whether you are designing a jewelry box, a chair, or a cabinet. Extra information may be required in certain cases. With a chair, for example, it might be ergonomic factors, such as the angle of the back, the height of the seat, and whether arms are required—all of which are important considerations. With a cabinet, however, the important issue is the volume and nature of things to be stored or displayed.

One thing common to all furniture is that both the structural requirements and the safety of users are very important considerations.

The design process *Problem*

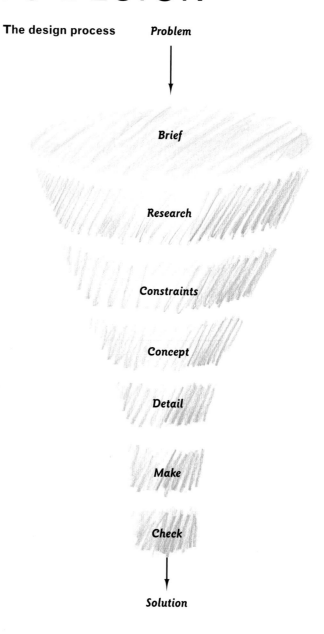

Brief

Research

Constraints

Concept

Detail

Make

Check

Solution

The design process

Think of the design process as a funnel: all the available information and known requirements are poured in, and this mix is filtered through to result in a solution. Thus the design process involves many separate elements that interact during the process.

The basic phases of the design process

Design is about solving problems appropriately rather than being over-concerned with originality.

1 Definition of the problem

This phase is initiated either by someone approaching you with a problem that needs to be solved or by your own identification of a problem that requires a solution.

2 Research

This stage involves the gathering and collating of as much information as possible about the problem.

3 Identification of constraints

Next, any inherent constraints such as safety, materials, time-frame, or cost need to be highlighted.

4 Concept and exploration

This phase entails proposing conceptual solutions based on knowledge of the problem. This refined information is commonly known as a "brief." The brief is used as a guide, so that when proposing solutions the designer does not stray too far from the problem and solve a completely different problem instead. After all, if the brief was for a simple, free-standing cupboard, your design for a built-in wardrobe might not be entirely appreciated!

5 Design detail and development

You now choose one or two of the best concepts and develop them by working to more detail; remember to check these ideas against the noted constraints as you go along. When a suitable solution has been found, it is time to produce the working drawings.

6 Realization

This is the phase in which the design is produced to scale or as a full-scale prototype. The quality of the result depends largely on how thoroughly the design phases were undertaken and how carefully the model or prototype is produced.

7 Evaluation

At this stage the proposed solution is compared with the original brief. It is also where final improvements can be decided on before you commit yourself to the production of the finished piece of furniture.

RIGHT *A selection of useful drawing and drafting equipment. Other useful items include a drawing board of some sort; a hard-backed sketchpad and tracing paper; a variety of pens and markers; plastic templates for drawing circles, ellipses, and curves; a compass/ divider set; a scale rule and adjustable protractor; a scalpel or break-off craft knife, and a glue stick*

Design activity

Function

Market

Standards

Time

Constraints

Production

Research

Design

Cost

Materials

Environment

Ergonomics

Safety

Manufacture

Transport

Packaging

Appearance

SKETCHING AND DRAWING TECHNIQUES

When you have successfully worked through the first three phases and derived the brief, you are now at the stage at which you need to communicate your ideas, usually at first through sketches. As with the first three phases, in which you started with general information and then, through analysis and research, made this information much more specific, the same applies now with drawing. Start with quite general ideas and gradually develop the concept sketches with more detailed information, such as tone, texture, and shading.

Freehand drawing

Everything you see can be drawn or represented by fitting the object to be drawn into one of the following solid shapes: a cube, sphere, cylinder, cone, or rectangular box (Figure 1). As with any other skill, it takes practice and, as you begin to master it, it becomes even easier and therefore more pleasurable.

There are a few simple things you need to learn to improve your drawing skills:
a) Freehand vertical and horizontal lines (parallel);
b) Freehand rectangles, squares, and parallelograms;
c) Freehand circles (inside squares); and finally

d) Freehand ellipses (inside parallelograms and rectangles) (Figure 2). The emphasis is on "freehand" because there is a natural tendency to turn to a ruler, which actually takes longer and does not in fact improve your skill.

Keep practicing

Keep all your sketches, preferably in a hard-backed sketchpad with non-removable pages, since this removes the temptation to scrap the bad drawings and keep only the good ones. By keeping all of the early sketches you can chart your progress, which is very instructive and also serves to show you where best to concentrate. This invaluable practice will help you to draw with some degree of accuracy relatively quickly.

These essential first exercises will give you the skill to draw, for example, a paint can or a jewelry box (Figure 3).

FIGURE 1

Freehand drawing solid shapes: cube, sphere, cylinder, cone, and rectangular box

Using drawing as a tool

Now that you have derived a brief and have had some practice at sketching, you are at one of the most exciting phases in design; the concept and exploration phase. Whether or not any ideas have yet sprung to mind is not that important, as you should have a mine of information to work with from your brief.

Looking at the brief will provide some immediate pointers such as scale. Are you going to design a chair, a jewelry box, a cabinet, or a music stand? Look around you at nature for a potential solution, either as a structural offering or as an aesthetic suggestion. The human body is a mine of information, especially when looking at movement such as that of the knee or

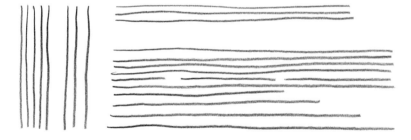

FIGURE 2a

Vertical and horizontal lines

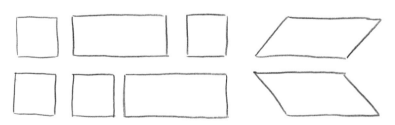

FIGURE 2b

Squares, rectangles, and parallelograms

EIGHT **DESIGN AND DRAWING**

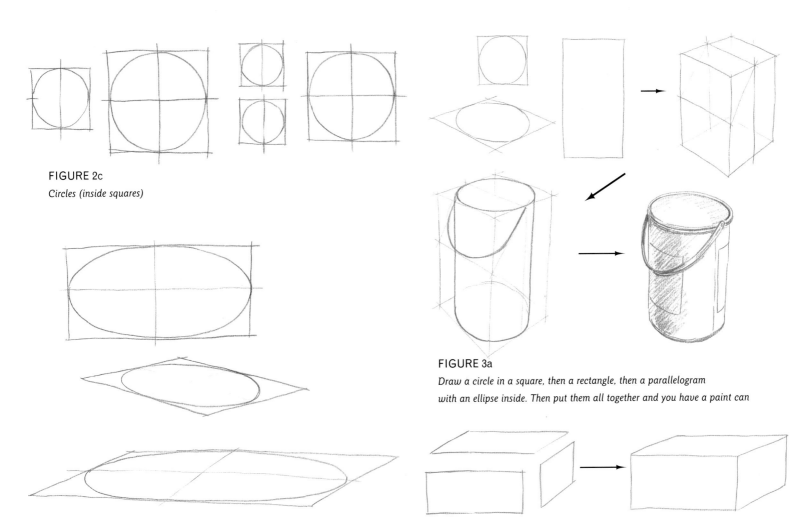

FIGURE 2c

Circles (inside squares)

FIGURE 2d

Ellipses (inside rectangles and parallelograms)

FIGURE 3a

Draw a circle in a square, then a rectangle, then a parallelogram with an ellipse inside. Then put them all together and you have a paint can

FIGURE 3b

Draw two parallelograms and a rectangle, then put them all together. You now have the basis for a jewelry box

fingers, which inspired the classic "knuckle" joint; or look at an umbrella—such a lightweight yet strong structure, perhaps inspired by a bat's wing or a leaf.

Another way to start the concept stage is through what designers often call "form generation." This can start with simple sketches of squares, rectangles, circles, and so on. By adding to them, subtracting from them, subdividing them or rearranging the subdivisions, a whole series of potential new paths to explore can be created.

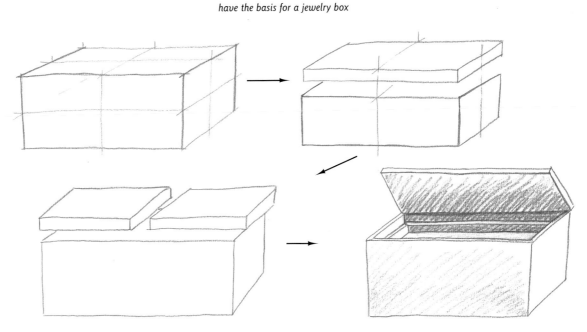

FIGURE 3c

By addition to or subtraction from the space you have drawn, you can quickly add shelves, trays, or lids, and so on

Sketching and drawing techniques

TWO SAMPLE DESIGN BRIEFS

The areas in design already covered are reinforced here by cementing the sketching techniques and providing you with two sample design briefs to work through. These briefs give you an insight into how the design process works—in a simple and enjoyable fashion.

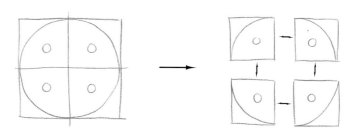

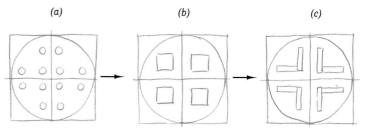

FIGURE 5
The concept is fine as a whole, but becomes unstable if separated

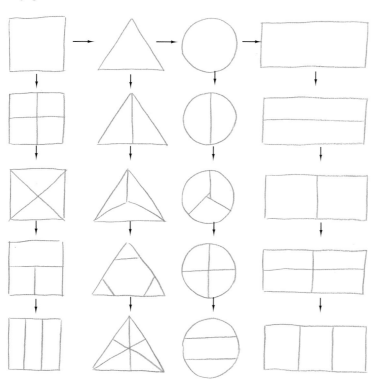

FIGURE 4 *Begin with simple shapes and develop them so that each of the above becomes a potential table top*

(a)   (b)   (c)

FIGURE 6
Alternative solutions are required (see text for details)

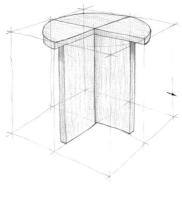

FIGURE 7
Your solution can be represented three-dimensionally

BRIEF 1
To design a low table that can act as a whole, or as a set of separate tables

Start with squares, triangles, circles, and rectangles. Then start to explore options by adding, subtracting, and sub-dividing. As Figure 4 illustrates, each of the shapes created is a potential table top (or tops). Now look at the elements as

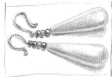

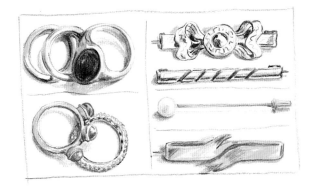

FIGURE 8 *First consider the items to be stored: their shape may suggest the perfect way to store them*

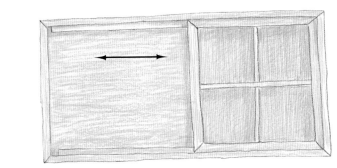

Plan showing sliding tray

Side elevation showing tray on runners

FIGURE 9 *Sketch further boxes incorporating different storage ideas*

a whole and as a set, and pick one or two ideas to work with. If legs are added, it is evident that as a whole the concept is fine, but if separated, each table top and leg would be unstable (Figure 5).

Explore your designs further, solve any new problems, and sketch in more detail. Look at further possibilities for legs that work separately. Draw a sketch of the proposed solution (Figure 6).

a) By adding two legs to each quarter, each section can stand alone, but there are too many legs.
b) By adding boxes underneath each section, again, each quarter can stand alone, but it will look very "boxy" or heavy.
c) By adding an "L" to each quarter, the separate tables become stable. Because the "Ls" are open at the outer faces, they are visually less heavy. They follow the natural split lines, and are therefore less obtrusive.

From some information and exploratory sketches, you now have one potential solution that can be further detailed and developed. Since it is a circular table, you know it fits into a

square; it therefore follows that if the height is the same as the width and the length, it can be represented three-dimensionally by putting it in a cube (Figure 7).

BRIEF 2
To design a jewelry box

First consider what needs to be stored: necklaces, earrings, bracelets, rings, cufflinks, brooches, and so on. In terms of scale or similarity of shape, see if you can categorize the list into sets. This may help you to decide on the divisions within the box. The necklaces can be stored either longitudinally or in a small bunch, though there is less likelihood of them getting tangled if they are not bunched up together.

Earrings and cufflinks could be put together, as could brooches and rings.

Lay each item of jewelry on a surface so that you can see how they lie, the space they take up, and the easiest means of access, etc. This should automatically suggest a path (or four!) for you to explore. The shape of the items may suggest the perfect way to store them (Figure 8).

With this information, and starting with the simple idea of a box, sketch further containers of appropriate proportion and start looking at how you might separate the different stored items (Figure 9).

It is important to keep an eye on each concept, its relevance to the brief, and whether or not you can

make it within your budget. If, as in the sketch, you go for a long rectangular box for the necklaces and bracelets, but with the simple addition of a slip of wood halfway up the sides, you can then fit a tray that can slide to either end of the box or be lifted out easily for smaller items of jewelry. A flat piece of wood drilled with an appropriate Forstner bit can quickly make a simple, yet effective, tray for the smaller items. Lining the bottom with felt, velvet, or suede makes it more luxurious; it also provides a softer surface for the jewelry and makes it quieter when items are returned to their places.

You now have the basis of a good concept: a box of

the right proportions, a method of storing the various items separately, and ease of access. This leaves one last major consideration—a cover for dust protection and to keep the items out of sight. (You could look at ways of locking the cover to protect the items inside from theft, but since a box of this size is so easily portable, it is hardly worth considering.)

How could you design this cover? A lid? Folding or sliding? A tambour? Running? A lift-off panel? Locating? This process can be very exciting, so do not go for the obvious and first idea that enters your head, but explore the different possibilities. You may come up with something that is more appropriate and aesthetically pleasing and which involves the user to a greater extent.

Quickly sketch all the designs you can think of for a cover for the jewelry box (Figure 10). See if any solutions spring to mind from nature (a clam shell, for example). Examine each possibility for ease of making, safety, ease of use, and so on. Does it need a stop, or need to locate in a particular way? Might it fall,

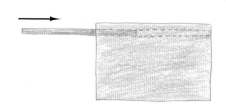

and dent or break? Could it serve any other useful purpose? Perhaps a mirror incorporated into the cover would be useful.

You are now at the stage of choosing one or two of your most promising solutions, and starting to detail and develop them to a stage in which working drawings can be produced so the box can be made.

Start by looking at each of the faces or, in drawing terms, "elevations." Draw a freehand sketch of each face—front, side, top—and consider refining the shape, looking at edge details, and whether you want to use any decoration such as moldings, inlays, veneer pattern, or simply a lovely piece of wood (Figure 11).

FIGURE 11

Draw elevations of your box, refining the shape and edge details

It is always important to try to keep any detailing or choice of material relevant to the function and nature of the design. For example, jewelry is associated with being precious and fine, so select a fine wood and lining that will enhance rather than conflict with the contents. If you choose a simple and elegant shape, try to keep any detailing sympathetically simple and unfussy. The other route is to detail the box in sympathy with its contents rather than its function. Consider the detailing, therefore, in terms of fine inlays and the addition of reflective materials such as mother of pearl or brass. Although these options may seem to offer conflicting advice, the purpose and result show that both approaches are equally valid.

It is important at this stage to look at the finish you intend to use, to check

FIGURE 10

When defining any problem, try to keep the language loose rather than specific to avoid preconceptions: e.g., "container" rather than "box," "cover" rather than "lid," and "fold" rather than "hinge." The above are ideas for a cover

how appropriate it is—not only in terms of feel, but also in practical terms, i.e., that it will not react with the jewelry. You may decide to texture the container by sandblasting or scorching it so that the box belies its function. The choices are endless and each may be right in a given situation, but the function of the piece does not change.

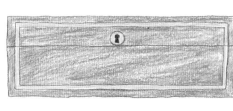

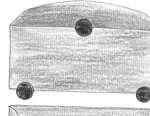

Two sample design briefs

NINE **VENEERING**

The benefits of using veneer in the construction of furniture have long been appreciated by the cabinetmaker. The increased stability, the huge range of high-quality veneers, and the endless decorative possibilities have contributed to some of the finest furniture made over the past 300 years. More recently, there has been a fresh enthusiasm for veneering as solid lumber becomes a more valuable commodity. In addition, equipment such as the portable vacuum press has given the woodworker the facility to exploit the exciting decorative potential of this material.

BASIC TOOLS AND EQUIPMENT

More and more woodworkers are exploiting the structural benefits and endless decorative potential of veneering. Veneers can be laid by hand the traditional way, or by the simple caul press and now by the recently introduced portable vacuum veneering press. Only a few other tools are required.

Veneer saw

Veneer hammer

Traditional glue pot

Veneer trimmers

Hand-held glue spreader

The knife

Although there is an excellent range of good craft knives, unfortunately none are made specifically for veneering, and those selected will benefit from reshaping. The three essential elements when choosing your blade are thickness, shape, and bevel.

Thickness For intricate work like marquetry or when patching veneers, a fine scalpel blade is preferred. However, for general cutting and trimming, a slightly thicker, stiffer blade is best.

Shape A straight, pointed blade cuts well across the grain but is less suitable for

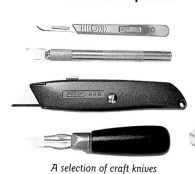
A selection of craft knives

straight edge cutting with the grain, when it has a tendency to follow the grain and can also split the wood. A curved blade is better suited for this task.

Bevel For preparing veneers ready for jointing, blades ground on one side (the waste side) only will produce a good square edge on veneers when cutting with the flat face against the straight edge. In hammer veneering, where the veneer is laid with overlapping joints and then cut, a blade ground with bevels on both sides at very shallow angles will produce the best results.

Shooting board

This simple homemade device produces absolutely straight and square edges on flat veneer. It can be long or short depending on the length of veneer to be jointed. Made from MDF or

plywood, it consists of a base board, a straight edge made from ¼ in. (6 mm) or ⅜ in. (10 mm) thick board against which a hand plane runs, and finally a top board to hold the veneers flat. Accuracy in the jointing is dependent on the accuracy of the jig.

Veneer saw

The veneer saw is about 6 in. (152 mm) long with a curved blade. The teeth require no set as the saw is used only for shallow cuts. It can be used for standard knife-cut veneer (approximately ¹⁄₃₂ in./ 0.8 mm) as well as for saw-cut veneer (⅛ in./3 mm) where a knife is ineffective, and produces a square edge for close jointing.

Straight edge and spring clamps

A good-quality straight edge is necessary for jointing

veneers, thick enough to keep the knife from running over the edge and into your fingers. They are available in a choice of lengths—a 39 in. (1000 mm) length is useful for most work.

Spring clamps are inexpensive and useful for holding the straight edge in place when cutting veneer.

Glue pot and spreader

The traditional glue pot is used for heating animal glue and keeping it liquid without it overheating. It consists of an outer pot containing water with an inner pot containing the glue. It can be heated on a gas or electric ring. For occasional use, however, an

ABOVE *Using a shooting board to plane veneers that are difficult to cut*

Pearl (animal) glue before soaking

old saucepan and a tin can will suffice.

When veneering with PVA and UF resins a hand-held glue spreader is a great time saver and guarantees a thin and even spread of adhesive. A cheaper alternative, but just as effective, is a thin sponge paint roller.

Veneer tape

Veneer tape is used to joint the veneers together and is essential to prevent joints from shrinking and opening up. The best tape is made from a thin paper covered on one side with a water-soluble gum. After wetting, the applied tape can be easily removed from the job without tearing the grain.

Self-adhesive tapes are to be avoided unless they are of the low tack type, as they invariably tear the veneer when removed and can leave glue deposits in the pores of the wood which present problems with finishing.

Veneer hammer

The veneer hammer is used to squeeze excess animal glue out from under the veneer and can be bought or homemade. If you are making one, the metallic insert in the working edge should be made of a non-ferrous metal such as brass to avoid staining the veneer. For the same reason do not use oak for the head or the handle.

Veneer trimmer

This tool is used to trim the excess veneer overhanging the panel after pressing. The best types can cut in both directions to prevent breakout and splitting.

Adhesives

Animal glue Animal glue, or "scotch" glue as it is commonly called, is made by first soaking in cold water, until the glue absorbs all of the water, and then heated in a glue pot or double-boiler. Great care must be taken to ensure that the glue does not get too hot as its properties will quickly deteriorate when overheated. For best results mix the glue fresh each time, but with care the glue can be reheated a maximum of three or four times.

When prepared, the glue may require thinning by added hot water a little at a time so that it runs off the brush without any lumps.

Polyvinyl acetate PVA need only be applied to one surface, the groundwork, when veneering. It is important that a thin film only is applied as it has no gap-filling properties. On a large surface it can be spread with a wide (4–6 in./ 102–152 mm) comb spreader and then rolled out with a cheap sponge paint roller. However, it is more suited to smaller panels, and there is a danger of it pre-curing on larger areas due to the faster curing nature of this glue, especially when veneering onto particle board.

Work veneered with PVA must be held under pressure for at least one hour and it is advisable to put it aside for several hours to allow the moisture to fully evaporate.

Urea-formaldehyde UF resins can be bought in two forms: a one-shot powder requiring water to trigger the catalyst and a liquid resin with a powder or liquid hardener. Of the two, the one-pack powder Cascamite is the most readily available.

UF resins are excellent wood glues with considerable gap-filling properties. Jobs veneered with UF resins must be held under pressure for the recommended period but usually require a longer pressing time than PVA.

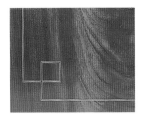

Decorative stringing on a mahogany curl veneer

A selection of inlaid lines

Parquetry motif

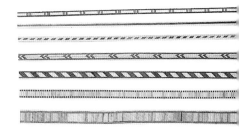

Assorted inlays/bandings

Part of a diamond-quartered panel with bird's eye maple

Shaded marquetry

Basic tools and equipment

PREPARING AND LAYING VENEER

Veneer used to be sawn to a thickness of about ⅛ in. (3 mm), whereas most veneer available today is knife-cut in the mill to a thickness of between ½₂ and ¾₄ in. (0.6 and 1 mm) from only the best-quality logs. It can be bought as a single leaf, pairs, or a whole bundle from most suppliers.

There is a huge range of woods offering many decorative features from crown-cut, straight-grained, or figured veneers to burrs and curls.

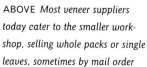

Flattening veneers

Before any cutting or laying of veneers can occur, the veneer must be flat. Most veneers lie flat naturally and require no extra work; however, curls, burrs, and highly figured veneers require preparation to remove any distortion.

To flatten the veneer, dampen it on both sides, put it between two boards, and place a weight on top. After a few hours the veneer will become more pliable and flat and should be cut and jointed and laid immediately to prevent it from drying out and buckling again.

BELOW *The range of veneers available provides endless possibilities for decorative woodwork*

ABOVE *Most veneer suppliers today cater to the smaller work-shop, selling whole packs or single leaves, sometimes by mail order*

The groundwork

Veneer can be laid onto both solid wood and man-made boards, but there are a few rules which apply according to the choice of groundwork.

Solid wood must be stable and free of knots and defects which will shadow through the veneer after laying. When using solid wood, lay the veneer with the grain direction matching that of the groundwork. This will allow the veneer to move with the wood.

When using plywood as the ground, it is important to veneer across the grain of the board to prevent surface cracks occurring later. Plywood and particle board are both fine for veneering as they have no grain direction to worry about, but use good-quality board.

Lippings are usually applied to man-made boards to give the impression of solid wood. They are generally applied before veneering for best results. Unless the lippings are to be molded later they need only be about ¼ in. (6 mm) thick to provide adequate protection against knocks. They can be clamped on or even applied using masking tape every 4 in. (102 mm) until the glue sets.

Balancing

Groundwork veneered on one side only is susceptible to distortion or cupping as the glue and veneer dry. To counter this reaction it is necessary to veneer the opposite side with a veneer of a similar thickness to the face veneer, although a cheaper veneer can be used where it is not seen.

Taping

When using a press or in caul veneering, all joints must be taped up before laying the veneer. The edges of the veneers should meet together perfectly before taping together. Strips of tape, 4 in. (102 mm) long, are dampened and applied every 6 in. (152 mm) across the joint, finishing with one long strip laid down the

Hammer veneering

1 Apply the hot glue.

2 Reheat the glue with an iron.

3 Squeeze out the excess glue with a veneer hammer.

4 Use the hammer, working from the center outward.

5 The overlapping joint is then ready for cutting.

6 Cut the joint using a straight edge.

7 Remove the waste.

8 Apply glue under the veneer before taping.

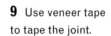

9 Use veneer tape to tape the joint.

10 Use a cutting gauge to trim the veneer for the crossbanding.

11 After reheating the glue remove the waste.

12 Cut the miter for the crossbanding.

13 Rout a channel to take the stringing.

14 The finished corner.

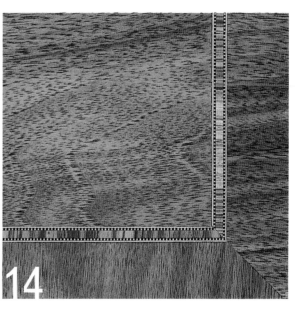

length of the joint.

The taping procedure is the same for hammer veneering; however, the veneers are laid first and the overlapping edges are then cut. In both press and hammer veneering, the tape prevents the joint from shrinking open.

Methods of pressing veneers

Hammer veneering The process of hammer veneering has been used since the last century and is still used today, although mainly by furniture restorers and enthusiasts who make it their hobby. It requires few tools but considerable skill and know-how, and is suitable for knife-cut veneer in relatively simple built-up designs.

After preparation of the groundwork and veneer, animal glue is applied to both surfaces before bringing them together. At this stage the glue will have cooled, leaving a thick glue line, and will require reheating with an iron before squeezing the glue out. The veneer is dampened first to prevent the iron from sticking, and after heating the veneer hammer is used to squeeze out the excess glue, leaving the veneer in close contact with the groundwork.

Jointing veneers is done by overlapping the edges and cutting through both veneers with a knife against a straight edge. The waste is then removed before finally taping up the joint to prevent shrinkage while the glue dries.

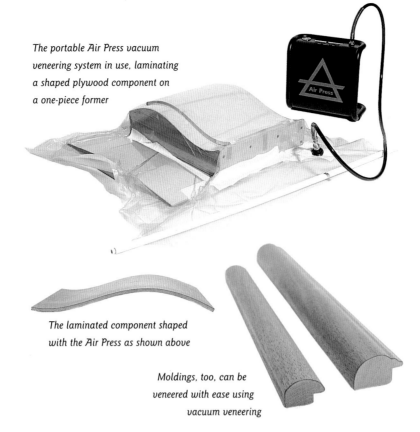

The portable Air Press vacuum veneering system in use, laminating a shaped plywood component on a one-piece former

The laminated component shaped with the Air Press as shown above

Moldings, too, can be veneered with ease using vacuum veneering

ABOVE *A veneered panel in the caul press*

Caul veneering When using thicker veneers or in more elaborate pattern work such as marquetry or parquetry, it is not practical to use the veneer hammer as this method has a tendency to displace the veneer pieces and break up the patterns. This kind of veneering requires pressing. In the absence of a press, caul veneering may be practiced with a certain degree of success.

This method uses cauls— stiff boards, usually man-made—with stout cross bearers top and bottom to press the veneers onto the groundwork, and pressure is applied by clamps. The top bearers should be slightly curved so as to apply pressure at the middle first, to prevent trapping air and

glue between the groundwork and the veneer. Most glues can be used for caul veneering. When using animal glue, however, it will be necessary to heat the cauls first with a warm iron, as before, to melt the glue and make it adhere.

Vacuum veneering

There is now a practical option to both caul veneering and hammer veneering, in the form of portable vacuum veneering systems (pictured left). This low-cost equipment gives the small workshop the facility to veneer flat boards and laminate shaped components without taking up valuable workshop space.

The system uses a small vacuum pump to extract the air from a plastic or rubber bag containing the work-piece. As the vacuum is produced the atmospheric pressure outside the bag exerts a force in excess of $\frac{3}{4}$ ton/ft^2 (8 tonnes/m^2) on to the work-piece. This pressure is uniformly achieved over the whole panel.

Preparation for finishing

After veneering the groundwork, leave the glue to harden fully before preparing the surface for finishing since the glue, particularly animal glue, can shrink as it dries out. The surface can then be sanded smooth with a finely set smoothing plane or cabinet scraper. Finally, use abrasive papers starting with 150 grit.

PARQUETRY SHELF AND WALL MIRROR *see plan page 220*

Parquetry work uses veneers cut into geometric shapes such as squares, diamonds, and triangles, and fitted together to make a repeat pattern. The pattern can be made from the same wood using changes in grain direction to give the effect, or it can use different woods to give a checkerboard effect. There is a wide range available from which to make your choice.

The core material recommended is plywood with solid wood lippings to complement or contrast with the veneer. The shelf slots into the wall mirror, supported by the wedge-shaped sections, and requires no glue to hold it in position. This project was veneered using a vacuum press (see opposite).

This straightforward construction uses plywood, laminated to give the thickness, and then bandsawn to give the tapered profile. The shelf is made first so that the top and bottom wedge supports can be butted up to the shelf and glued into position on the ¾ in. (19 mm) plywood backboard. The veneer is a bookmatched, quilted maple veneer with a parquetry pattern of diamond shapes cut at 60° from a combination of natural and dyed sycamore.

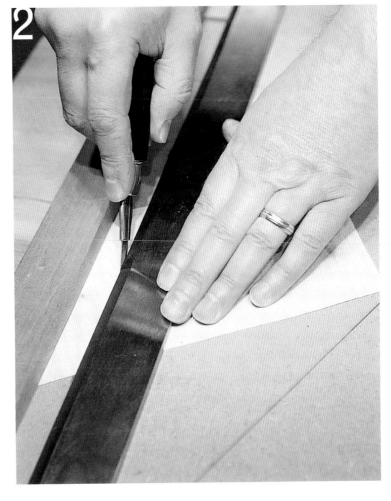

Cutting the veneer strips

1 To produce the parquetry pattern make the first cut at 60° to the direction of the grain of the sycamore.

2 Using the cutting jig with stops set for the correct width, cut the strips parallel to the 60° cut.

3 Then cut the dyed veneer to the same width but with the cuts running parallel to the grain.

NINE **VENEERING**

Forming the parquetry pattern

4 Tape the strips together using a low-tack adhesive tape, gently stretching the tape to pull the strips together.

5 Turn the veneers over and spread a thin bead of fast-setting PVA glue between each strip. Hinge the veneers open to spread the glue. Tape up the glued side and weight down under a flat board.

6 When the glue has cured, remove the tape and cut into strips again.

7 Set out the strips in checkerboard fashion; tape and glue as before.

8 Finally, cut the assembled strips into the required triangle shown in Figure 9.

9 The parquetry pattern triangle is now complete. To inset the triangle in the shelf, cut through the background veneer using the parquetry as a pattern and tape into position before pressing.

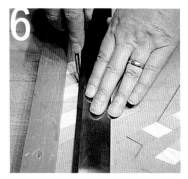

Project: Parquetry shelf and wall mirror

TEN **WOODTURNING**

Woodturning is a popular area of woodworking that requires a relatively small working area. It involves rotating, or turning, wood into a circular form either by faceplate turning—for example for making bowls and round boxes, or by spindle turning—for making round or partly round items such as chair and table legs, lamp stands, and tool handles.

TURNING TOOLS AND EQUIPMENT

The basic requirements for turning wood are a lathe, a bench grinder, a set of turning tools, eye protection, a dust mask, some wood, and a workshop. What sort of lathe and tools you need depends on what sort of things you want to make and how much you can afford to spend. If you do not have clear ideas about this, it may be a good idea to join a woodturning club or attend a class.

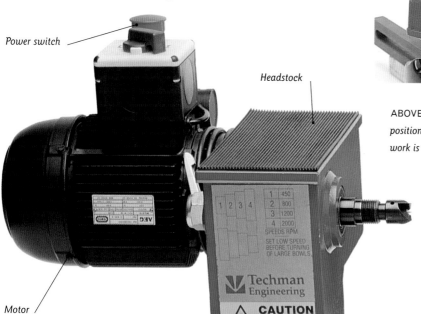

Power switch

Headstock

Motor

ABOVE *The headstock with a small faceplate inserted. The tool rest is positioned so that small bowls or other faceplate products can be turned. The work is screwed to the faceplate*

Adjustable tool rest

The lathe

If you want a lathe for normal bowls and spindles there is a wide range available, but beware of very cheap lathes which can be so poorly made that they make turning difficult. If you are mainly interested in miniatures, it would be better to buy one of the small lathes that are made to a high standard rather than a cheap, large lathe.

A lathe consists of a motor which powers a spindle in a headstock at varying speeds. The lathe rotates the wood, which is shaped by tools held by hand on a tool rest that is supported on the lathe bed.

To make spindles, wood

ABOVE *The drive center inserted in the headstock which is used to turn between centers to make spindles or other cylindrical objects. The sharp spurs grip the end of the work to make it turn*

with its grain running parallel to the axis of the lathe, is rotated between two centers: a drive center in the spindle in the headstock and a "dead" or "live" center in the tailstock.

To make bowls, a circular blank of wood with its grain running at right angles to the lathe is held on one face on the spindle by means of a faceplate or chuck.

Turning tools

Turning tools are specially designed to withstand the stresses of being held against a rotating piece of wood. There are special tools for faceplate work and for spindles and it is best to use the designated tools for their intended purposes only. Miniature versions are available for use with a small lathe. A basic full-size kit could consist of the items shown here.

Always keep your tools sharp and the bevel concave.

For spindles

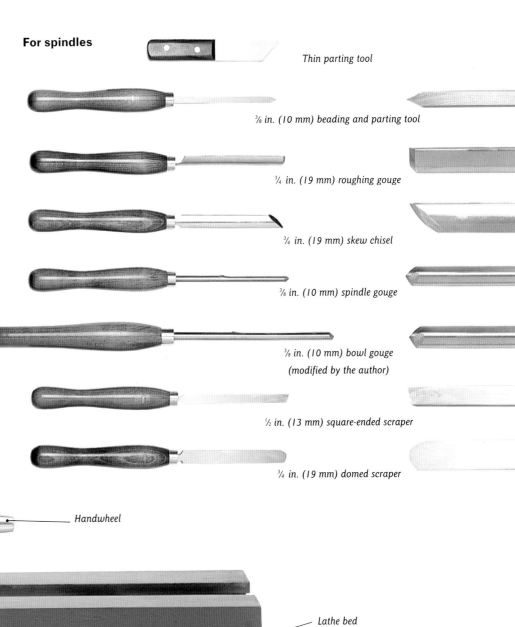

Thin parting tool

⅜ in. (10 mm) beading and parting tool

¾ in. (19 mm) roughing gouge

¾ in. (19 mm) skew chisel

⅜ in. (10 mm) spindle gouge

For bowls

⅜ in. (10 mm) bowl gouge (modified by the author)

½ in. (13 mm) square-ended scraper

¾ in. (19 mm) domed scraper

Tailstock

Handwheel

Lathe bed

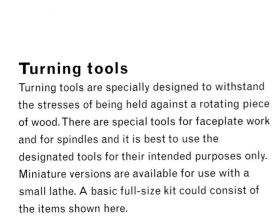

LEFT *The adjustable tail stock with a live center installed. This has ball bearings that enable the work to revolve freely; if you do not have a live center, a dead center will work provided it is lubricated with wax or grease*

TEN **WOODTURNING**

Turning tools and equipment

FACEPLATE AND SPINDLE TURNING

Faceplate turning mostly means producing bowls, but also includes breadboards and other flat ware where the principles are the same. The best way to learn about this is by making the bowl in the next section. It is fairly easy to obtain the lumber to practice spindle turning because of the small thicknesses required.

Faceplate turning

This entails fixing one face to the lathe with either a faceplate—usually supplied with the lathe—or a chuck. The faceplate holds the wooden blank by means of screws which pass through it into the wood. This is a safe method provided the wood is sound and its surface flat, that the screws are at least ³⁄₁₆ in. (5 mm) (No. 10) or bigger, that they project into the blank by at least ½ in. (13 mm), and have been screwed in tightly.

Faceplate blanks are usually cut from planks with the grain running along them, since this is the way most wood is prepared for seasoning. It also means that the screws hold more strongly because they are going into side grain. As in all woodwork it is most efficient to cut with the

grain and this grain direction makes it easier because it enables you to hollow by working from the outside inward. You can buy ready-cut blanks from turning suppliers or you can buy planks and cut your own with a bandsaw. In any case, until you are well practiced it is wise to use cheap wood provided that it is sound. You can even practice on wet (unseasoned) wood, which is easier to cut, as long as you realize that it will change shape and possibly crack as it dries.

Mounting the faceplate blank

In faceplate work the blank is generally mounted on the face that will eventually be the top of the piece so that you can turn the base easily, and if you have an expanding chuck make a recess to remount it on. You therefore need to decide which will be the top and bottom of the piece before you start. This is done by examining the blank for features you wish to either incorporate or omit from your finished piece—for example, you might want to lose a crack or include an attractive bit of grain.

Take care to mount the blank securely and always check that the lathe is set to the appropriate speed. As a general rule, the larger the piece the slower the speed, so if you are not sure start slow and speed up later. Before starting the lathe adjust the tool rest so that it is at the right height for the tool to cut through the center of the work at the proper cutting angle, and rotate the wood by hand to make sure it will not catch on the tool rest. If the blank does come off the lathe the likeliest trajectory is at right angles to the faceplate, so when you start the motor it is best to stand to one side.

Spindle turning

Before spending money on raw materials, practice the techniques on the cheapest wood available, which may be branches lopped from trees—these have the advantage of being roughly circular in cross-section and "wet." Short lengths about 2 in. (51 mm) in diameter, are good, but rotate them by hand before starting as they will not be exactly round. Waste skips are also a good place to look for unwanted lumber for practicing on or for a project. Beware, however, of hidden nails and avoid pieces with splits or knots. Never use wood that has been treated with preservative as this will be toxic.

Spindles are rotated by the lathe through a drive center that has two or four

ABOVE *The faceplate is screwed to the blank, then mounted onto the lathe, with the tool rest just beneath the center of the blank. Stand well back when first starting the lathe*

sharp edges that bite into the end of the blank and therefore need to be kept sharp. The other end is supported by a center, a cone that engages in a hole in the end of the blank. A "dead" center does not rotate with the wood, so needs lubrication with wax to prevent it from burning, whereas a "live" center rotates and is easier to use.

Mounting the spindle blank

To mount the wood you need to find the center of each end. If the blank is perfectly straight and square in section you can mark diagonals that will meet in the middle, but if the wood is irregular in section, use a pair of dividers. Guess the center and put a point there, then twirl the other point around to see whether you have guessed correctly—press the point home if you have, or move it if you have not. The driving center should be removed from the lathe and forced into the end of the wood using a wooden mallet. The wood is put between the centers, and the tailstock moved up to nearly engage in the end of the spindle. The tailstock should then be fixed, the center wound up into the end and then slackened off slightly so there is not too much pressure on the bearings.

Which woods to use?

Most woods can be turned and your choice depends on various factors in addition to suitability for the project.

Certain woods, such as yew, are toxic and great care must be taken not to inhale the dust. Others such as elm and beech have been found to be carcinogens. You may even find that you are sensitive to a particular wood or become sensitized by frequent use. Contact dermatitis can develop in this way and can be serious.

Woods which are soft, such as conifers and poplar, are rarely used for bowls because the bowls are easily damaged after completion. Softwoods do, however, have a tradition of being used for spindles. Woods with curly grain or burrs are sought after by experienced bowl turners but should be avoided by the novice on the grounds of expense and difficulty of

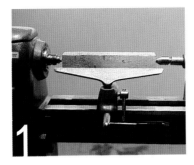

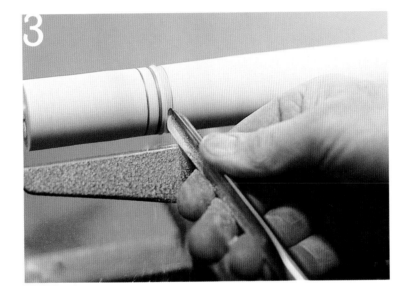

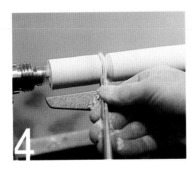

use. They are also not suitable for normal spindle work because they are hard to finish and do not have the longitudinal strength required in a spindle.

Preparing to turn a spindle

1 Move the tool rest as close to the work as possible and level with or just below center height. The exact position will depend on your height relative to the lathe, but always ensure that the work will not snag the tool rest before you start the lathe. Spindles are generally turned at faster rpm than bowls because they are usually smaller in diameter, but always start slowly and then work up to faster speeds as you feel

confident. In any case, if you are roughing out a square section piece you will need to start at a slower speed because of the larger effective diameter and the irregular surface.

Roughing out

2 Roughing out is done as shown with a roughing gouge, while spindle gouges and skew chisels are used for shaping. The skew chisel is used for planing straight cylinders or gradual curves by cutting with the edge just behind the point.

Decorating spindles

3 When the spindle has been turned to a cylinder, decorative shapes can be added using a spindle gouge.

4 Roll the spindle gouge to cut in the other direction.

5 More of the wood is removed as you progress.

If the marks made by the lathe centers should not be seen in the finished piece, allow extra wood at each end of the blank so that a short length of waste (a spigot) can be left. This is turned with the beading and parting tool while turning the shape and eventually turned off when the spindle is finished, using a skew chisel or a parting tool.

TURNED WOODEN BOWL *see plan page 222*

A good size bowl for the beginner to make is one that is 8 in. (203 mm) in diameter by 2 in. (51 mm) deep, since it is big enough to be useful but not too big to break the bank if you mess it up!

Choose a straight-grained piece of a medium-hard wood such as sycamore. Burrs are not a good idea for a first bowl because of cost, their relative difficulty to work with, and the fact that they can contain flaws which might make working them dangerous.

LEFT *Detail showing a very slight overhang inside the top of the rim which adds mystery to the bowl by enhancing the impression of depth*

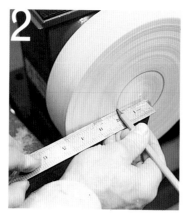

Mounting the blank
1 Mount the blank on the faceplate as described in the previous section.

First make the bottom slightly concave by using the gouge on its side, cutting with the part of the edge between the nose and the extreme end of the edge going from the outside to the center. Gouges are usually used with the flute pointing in the direction of cut.

Marking the base of the bowl
2 Draw a circle the size of the faceplate plus ½ in. (13 mm) on the base with a

pencil. This will be the size of the base.

Shaping the outside of the bowl
3 Start shaping the outside of the bowl with the gouge on its other side, working from the center toward the outside. At this stage the tool rest will be parallel with the original face.

4 As the bowl takes shape you will need to stop the lathe and adjust the position of the tool rest from time to time.

5 As the tip of the tool goes around the bowl, the end of the handle should move around, too, to keep the bevel rubbing.

6 As the shape nears completion, work the base into the curve of the side.

7 When the shape is right, sharpen the gouge and make a thin cut to get rid of any rough grain.

Finishing the outside

8 Use abrasive paper on the outside with the tool rest well out of the way. Start with a coarse grit such as 100, moving it in and out to avoid creating lines

on the surface, and only progress to the next grit when you have removed all the rough grain.

9 Then re-mark the faceplate diameter on the

base so that you can mount it accurately.

Remove the faceplate and bowl from the lathe and take out the screws.

10 Put the faceplate on the base of the bowl and attach it with the screws, making a note of how far they penetrate into the blank.

11 Put the blank back on the lathe and true up the top using the gouge as you did on the bottom.

12 Measure the depth of the blank, subtract the length of the screw penetration plus ¼ in. (6 mm) and, using a ¼ in. (6 mm) drill bit, make a hole in the center of the bowl to tell you how deep you can go.

Shaping the inside of the bowl

13 Make a cut in the top of the bowl with the corner of the square-ended scraper to mark the thickness of the bowl's rim.

14 Then hollow with the gouge, working from the rim of the bowl into the center.

15 Continue this process until the shape is near to that which you intend.

16 When the wall thickness is even, except for a little overhang at the top, use the domed scraper to get rid of any unevenness inside.

17 Finish with abrasive paper and apply some vegetable cooking oil with the bowl stationary. Remove from the lathe, take out the screws, and fill the holes with plastic wood.

LEFT *Common woods such as the ash used in this project make useful and attractive bowls, but the experienced turner can invest in more expensive woods such as burr elm to produce something really special*

Woodcarving can be described as three-dimensional drawing. It requires basic manual skills and is aided by natural artistic flair. Almost anyone can learn the skills required for basic carving and as long as the fundamental rules are understood and followed, a satisfactory result can be obtained. The simpler your first projects, the more success you will have. This will encourage you to attempt more ambitious projects as you progress. Instructions are given here for carving a scallop box, which is an ideal first project.

ELEVEN WOODCARVING

TOOLS, EQUIPMENT, AND LUMBER

Carving is a very rewarding aspect of woodwork with which you can develop fine skills. You will be able to explore your own ideas, free from the structural constraints of cabinetmaking in areas in which form, shape, and detail are paramount.

Hand tools

Carving tools come in a variety of shapes and sizes that provide endless possibilities for shaping wood. Large high-sided gouges, larger open-radius gouges, and near flats are used mainly for heavy work such as roughing out and bulk shaping. Parting, or "V," tools can also be used for this process, in which a definite and fine, deep division is required. As the carving progresses, smaller versions of the tools are required for the refined sharpening and modeling.

There are a large number of carving tool suppliers, most of whom carry a comprehensive list of different types of tools. Well-balanced, high-quality steel, finely ground tools are required for good

woodcarving. Old second-hand tools of well-known makes are a good purchase —often being of a standard as yet unsurpassable in all-round quality to anything available today.

Most manufacturers supply tools with ash or box wood handles with or without steel or brass ferrules. Separate replacement handles can be purchased. Hexagonal- or octagonal-shaped handles ensure the tools lie steadier on the bench.

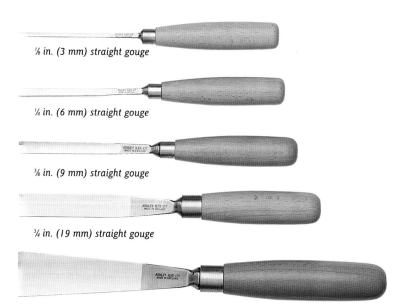

⅛ in. (3 mm) straight gouge

¼ in. (6 mm) straight gouge

⅜ in. (9 mm) straight gouge

¾ in. (19 mm) straight gouge

1½ in. (37 mm) alongee gouge

Rasps, rifflers, and files

A good range of abrasive tools are useful, especially when working on large sculptural pieces. Rifflers and rasps will quickly

ABOVE AND RIGHT *A small selection of the wide range of sizes and sweeps of carving chisels and gouges available*

Species of lumber	Assets for carving	Pitfalls
Lime	Good all-round	Plain grain
Yellow Quebec pine	Soft, straight grain	Brittle
Russian red	Soft, tight, straight grain	Slightly brittle
English oak	Character grain	Hard, open grain
English walnut	Good all-round	Slow to carve
Jelutong	Tight, even grain	Slightly, brittle—bland
Cherry	Nice to carve green	Sticky when dry
Apple	Nice to carve green	Sticky when dry
Pear	Nice to carve green	Sticky when dry
Plum	Nice to carve green	Sticky when dry
American white maple	Interesting grain	Very slow carving
Sycamore	White, nice polished	Slightly curly
Mahogany	Good for furniture carving	Slightly brittle
Ebony	Very good finish	Slightly brittle and very hard
Box	Takes excellent detail	Limited dimension and hard

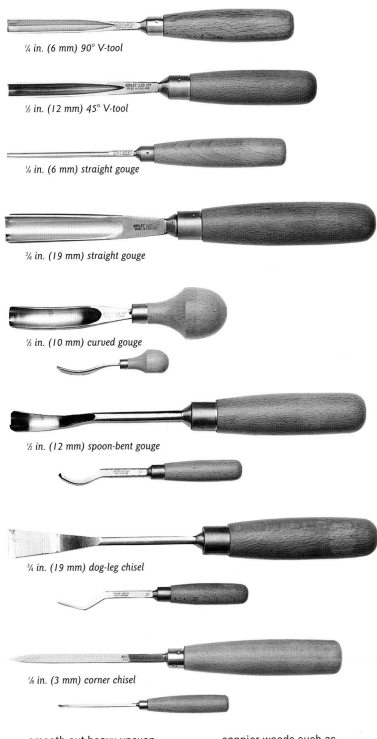

¼ in. (6 mm) 90° V-tool

½ in. (12 mm) 45° V-tool

¼ in. (6 mm) straight gouge

¾ in. (19 mm) straight gouge

½ in. (10 mm) curved gouge

½ in. (12 mm) spoon-bent gouge

¾ in. (19 mm) dog-leg chisel

⅛ in. (3 mm) corner chisel

smooth out heavy uneven surfaces. They have more of a ripping action than a cutting one, and although they remove heavy bumps, finishing will still have to be done with the finer rasps and files before any glass-papering can be done.

When used often on some of the more oily or sappier woods such as Scotch pine, teak, or lignum, rasps and files have a tendency to clog up. A wire brush will help here or, for the more stubborn ones, a blow torch will do the trick.

The Surform is a more advanced type of rasp with holes in the teeth so that it does not clog up.

Inexpensive and extremely useful, Surforms are available in a variety of shapes and sizes.

Power tools

Angle grinders Since the invention of the Arbortech cutter, the angle grinder has become invaluable to many experienced carvers. The Arbortech has six offset alternating teeth, with a ridge spacer between the teeth for a smoother cut. It is especially useful for roughing out but is noisy, messy, and dusty, and it also has a tendency to snatch when cutting with the wrong side of the blade. It is very important to read the manufacturer's guide before use.

Hand-held power carvers (routers) Such tools are also useful for carving and their application is vast. With a comprehensive range of makes and sizes and a variety of cutters and burrs, they negotiate the grain faster and more efficiently than any riffler or rasp.

Miniature rasps and files

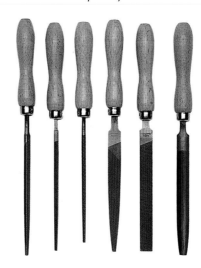

Miniature power tools

With various high-speed and diamond cutters, miniature power tools enable the carver to create some very fine and detailed carvings in a fraction of the time taken by other conventional tools.

Holding devices and clamps

Your hands are the best holding device, but since both hands are required for carving, a variety of devices have been invented. These range from simple spot gluing, bar and C-clamps, and vises, to sophisticated hydro-clamps, where pressure is applied via an oil-filled chamber.

Woods suitable for carving

"Which is the best wood to use for carving?" is a question often asked. The answer is that it depends entirely on the type of carving to be undertaken.

In the past, oak was used for church carvings, mahogany for polished furniture, and lime and carving pine (yellow Quebec) for items that were to be gilded or painted. These days jelutong is used for pattern-making, and box for fine and intricate detailed carvings. Lime is ideal for the novice to use: easily obtainable, it is soft and easy to work with and holds good detail.

GENERAL CARVING TECHNIQUES

Woodcarving has progressed historically from very primitive carving through to the present day. As with anything, practice will perfect your skill. Some of the techniques shown here are used in making the scallop box in the next section.

LEFT *Prior to veining, it is necessary to mark out with a pencil exactly where you wish to cut*

Marking out and measuring

Marking out devices are as essential to the carver as his chisels. This is most important in the case of repetitive carved moldings evident in classical and architectural woodcarving, as well as in geometrical designs for chip carving.

BELOW *Detail depicting a George III dining chair leg, finely tapered with five-tiered husk drop, crested by a decorative interlocking band, typical of Chippendale furniture*

Accurate marking out of the pattern is essential—this is the groundwork for making stencils.

Making stencils A variety of materials can be used, the most temporary being paper or card. Thin plastic sheets can be used if something more permanent is required. The most versatile material is copper sheeting—a good tip is to use metal toothpaste tubes, which are ideal. (See Scallop box project.)

Carving techniques

The practical processes of carving are relatively straightforward. What is important is that your tools are sharp.

Most carvings are constructed from sections of circles and ovals. A combination of the two produces "S" shapes, which create the high and low points of the carving to round over and scoop out. Coping with changing grain direction requires some practice. Slicing helps to deal with this problem when cutting against or across the grain: slightly curl the tool to the left or right to give your work a cleaner cut.

Paring is the action of pushing along the tool while

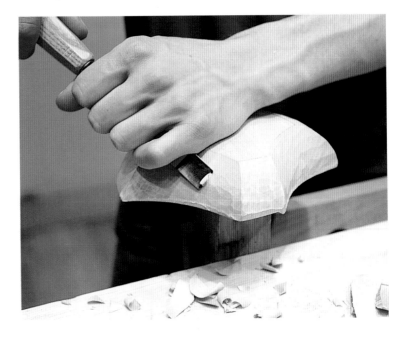

ABOVE *Intermediate modeling using a slicing action, prior to decorative detailing*

keeping the blade flat to the surface of the wood, skimming off small amounts of wood. Scalloping comprises making a series of shallow scoops adjacent to one another, giving a fine, rippling texture to the surface.

It will obviously take practice to become proficient, but the more you practice, the more this will be reflected in your work. Natural drawing skills are an asset and drawing practice is recommended. Obtain as much reference material on your chosen subject as possible. Clay

modeling is also of great benefit to the woodcarver, allowing you to create a relatively quick, three-dimensional form from which to copy.

Veining Veining is a finishing or decorative process, executed with a combination of straight and bent tools in the smaller sizes. It is often used as an aid to create shade and depth, as on a shell (see Scallop box project), or to enhance the flow and movement of leaves. Some characteristic shapes are elongated tear drops, which normally radiate from a visible or invisible point.

grade steel wool. Apply a second coat with a soft brush. Once dry, several coats of polish may be applied using a polishing pad to attain a high sheen, or simply apply a coat of wax after sealing, buffing to a shine when dry.

The simplest finish is probably a light coat of natural mineral oil. On some woods, however, this can remain slightly tacky.

Painted finish

On some of the plainer woods, a sensitively applied painted technique can make the carving come alive. Thin acrylic washes are ideal for this purpose, blending with the wood but still allowing the texture and the grain to show through. Sealing your painted surface using an acrylic sealer or light waxing is recommended.

Traditional finishes such as gilding or lacquer work are highly skilled processes, and require mastering. When expertly executed, such finishes complement many decorative carvings.

Finishing your work

When preparing for your decorative finish, sanding is usually necessary to some degree. If a smooth sanded finish is required, it is recommended to work through grades of paper, from coarse 100 grit to very fine 500 grit.

Scrapers can also be used to remove any heavy dents or blemishes. Home-made scrapers can be made by heating old screwdrivers and hacksaw blades and bending to shape—these make excellent additions to your kit.

Stamping

A variety of textures may be attained by stamping the

ABOVE *Roughing out radiating flutes which have been previously marked out using a pencil, either freehand or with a stencil*

RIGHT *Using a spoon-bent gouge to carve concave surfaces*

wood, or wetting and stamping. There are a variety of stamps and punches available on the market. Stamping the background on a relief panel can help to even out a rough surface, and also fetch out your carving, making it more prominent.

Seal and polish

Apply grain filler and sanding sealer to the surface. When dry, rub down with abrasive paper or 0000

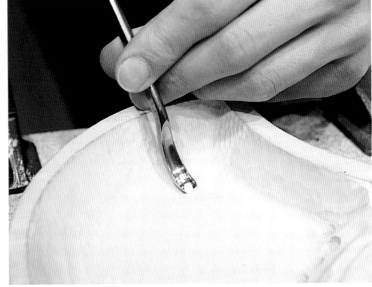

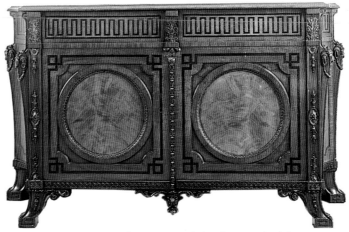

ABOVE *This George III mahogany commode is a fine example of the Chippendale style, with its Acanthus leaf caps, paterae, husk swags, interlaced band, and center spray motif*

SCALLOP BOX *see plan page 223*

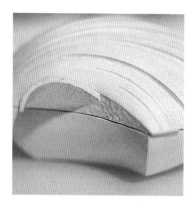

ABOVE *The fluting on the scallop top can be marked out freehand or by using a stencil (see below)*

Stencil for the fluting

Stick a tracing of the half stencil provided with the project plans onto a piece of copper foil. Using a craft knife, cut out the segments which will be the fluting, leaving some small connections between the remaining foil. Bend the foil over the smooth, shaped top of the scallop. Draw inside it with a pencil to mark the fluting.

FURTHER INFORMATION

This is an interesting project that incorporates many of the basic skills required in woodcarving.

There is no international standard for shapes and sizes of carving tools; for example, one manufacturer's ¾ in. (19 mm) roughing-out tool will be a slightly different shape from another's. This makes it difficult when specifying to beginners which size tool to use for which stage. For this reason, the tools suggested here are for general guidance only. The important thing is to use good-quality tools. As with any aspect of woodworking you will, in time, discover for yourself which tools you feel most comfortable with.

Materials and tools list

Materials
1 piece lime measuring 5⁹⁄₁₀ x 6¹¹⁄₁₆ x 1½ in. (150 x 170 x 38 mm) for the top

1 piece lime measuring 5⁹⁄₁₀ x 6⁵⁄₁₆ x 1⁵⁄₁₆ in. (150 x 160 x 33 mm) for the bottom

Small block of scrap wood plus sheet of MDF or chipboard for mounting work.

Scrap stock to form holding cradles (see Figure 16)

1 x ⁷⁄₁₆ x ³⁄₆₄ in. (25 x 11 x 1.5 mm) solid brass butt hinge

Tools
Hard pencil or pen

Tracing or carbon paper

Bandsaw

Hot glue gun

1³⁄₁₆ in. (30 mm) flat

Abrasive paper

Drill and ⅜ in. (9.5 mm) HSS drill bit with depth stop or masking tape

½ in. (13 mm), ⁹⁄₁₆ in. (14 mm), ⅝ in. (16 mm) and ¾ in. (19 mm) spoon-bent gouges

¼ in. (6 mm) V-tool

⁹⁄₁₆ in. (14 mm) and ¾ in. (19 mm) modeling tools

³⁄₁₆ in. (5 mm) and ⅜ in. (10 mm) gouges

¹⁄₁₆ in. (2 mm) veiner

⁹⁄₁₆ in. (15 mm) joiner's paring chisel

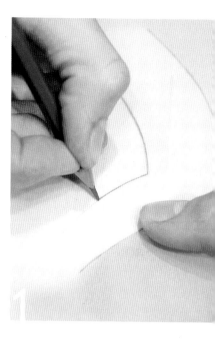

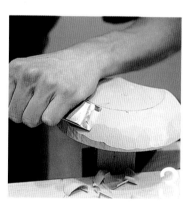

Preparation
1 Transfer the plan drawings of the top and bottom of the box onto the pieces of wood with the use of a pencil and tracing or carbon paper. Cut out each profile as accurately as possible with a bandsaw.

Holding the scallop

2 Place a piece of scrap wood in a vise, and apply some glue from a hot glue gun. Mount the box bottom on this to hold it firmly.

tape on the drill bit to mark the depth). Take care toward the edges, where the depth is less, not to drill all the way through.

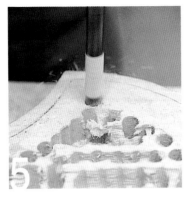

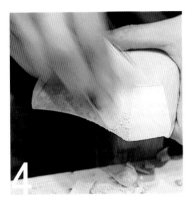

Forming the bottom

3 With the use of a 1³⁄₁₆ in. (30 mm) flat, start from the pencil line and cut outward to round over the edges. The aim is to create a smooth, even surface on the bottom.

4 Sand down the sides and base for a smooth finish.

5 Remove the bottom from the scrap wood mounting, turn it over and spot-glue it to a sheet of MDF or board, clamped to the workbench.
Mark out the perimeter of the hollow to leave a ⁵⁄₁₆ in. (8 mm) wall. Start hollowing out the bottom by drilling a series of holes to a depth of 1 in. (25 mm) (using masking

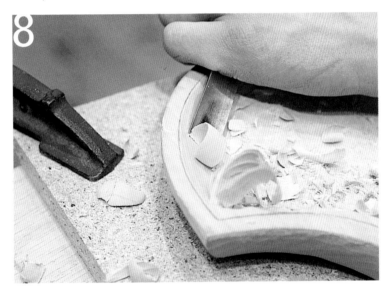

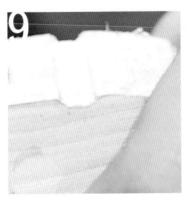

6 Remove the remaining wood using various sizes of spoon-bent gouges—½ in. (13 mm), ⁹⁄₁₆ in. (14 mm), ⅝ in. (16 mm), and ¾ in. (19

mm)—working with the grain using scooping and slicing actions. Work from the outer edge to the center using radiating cuts.

7 Now comes the precise process of finishing off the inside, which requires sharp tools.

8 Fine, even, shallow scoops in a slicing action will help to prevent tearing the grain. Use ⁹⁄₁₆ in. (14 mm), and ½ in. (13 mm) spoon-bent gouges for this process. When the bottom of the box is finished, remove it from the board.

Forming the top

9 Bandsaw out the previously marked undulating outer edge of the scallop top. This will create the ends to your radiating flutes.

10 Glue the top to the clamped sheet of MDF, as you did for the bottom, and rough out the curved shape using a 1³⁄₁₆ in. (30 mm) flat.

15 Using ⅜ in. (10 mm) and ³⁄₁₆ in. (5 mm) gouges and working towards the center, start at the highest point to cut in the flutes. Start lightly, getting progressively deeper (¼ in./6 mm) toward the outer edge.

Now add finer veining using a ³⁄₁₆ in. (5 mm) gouge and a ¹⁄₁₆ in. (2 mm) veiner.

11 Next use a ¼ in. (6 mm) V-tool to divide the scallop's side wings from the main body, lowering them to the required height.

12 Shape and model the wings using ¾ in. (19 mm) and ⁹⁄₁₆ in. (14 mm) modeling tools. View the piece from all angles to ensure a correct balance.

Fluting

13 Having attained a good basic shape, mark the centers of the flute lines at the base of the shell.

14 Start with the central undulation and, working out toward the sides, mark the fluting lines with pencil.

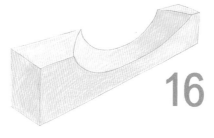

Finishing

16 Remove the scallops from the board and remove any glue, fuzzy bits, or blemishes. The top needs to be held at both ends in cradles of scrap stock.

17 Repeat the hollowing-out process that you used for the bottom. The wings should be scooped out and thinned toward the edges to a depth of ⅛ in. (3 mm). Their undersides may also be tool cut or sanded.

Let in the hinge with a ⁹⁄₁₆ in. (15 mm) joiner's paring chisel. Mark out its position, paring out flat to a depth of ³⁄₆₄ in. (1.2 mm) in both the top and bottom. Fix on the hinge, then apply your chosen finish.

LEFT *Your finished scallop box makes a fine storage piece for jewelry and other trinkets*

TWELVE
WOODS AND MATERIALS

These days there are many different types of wood and board materials available to the woodworker, each with its own specific qualities, properties, and uses. Selecting the material you wish to work with depends on its intended use, understanding how it has been sawn and stored or manufactured, and looking for defects, whether natural or man-made. You will find there is a constant joy in discovering something new about wood and its behavior, even after years of working with it.

CHARACTERISTICS OF HARDWOODS AND SOFTWOODS

All lumber is categorized as either a hardwood or a softwood. The majority of hardwoods happen to be hard and heavy; correspondingly, most softwoods are less dense and lighter than hardwoods. The only way to discover the difference is by viewing a small end-grain section under a microscope, which one can hardly undertake at a lumber yard! However, most species have already been identified for us.

The coniferous or cone-bearing trees are called softwoods, and have needle-pointed leaves, whereas the broad-leaved trees are called hardwoods and many species lose their leaves in winter, especially in temperate climates. A coniferous tree matures in about one-quarter of the time taken by a hardwood tree, but the term softwood can be misleading since some softwoods such as pitch pine and larch are actually much harder, denser, and tougher than some hardwoods, for example balsa wood. This is an extreme comparison, but it demonstrates you cannot rely on the simplistic view that all hardwoods are hard and all softwoods are soft.

The term softwood means that the tree cells are hollow and spindle-shaped, and along the sides of the cells are small holes which act as connecting passages and through which the food passes on its way to the leaves. Some common softwoods include spruce, fir, pine, yew, giant redwood, and the mighty sequoia.

The hardwood structure relies on each cell or fiber being very long and needle-shaped, and these, lying side by side, tend to make the hardwood lumbers more elastic than softwood lumbers. Some common hardwood species include oak, elm, chestnut, lime, sycamore, walnut, pear, apple, and many others.

There are the occasional odd species as already mentioned, such as balsa wood, which is classified as a hardwood; but generally, long-term usage has given us sufficient experience to know which lumber is suitable for our specific requirement.

ABOVE *This shows the cut end of a tree trunk with the bark, or wane, still in position prior to conversion*

LEFT *A forest of softwood trees, showing the straight trunks and the needle-type leaves*

RIGHT *The softwood cell, or tracheid, and the holes through which food passes*

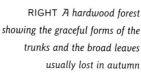

Pits | Cellulose wall

Round end

About ⅛ in. (3 mm)

BELOW *A hardwood cell or fiber, which lies side by side with its companions*

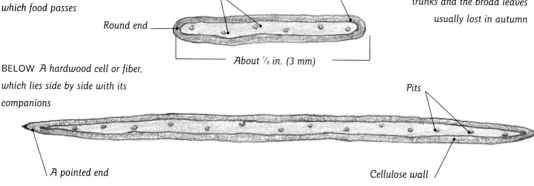

Pits

A pointed end

Cellulose wall

RIGHT *A hardwood forest showing the graceful forms of the trunks and the broad leaves usually lost in autumn*

Making your choice: hardwood or softwood?

There is a greater range of hardwoods available for furniture-making than there are softwoods. As most softwoods grow much faster than hardwoods they are less dense and durable and, although much cheaper, are used less than the more robust hardwoods.

When buying lumber, consider the environment to which it will be exposed; for example, for outdoor use iroko, bubinga, jarrah, or cedar are all excellent. For decorative indoor furniture, walnut, yew, mahogany, sycamore, and satinwood will look very handsome. Sports goods are often made of ash and willow, whereas balsa wood is best for model-making. The list is endless, but experience and observation will guide you.

Some woods contain a much higher wastage factor than others: English walnut, holly, and yew have a 400% wastage, whereas others such as beech, mahogany, chestnut, and most pines have less than 100%. This is due mainly to the manner in which some species have evolved. Some lumbers have a strong scent, such as camphor wood from Kenya and cedar of Lebanon, both highly prized for making small boxes. Others, such as greenheart and Burmese teak, are excellent not only for outdoor use but also for their ability to withstand water immersion without detriment to their strength. It is essential to use teak when there is a risk of iron corrosion. Ferrous metals can cause nasty stains in woods such as oak and chestnut that have a high tannic acid content.

Mahogany is one widely used species that has many different sources, and identification can be difficult. The species includes Brazilian, Cuban, Honduran, Costa Rican, Guatemalan, Nicaraguan, Mexican, Australian, and six types of African mahogany. Besides these, there is also sapele, which is not strictly

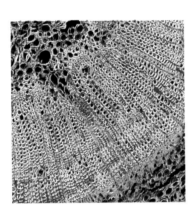 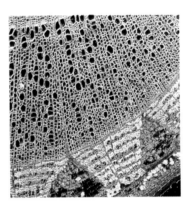

ABOVE *Microscopic sections of the structure of a softwood (left) showing tracheids and the annual rings, which illustrate the change between dense winter growth and open summer growth, and a hardwood (right) showing the fibers and large pores through which food travels up to the leaves. Some hardwoods have clearly defined annual rings (ring porous), others have regular growth all year round (diffuse porous)*

from the mahogany species but is widely used as a substitute. Similarly used are meranti from Malaya, and also lauan stained to look like mahogany, but their use is really more for general joinery such as window and door frames.

Lumber suppliers tend to refer to a species not by its Latin name but by its general name, such as "oak." This one species, however, covers a range of oaks such as American white, American red, European, Japanese, and English, each with its own characteristics. For example, you can stain all but American red oak; American white oak is often sold with one face showing a high percentage of sapwood, due to the way it is converted (see later); English oak generally has beautiful grain patterns, whereas European oak is straighter, and produces less wastage.

If a species is new to you, buy a small quantity first and experiment before buying more. There is the story of an excited buyer of a large amount of iroko bought very cheaply, whose excitement evaporated when, during machining, the pungent aroma emptied his workshop of employees. He had not realized how irritating the dust can be!

Other considerations

Some species are very hard on your cutting equipment. For example, Burmese teak has calcium pockets and grit within its fibers that dull a keen edge, even a tungsten carbide-tipped blade. Bog oak from Ireland, jarrah wood from Australia, and lignum vitae from South America all require exceptionally sharp tools due to their density.

Apart from color, grain is probably the predominant aesthetic reason for choosing a particular species. Some species have a large pore or open grain, such as oak, chestnut, wenge, and teak. Others have a fine grain or small pores, and polish easily with a deep luster; for example sycamore, holly, maple, and tulipwood.

Some species, such as sapele, have interlocked grain. This gives a stripy effect, and planing tears the grain on alternate stripes. The ultimate beauty in any species is perhaps that produced from a quartered board showing the medullary rays—terms that are explained later.

SEASONING AND CONVERSION

When a tree is felled, the majority of its weight is water. To convert a trunk into usable lumber, the sawmill cuts it into various board thicknesses. This method involves starting on one side of the trunk and, as each pass of the saw cut is complete, so the trunk will be moved for the next cut, until the entire trunk has been sawn.

Drying lumber

Once sawn, the individual boards are re-assembled using small strips of wood, about ¾ in. (19 mm) thick, called "stickers." These are placed between each board, and the entire log is stored in the open air. The time required to air season the wood will depend on the thickness to which the boards have been cut. A rough guide is 1 year per 1 in. (25 mm) thickness of board. Air flowing over each sawn board draws the water to the surface by capillary action; this then evaporates, reducing the moisture content to about 25–30%.

This system worked reasonably well before the advent of central heating and air-conditioning.

However, the climate in many countries means that even the best air-dried lumber retains about 26% moisture content, no matter how long it has been dried.

Today any wood used indoors must be able to remain stable, even when the central heating system is on. In order to achieve this, air-dried lumber is placed in a kiln to extract most of the remaining moisture until it achieves an average of 15% moisture content. In the USA this level is even lower, and the lumber is kilned down to an average of 11%. One word of warning: beware of the term, "average moisture content of 15%." This could mean some boards retain as much as 19% and other boards from the same kiln could be as low as 12%.

The general rule of thumb is to assume that the best moisture content for lumber in today's well-heated homes should be 10–12%. This is difficult if

the merchant supplies only lumber averaging 15%! Most good cabinetmakers will rough machine their wood and then expose it to a well-heated workshop for some time prior to finishing the piece to its final dimension.

Always ensure that you ask whether the wood you buy has been kiln dried. The letters "KD," which conform to most trade description acts, should be printed upon your receipt. In the event of subsequent extreme movement in your lumber, it may be necessary to prove

that your lumber was sold as kiln dried. Most lumber merchants are conscientious and will replace the odd board that appears to have too high a moisture content despite being kiln dried.

For outdoor use it is possible to buy and use air-dried lumber, but do not assume that buying this less expensive lumber and leaving it in a warm room will reduce the moisture content. It will not, and if used for furniture the result will be very bad shrinking and distortion.

BELOW *The sequence of stacking a log "in stick" is shown: the sticks are placed on the plank and the next plank placed on top of them*

Sometimes the kilning process leaves surface splits across the board face that can cause problems. It means the drying took place too rapidly, leaving the inner part of the board wet with the outer part too dry. This is called case-hardening. Avoid such boards; otherwise after you have machined the surface the wet inner fibers will distort the board when subjected to the heat in your workshop.

Sawing and storage

There are two important points to remember when choosing and purchasing wood. The first is to see what method of sawing has been adopted in cutting the log. The second concerns the condition of storage while the lumber stocks are air drying in the merchant's yard. More detail on these two points is given in the next section.

LEFT *A stack of lumber emerging from a kiln*

ABOVE *The moisture content of the lumber is checked with a special electronic meter*

SAWING METHODS AND CHOOSING WOOD

The different methods of sawing lumber yield different types of board with regard to stability, attractiveness, and cost. It is these factors which will affect your choice of lumber, depending on the requirements of your project.

Quarter sawing

Years ago when the cost of labor was not as high as it is today, lumber merchants would be prepared to saw a log in half down its length and then saw the two halves in half again. This gives a quadrant or quarter circle at the end of the log. The reason for sawing this way, called "quarter sawing," was to show the best surface of a board, since the sawn face shows the medullary rays that would otherwise be lost. The most well-known medullary rays are seen in some oak boards that have light, almost silver, flecks dancing across the grain. These rays or flecks, which make boards with this type of detail highly prized, are in all trees to a greater or lesser extent.

This quarter-sawn method is very wasteful because it involves turning the lumber frequently before the next saw cut, so it is very rare to find a merchant converting a tree to boards in this way. Since quarter sawing is so rarely done, if an occasion arises when you can choose a board showing medullary rays, then you should buy it.

ABOVE *A piece of oak showing the flecks produced by the radial medullary rays*

RIGHT *A log sawn through and through prior to being put "in stick"*

Through-and-through sawing

The method of "through-and-through" sawing or "plain" sawing is the most common, and although there are other methods of sawing such as wainscot cutting, where there is one sawn square edge and the other left with a waney (bark) edge on the board, it can be confusing to try to describe all the different types of conversion.

The through-and-through method simply involves the trunk being

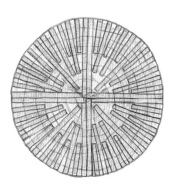

A *A quarter-sawn plank in the old method, whereby all of the planks are sawn on a radial line*

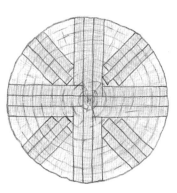

B *Modern quarter sawing: less labor intensive and wasteful. Most planks have some quarter grain*

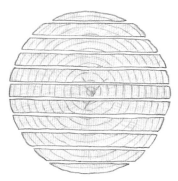

C *Simple through-and-through sawing, where the lumber yield is maximized*

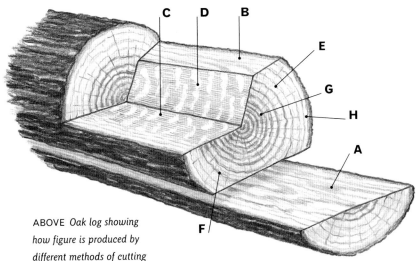

ABOVE *Oak log showing how figure is produced by different methods of cutting*

Key

A *A face that has been tangentially cut*
B *A face that shows partial quarter grain*
C & D *Both these faces have been sawn radially and show quarter grain (medullary rays)*
E *Rays that radiate from the center*
F *Boundary between heartwood and sapwood*
G *Annual rings visible in heartwood*
H *Sapwood*

Wastage

The other very important point to remember when buying lumber is wastage. On average, allow for 100% wastage when buying any waney-edged boards. There are a few exceptions, however, and some of the worst (financially) and, sadly, the most beautiful lumbers are holly, yew, and English walnut, for which you should allow a wastage factor of at least 400%, as described earlier.

It is advisable to buy slightly more lumber than required for your project, not only because this can often reduce the cubic area cost, but also because when you have machined a number of boards and viewed the grain you will have a chance to match colors and figures. The excess lumber will always come in use and allows you to dry your stock fully to your conditions. Compare the additional cost of a few extra boards with a completed project which has color, balance, and harmony of grain structure, and you will not resent the slight extra outlay.

sawn from one edge, and, as each saw cut is complete, the log is moved the required distance to produce another cut until the trunk is sawn into a number of boards. Logically, the center boards will show the medullary rays and are produced without the costly quarter-sawn method.

Tangential sawing

In some countries, especially the USA, the log is cut to produce maximum wood from the trunk, despite the fact that this method does not produce the attractive figure of other methods. This system of sawing around the log is often referred to as "tangential" cutting because each cut forms a tangent to one of the annual rings. Often this results in one face having sapwood included— American cherry is very prone to this.

It is advisable to reject any sapwood in your finished cabinet work, regardless of the fact that some merchants will try to convince you otherwise. It is prone to beetle attack, it shrinks badly, and its immature

Note the high wastage on this waney-edged board of walnut, which has very little heartwood

fibers do not accept glue or polish as well as the heartwood section.

Problems to avoid when choosing lumber

When buying lumber, choose your board carefully if you want to avoid problems later. The further the board is away from the heart, or center, the more it is prone to movement.

Remember, wood always warps away from the heart; therefore, if you are using outside boards it helps if you are converting them into small sections. The basic rule is only to use heart boards when requiring wide boards. The best possible board is, of course, the center one. It is the most stable board as it cannot warp away from the heart because it *is* the heart board! Not only that, but it is the *only* board which, on the through-and-through method of cutting, shows the medullary rays. There will be some wastage because of the split and distorted section in the middle of this center board, but this is a small price to pay to see the full figure.

If the end of the board does not show the growth rings clearly, because of heavy saw marks or paraffin wax sealing the end grain, then you must rely on looking at the board's face to judge from where in the sawing process the piece would have been in relation to the complete log.

BUYING WOOD AND AVOIDING LUMBER DEFECTS

Your failure to identify a defect could result in many hours of work wasted. For example, it is quite possible to spend a considerable time shaping a complex table leg only to discover, upon polishing, a hairline crack around the whole leg known as a thunder shake. If the trunk bounces on the ground when it is felled, it may shatter across its grain, causing a fracture that is so fine you really have to look hard for it. Although this might be an extreme defect, it certainly pays to inspect for thunder shakes, especially in mahogany. Many defects are obvious and are in the form of knots or star and cup shakes on the end of the board.

Calculating the cubic content

Bad defects such as knots, splits, and shakes should be marked out and deducted from the cubic foot or meter calculation. The easy way of calculating the cubic content is to multiply the length by the width and multiply that figure by the thickness. All lumber yards in the USA and most in the UK still calculate using the imperial measure, which is a cubic foot. As there are 1728 cubic inches to a cubic foot you can see how easy it is to check yourself. For example, six boards 10 feet long, 6 inches wide, and 2 inches thick works out at 120 x 6 x 2 in. = 1440 cubic inches x 6 = 8640 cubic inches. You know there are 1728 cubic inches to a cubic foot, so just divide 8640 by 1728; the result will be 5, which means your six boards contain 5 cubic feet. (Similar sums can be done for metric measures.) If you buy your wood with two waney edges and the board is not the same width at both ends, the lumber yard will measure the width at both ends and in the middle of the board and calculate an average width. The lengths and thickness do not change whether you buy waney-edged or sawn-edged boards.

The majority of wood with splits and shrinkage

defects should have been marked with a wax stick or removed from the merchant's purchasing stock. It will be to your cost if you fail to spot any split or shake in the length of a board. Often a split will continue following a growth line and can reappear on the opposite face on the opposite edge! This will render the board worthless for part of its length.

Always look on both faces of a board. Often the best face is presented, but inspection of the opposite face may reveal larger, additional knots and wild grain, which means that some areas cannot be used for structural purposes. Although these defect areas are often marked out in the calculations, for what you save you may feel it not worth the inherent problems later, so select another board. When buying wood you should always be aware that others may have

ABOVE *A stack of planks immediately after sawing, prior to being put "in stick" to undergo air drying. Sawn by the through-and-through method*

LEFT *Large racks containing kiln-dried lumber being selected and checked prior to purchase*

RIGHT *The cross-section of a felled tree shows radial splits, the annual rings and the bark*

TOP RIGHT *Base of a Scots pine showing the trunk and roots*

already selected the best pieces and that what is left may contain defects that will present problems when you start your project.

A good tip is to get on friendly terms with your lumber merchant. It is amazing how a good relationship can yield special offers, or invitations to inspect a new delivery.

Shrinkage

First, the good news: lumber never shrinks in its length. Now the bad news: it more than makes up for it by shrinking in its width! Not only will wood warp or cup away from the heart, but if, for example, the tree grew on a steeply sloping hillside, the trunk may have had undue strain placed upon one side while being in compression on the other. The effect will be a banana-shaped board that has also cupped. This emphasizes just how important it is to inspect each board along its length and width before purchasing it.

Buying wood and avoiding lumber defects

Other natural defects

There may be knotty problems with the lumber, too. If a branch dies while the tree is still growing, the result is a dead knot that will shrink and eventually fall out. If, on the other hand, the living branch and the living tree are felled at the same time, then the knot is live. This means that it will stay firmly within the board when converted or seasoned.

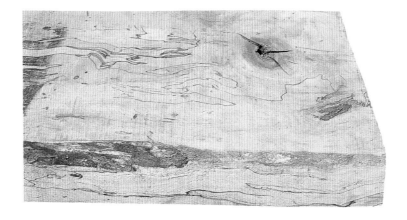

A board with a dead knot, part of which will fall out. The hole will need filling or disguising with a plug

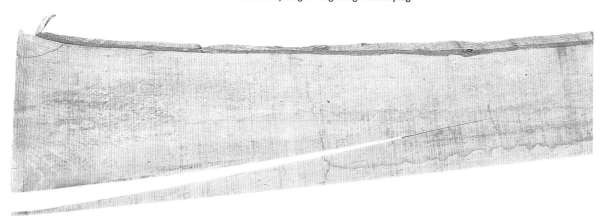

A board with a shrinkage split which cannot be closed and will have to be removed

Some species become infected by disease while they are growing. This can sometimes be attractive, as in spalted beech, and is sought after, while others are so affected that the wood's inherent beauty is spoiled forever.

The biggest enemies of wood are fungi and insects. The initial selection process will have removed much of this type of defect, but look out for beetle holes. If the beetle has flown, as evidenced by the flight holes, beware the grubs left behind. They can eat happily for some years before they also leave the

The maze of tunnels provides evidence of beetle activity under the bark

nest! Look for fine dust that may have settled on the board below a flight hole. This will reveal current activity. Remember that, generally, when you spot a

Damage to lumber caused by bark beetle

hole it represents where the beetle has been, not where it is. The kiln-drying process usually kills most beetles, but they may return to any sapwood that is present in lumber awaiting purchase.

If you have the opportunity to visit your lumber yard, you will probably observe many pieces of wood for sale with stick marks at right angles to the boards' length. Mention has already been made of these small strips of wood separating the boards during air drying. Normally the sticks leave surface marks only, but in some cases, where the lumber merchant has not disinfected the sticks, a fungal infection can cause the stick mark to travel through the thickness of the lumber. This is disastrous as you cannot disguise it, especially in light woods such as oak, ash, or chestnut. If in doubt, scrape below the surface to check for the possibility of this fungus.

Man-made problems

Most lumber merchants are conscientious in spreading the load evenly when loading half a dozen fully sawn logs one on top of another. Others, however, are careless and may sell badly distorted boards to the next unsuspecting customer. If you are able, ask to view the lumber merchant's yard and see for yourself how well the lumber is stacked. You may be surprised at how many trunks have so much uneven weight placed upon them that the entire log bows considerably at one end or in the center! Be aware that stresses thus introduced will eventually cause a board to try to revert partly to its original form— probably once you have finished making your piece of furniture!

Generally speaking, much of the movement of each sawn board will have resolved itself in the air-drying process. Although lumber yards place cleats on the ends of boards to reduce splitting, you would be wise to let the wood move in whichever direction it wants to go. Very little can stop a growth line from shrinking, and it has been known for 6 in. (152 mm) nails to snap in half due to the force of shrinkage.

The basic rule when inspecting lumber is that the more parallel the grain, the less it will shrink. This is not to say that you should not buy a board with flowery and wild grain. Indeed, this may, to your eye, be more exciting than straight grain. It does mean, however, that you may have to saw a wide, figured board into widths of 6 in. (152 mm) and reglue them to give you a wide board with much of the tension removed.

ABOVE *Careless stacking leads to a degrade in board quality, giving poor performance and greatly reducing its value*

LEFT *An example of case hardening, caused by kiln drying too rapidly. The inner part is left wet while the outside is too dry*

Wood storage

Before buying wood for your own use, it is wise to inspect the way in which wood is stacked in your chosen lumber yard. Do not buy distorted boards for the reasons already mentioned. Check along the board's length, since it will not straighten once it has been distorted. The fibers will have been distorted in the drying process and the cell walls will remain permanently damaged.

Storing wood in the workshop In your workshop, leave long boards flat on the floor rather than at an angle against a wall, and do not expose them to direct sunlight as this will cause the natural color either to fade, as in the case of mahogany, or to darken, as in the case of cherry. Rub candle or paraffin wax on the end grain of all boards to prevent the ends from drying too quickly in a heated workshop.

A good maxim is always to "keep a long piece of wood as long as you can for as long as you can." All woodworkers tend to have workshops full of lumber just too small for use! Finally, keep all wood storage areas well ventilated and avoid damp conditions.

BELOW *Remember it is important to stack boards carefully in your own workshop*

BOARD MATERIALS

Modern technology has provided the woodworker with a vast range of board materials from which to choose. There are so many variations on the same type of board that it would be impossible to describe all of them, but there are a number of commonly used boards which are found in most lumber yards.

With each type of board detailed here there is a description of the defects or dangers to avoid. Be aware that some suppliers will argue that the problems you identify are outside their control. Although this may be the case, it may equally be due to the merchant's method of storage. Some merchants place large amounts of heavy sheet material on top of each other, all supported on perhaps two bearers. This causes all the boards to sag in the middle which, in time, permanently distorts the boards. If you buy a full sheet of any board material always look down its long and short edges once the sheet is free standing. Any banana shapes will clearly show. Bending the sheet overnight in the opposite direction to the curve does not work. Once tension has built up on a board it is very

difficult to reproduce the exact opposite tension to straighten it.

Laminboard

This is not often available. The inner core comprises softwood strips of about ¼ in. (6 mm) in width veneered over at right angles to the grain in a rotary-cut veneer such as gaboon. It used to be favored as a good surface upon which to veneer, but unless you can find a first-class supplier, beware: the inner softwood core is often not dried thoroughly, and eventually, when it does dry, a pattern showing the core strips is revealed through the polished surface, sometimes referred to as "telegraphing."

Blockboard

Also called lumber-core plywood, blockboard is similar to laminboard in construction, but the inner cores are generally ⅞ in. (22 mm) wide. This more robust board used to feature in carcass work but does so less these days, again due to the problem of the softwood cores

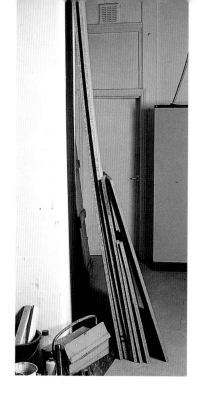

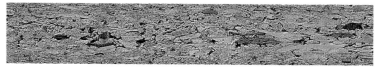

TOP *As evident here, some manufactured boards can sag, so good, flat storage is essential*

ABOVE *Section of a piece of chipboard showing the fine particles on the faces and the coarser material in the centre*

telegraphing. Undoubtedly there are some good manufacturers of these types of boards—it is a matter of finding them.

Chipboard

There is now a vast range of chipboards, which essentially comprise wood chips mixed with synthetic resin and placed in a heated press. Different layers in the thickness can be observed. For smooth surface chipboards, finer particles of chip are compressed on the outside faces and a coarser, looser

wood chip is trapped in the middle. Some chipboards are made for external use and some are specifically designed for kitchen work-tops to a thickness of 2 in. (51 mm). Chipboard is available with a resin paper-coated surface, plastic surface, or wood-veneered surface. When planing solid wood lippings (edging) level with the surface be careful not to break through the face of the chipboard—this will reveal a coarser chipboard which is very noticeable under a coat of paint.

Chipboard has little strength unsupported; it sags under its own weight, as observed when used in a long length to support books. All types of edge lippings are available: in plastic, metal, and wood. Many require simply either a sawn groove for attachment, or clamps and glue. Whichever you use, leaving a chipboard edge without protection not only is unsightly but leaves the edge vulnerable to chipping.

Hardboard

Although still available, hardboard is now often replaced with a range of similar thicknesses in medium-density fiberboard (MDF) (see below). To prevent thin sheets of hardboard buckling try dampening both surfaces before fixing to a frame.

This often resolves the problem.

Medium-density fiberboard (MDF)

Also called particle board, MDF has really taken over in the furniture industry due to its adaptability. It is available in a large range of thicknesses from 1/16 in. (2 mm) upward, and is an excellent surface on which to veneer, paint, polish, or stain. The edge can be shaped and spindle molded and it is the most versatile board available. The disadvantage of this board is that, like chipboard, it does not support its own weight. Steer clear of the MDF with a very shiny surface. The release agent used to clean the presses from which the MDF is made can sometimes remain on the sheet surface, and this agent or chemical can react with glue, paint, or polish. All these boards, MDF, and chipboard in particular, will require very sharp saws, and the high resin content

will blunt your sawing and planing edges at twice the rate of real wood. Also note that it is essential to use a good dust mask when machining MDF, as the dust is harmful if breathed in over a period of time.

Plywood

Originally the most widely used board, plywood is now being overshadowed by the likes of MDF. Many plywoods are made from veneer leaves which have been poorly dried and result in distorted boards. Initially, plywood was the most stable material around; nowadays the woodworker may be faced with a time-consuming selection process of finding undistorted boards, and experience finding the saw blade trapped by the plywood sheet contracting. Birch multi-ply can cause serious adhesion problems—probably due to the cleaning agent (as described in the MDF section) being left

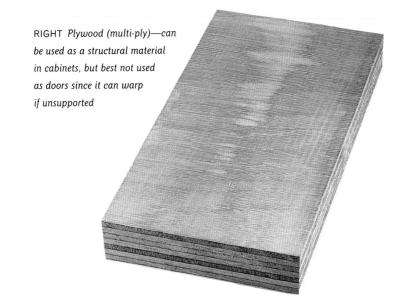

RIGHT *Plywood (multi-ply)—can be used as a structural material in cabinets, but best not used as doors since it can warp if unsupported*

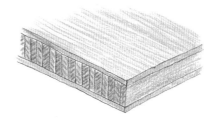

RIGHT *Laminboard (three-ply)—showing thinner cores than blockboard. A superior board is made where there is another layer of veneers on the face running in the same direction as the cores*

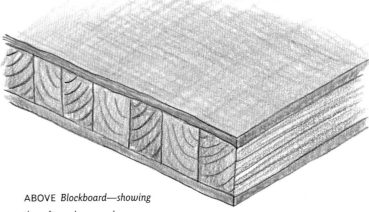

ABOVE *Blockboard—showing the softwood core and veneer surfaces*

RIGHT *"Telegraphing" shows how poor-quality core material can move and distort the final surface*

impregnated in the surface. It would be wise to thoroughly sand all faces before using this material.

Working with board materials

Where you see defects in a board's face try not to use fillers. These shrink in time and show below the surface. Always use the actual veneer material, such as birch for birch ply, gaboon for gaboon ply, MDF for repairs to MDF and so on.

Finally, do not rely on a glue face for heavy lippings;

LEFT *Plywood (three-ply)—very useful as a cabinet back or drawer bottom*

always put a tongue in the board edge, which vastly increases the strength of the gluing surface.

VENEERS

Veneers allow you to enter a wonderful fantasy world. The range is enormous, from exotic burrs to three-dimensional ripple and figured veneers. Many of the world's most unusual and magnificent trees are converted into veneers, as well as good examples of less exotic species.

ABOVE A veneer showing faults that have arisen from poor cutting (left) and a well-cut veneer with no apparent faults (right)

Producing veneers

To produce a veneer the log is generally cut square. It is soaked for some time in hot water before being placed on a massive guillotine which slices about ¾₄ in. (1 mm) of wood along its entire length. As the blade retracts the log moves forward by ¾₄ in. (1 mm) and the process is repeated. As each veneer leaf falls one upon the other the figure is visibly repeated on each leaf. Once the leaves have been dried and stacked, generally in bundles of 24 leaves (so the entire solid log is rebuilt but in bundles or parcels), each bundle is taped so the sequence of cut leaves is not disturbed.

When buying veneers always check for this—look through the leaves and any loss of sequence will be apparent. Hold a random leaf up to the light. If it has been badly cut daylight will appear through all or part of the leaf. Check that the leaf

ABOVE A well-stacked and sorted bundle of veneers

edges have not discoloured with ultraviolet light; the center of the leaf should match the color of the edge. Always store veneers away from direct light. Tape the ends to prevent splitting and store in a cool dry place, preferably flat.

Types of veneer

Veneers tend to fall into two categories. The first comprises veneered leaves produced from good, clean, but not necessarily highly figured, boards. For example, rotary-cut veneers are economical to produce and are used in the manufacture of plywood. Other slice- or guillotine-cut veneers are clean and representative of a species but without the sought-after highly prized

figure. These are suitable for areas such as the inside of a carcass. These straightforward veneers are often crown cut, which gives a wider leaf than the straight grain of a quarter-sawn log.

The second category relates to exotic or highly figured veneers. Although most hard and softwoods can be converted into veneers, it is an expensive process which should ideally be reserved for a good commercial log. A really unusual log is unique. It can take the form of fiddle-back rays dancing across the surface or examples of quilted maple where the surface literally appears to have the texture of a satin quilt. Often the figure and real beauty of a species can

only be found in veneer form, and it should certainly not be regarded as a cheap method of furniture-making.

A final piece of advice: on purchasing your bundle of veneers, before spreading out all the leaves, number each leaf in sequence. Once spread around the workshop to evaluate the best matching sequence, it is so easy to mismatch when trying to re-establish the original sequence.

BELOW Bookmatching veneer leaves creates beautiful patterns. Here a double bookmatch gives a quartered effect

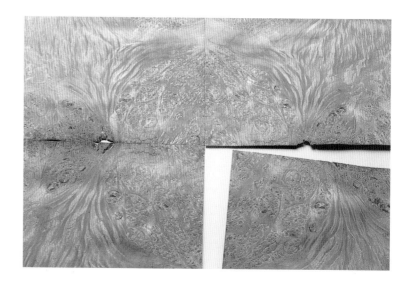

GLUES FOR WOODWORKING

Modern technology has produced a vast range of very sophisticated glues. Many of them require specific equipment, for example the application of radio frequency to set certain glues. Only those glues which are readily available are described here.

Standard PVA

A fast-drying PVA

Contact glue

A resin glue in powder form which requires mixing with water

Animal glue—now available as granules and placed in water to form a fluid. (Originally available in brittle cakes or sheets which needed overnight soaking.)

PVA

The most common glue available is PVA (polyvinyl acetate), which is a cold-setting glue. A good all-round glue with water-proofing properties in some types, its advantage is that it remains slightly flexible, even when set, thus allowing very slight movement of lumber. However, its high moisture content can make gluing larger areas of veneer difficult as the moisture is absorbed within the veneer, leading to curling. If using a cellulose-based polish, you will find the solvents mix with the PVA and can cause unsightly swelling on the glue line, called creep.

Contact cement

Contact cement is rubber based and relies on both surfaces being coated and meeting when touch dry, to form an instant bond. This glue should be avoided at all costs in cabinetmaking. The tension within the glue can pull veneers open in time and edges are likely to lift slightly, especially where high humidity is present. It is fine for laying plastic laminates over large areas, but where wood meets wood a more permanent glue is required.

Resin glue

The most permanent and reliable glue is synthetic resin glue—often sold as Cascamite One Shot, Aerolite 300, Aerolite 306, and Beetle Cement H. These glues are obtainable in the USA and most European countries—if in doubt look for the words "urea-formaldehyde." This glue can be used for hot and cold pressing. Many of these glues are in two parts: the glue and hardener. The glue is applied to one joining surface and the hardener to the other. Some resin glues, in powder form, have the hardener incorporated—simply add water prior to using. Many have a limited shelf life, so only purchase them in small quantities.

A general guide for shelf life, in dry conditions, is three months.

Animal glue

Finally, there is animal glue. Made from the bones and skins of animals, it has been used for centuries and is still preferred by antique restorers and those making reproduction furniture. The disadvantages of this glue have been especially noticeable in the USA where air-conditioning has reduced the humidity levels upon which this glue relies. Many genuine antiques have lost their marquetry veneer due to the dry environment in which they have been placed. If in doubt, leave a bowl of water under a radiator to maintain the humidity needed for this type of glue.

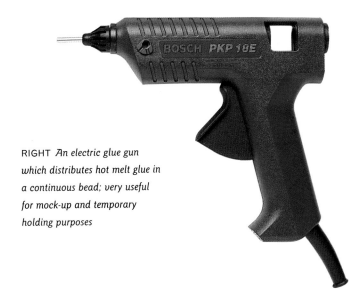

RIGHT *An electric glue gun which distributes hot melt glue in a continuous bead; very useful for mock-up and temporary holding purposes*

FURTHER INFORMATION

Joints and joint-making (Chapter 7)

ENVIRONMENTAL CONSIDERATIONS

Everyone can play a part with regard to helping to protect our environment. Although you may feel that your purchase is not significant in terms of affecting the purchasing opinions of local lumber merchants, it is possible that sufficient numbers of woodworkers could be a persuasive force. Certainly purchasers of commercial lumber have a duty to purchase responsibly.

Rainforest cleared by fire (left) or logging (above and below) leaves large tracts of open land where soil erosion soon takes a deadly hold (right)

Deforestation

The USA is the world's largest importer of Brazilian mahogany, the UK being the second largest. Even though Brazil's exportation in tonnage terms has reduced over the past few years, there is still immense damage caused in the areas where felling continues. For example, for every tree felled, 26 smaller trees are damaged, and this is apart from the suffering caused to the indigenous people by the loggers.

Over half of all the plant and animal species on earth are to be found in our fast-diminishing tropical forests, which cover less than 7% of the world's land surface!

Commercial plantations have covered nearly 60% of Sweden and 70% of Finland, leaving only 5% of the original forest. Over 60% of British Columbia's rain forests have been logged, and Canada's record for rain forest protection is dire.

Recent developments

Although Asia and the Pacific countries are threatened in much the same way, there is no doubt that governments are beginning to take notice. Question your lumber merchant closely as to the sources of his raw material and his policy on the whole environmental issue. Recently, the World Bank has begun to impose strict conditions regarding forest management on countries applying for loans. All this should have an influence on forest protection that will be for the good of our heritage.

FURTHER INFORMATION

Sawing methods and choosing wood 198

Buying wood and avoiding timber defects 200

THIRTEEN **PLANS**

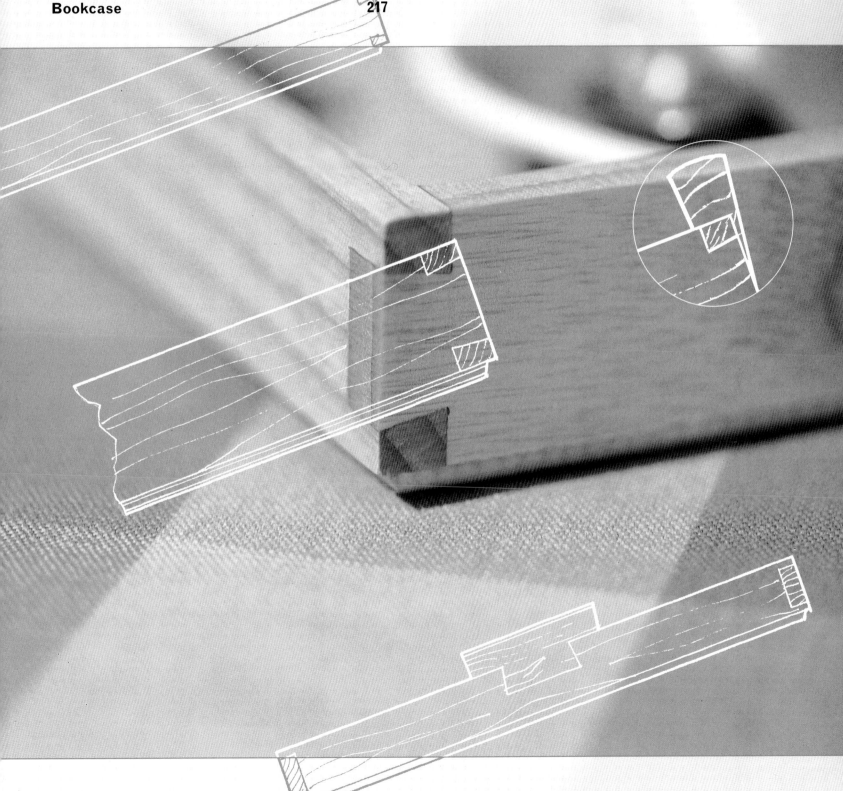

PROJECT 1: GLASS-TOPPED
TABLE *see page 102*

**This project is an attractive occasional table that
can be made in a weekend by an absolute beginner.**

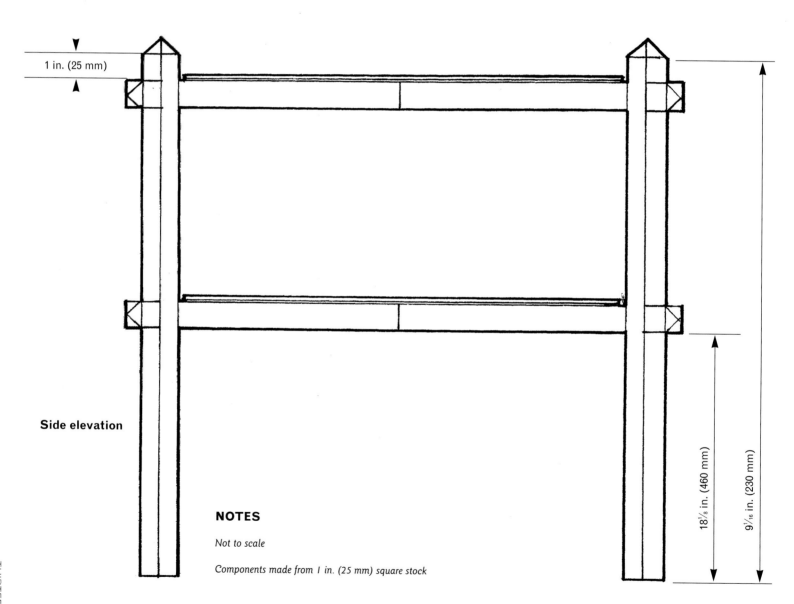

1 in. (25 mm)

Side elevation

NOTES

Not to scale

Components made from 1 in. (25 mm) square stock

18$\frac{1}{8}$ in. (460 mm)

9$\frac{1}{16}$ in. (230 mm)

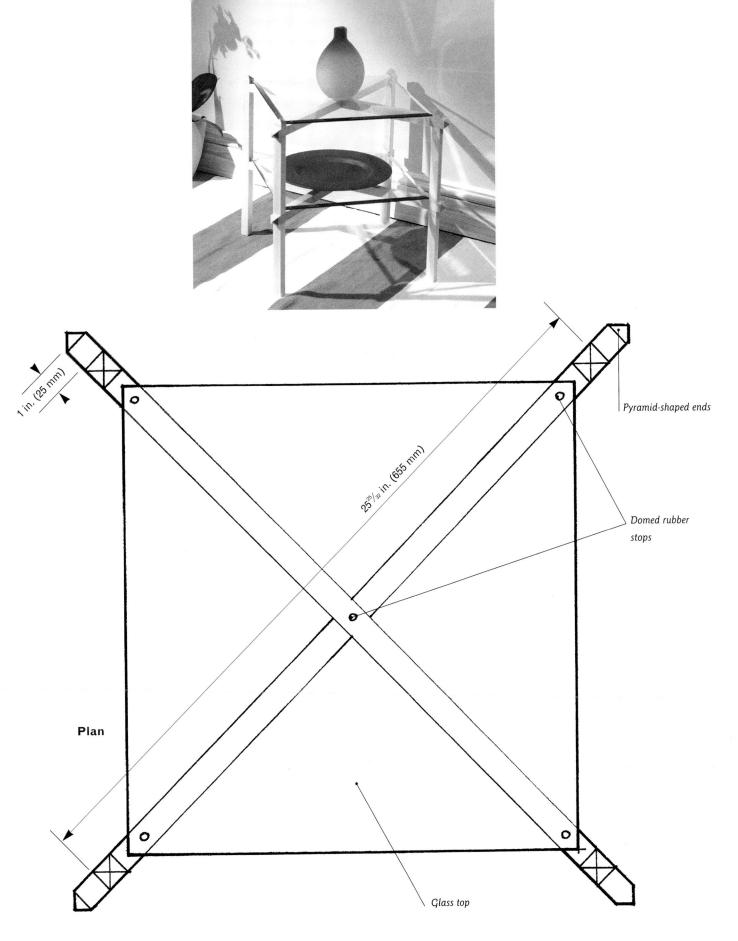

1 in. (25 mm)

Pyramid-shaped ends

$25\frac{25}{32}$ in. (655 mm)

Domed rubber stops

Plan

Glass top

PROJECT 2: CD STORAGE BOX *see page 112*

This small box for storing CDs exploits the use of dowels to join the components. This project can be made in two to three days by a beginner.

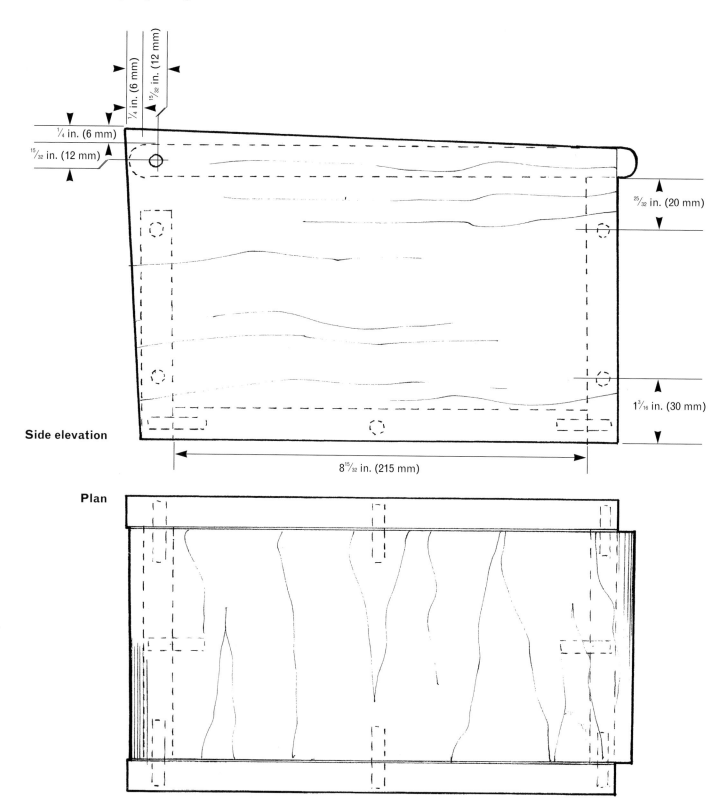

¼ in. (6 mm)

¹⁵⁄₃₂ in. (12 mm)

¼ in. (6 mm)

¹⁵⁄₃₂ in. (12 mm)

²⁵⁄₃₂ in. (20 mm)

1³⁄₁₆ in. (30 mm)

Side elevation

8¹⁵⁄₃₂ in. (215 mm)

Plan

$^{25}\!/_{32}$ in. (20 mm) radius

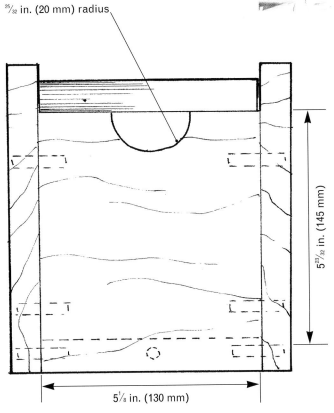

Front elevation

$5^{23}\!/_{32}$ in. (145 mm)

$5^{1}\!/_{8}$ in. (130 mm)

NOTES

Not to scale

All parts $^{15}\!/_{32}$ in. (12 mm) thick

*Use $^{3}\!/_{16}$ in. (5 mm) or
$^{1}\!/_{4}$ in. (6 mm) diameter
doweling*

*Not through doweled but
stopped ("blind"), drilled from
the inside*

Project 2: CD storage box   213

PROJECT 3: WORKBENCH *see page 122*

The dimensions shown in this plan drawing are suggested for guidance.

The bench height should be roughly half the height of the user.

The length and width may be adapted to suit individual requirements.

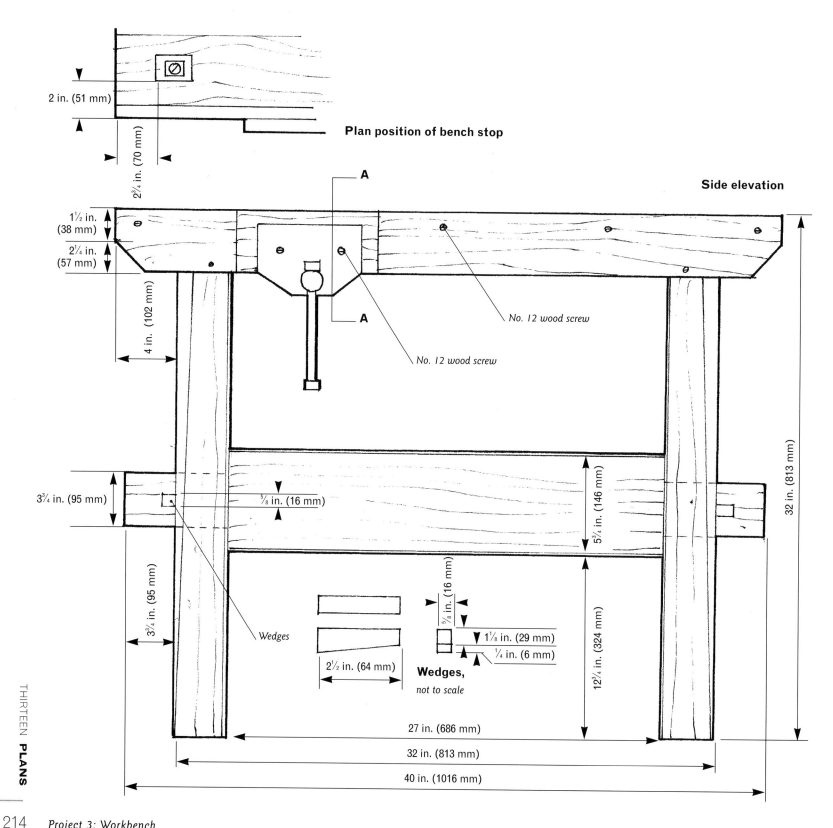

2 in. (51 mm)

2¾ in. (70 mm)

Plan position of bench stop

A

Side elevation

1½ in. (38 mm)

2¼ in. (57 mm)

4 in. (102 mm)

No. 12 wood screw

No. 12 wood screw

A

3¾ in. (95 mm)

⅝ in. (16 mm)

5¾ in. (146 mm)

32 in. (813 mm)

3¾ in. (95 mm)

Wedges

⅝ in. (16 mm)

1⅛ in. (29 mm)

¼ in. (6 mm)

12¾ in. (324 mm)

2½ in. (64 mm)

Wedges,
not to scale

27 in. (686 mm)

32 in. (813 mm)

40 in. (1016 mm)

A well-laid bench will quickly become the focal point of the workshop

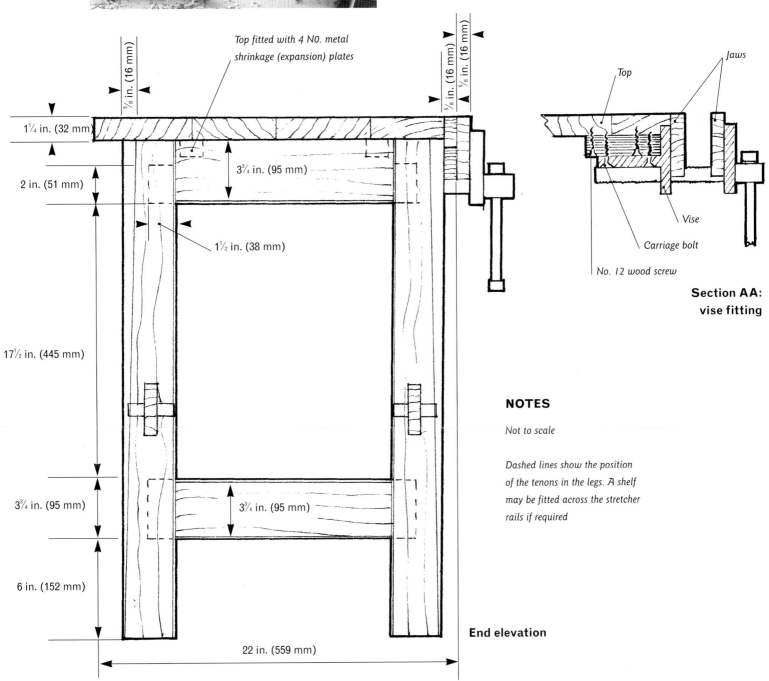

Top fitted with 4 N0. metal shrinkage (expansion) plates

⁵⁄₈ in. (16 mm)

1¼ in. (32 mm)

2 in. (51 mm)

3¾ in. (95 mm)

1½ in. (38 mm)

17½ in. (445 mm)

3¾ in. (95 mm)

3¾ in. (95 mm)

6 in. (152 mm)

22 in. (559 mm)

End elevation

⁵⁄₈ in. (16 mm)   ⁵⁄₈ in. (16 mm)

Top

Jaws

Vise

Carriage bolt

No. 12 wood screw

Section AA: vise fitting

NOTES

Not to scale

Dashed lines show the position of the tenons in the legs. A shelf may be fitted across the stretcher rails if required

PROJECT 4: MIRROR FRAME *see page 134*

The size of this project may be adapted to suit
individual requirements and choice. The proportions
of the frame section should remain similar to the
project as drawn here.

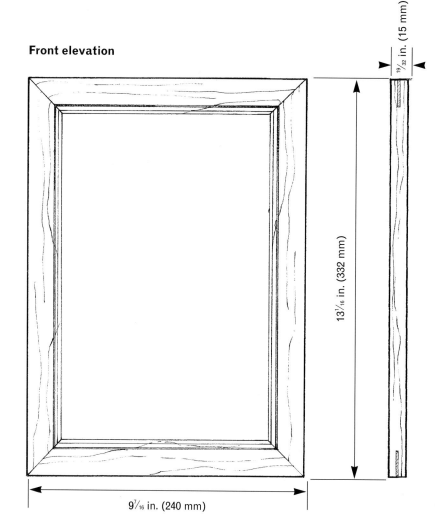

Front elevation

13⅟₁₆ in. (332 mm)

9⁷⁄₁₆ in. (240 mm)

¹⁹⁄₃₂ in. (15 mm)

Side elevation

NOTES

Not to scale

*The frame may be used
for mounting a picture,
in which case ¹⁄₁₆ in.
(2 mm) picture glass
should be used.*

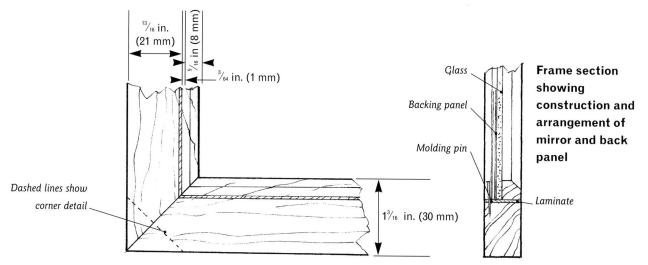

¹³⁄₁₆ in.
(21 mm)

⁵⁄₁₆ in (8 mm)

³⁄₆₄ in. (1 mm)

*Dashed lines show
corner detail*

1³⁄₁₆ in. (30 mm)

Glass

Backing panel

Molding pin

Laminate

**Frame section
showing
construction and
arrangement of
mirror and back
panel**

PROJECT 5: BOOKCASE *see page 142*

This bookcase requires more equipment and a little more time than some of the other projects but can be accomplished by a beginner in four to five days.

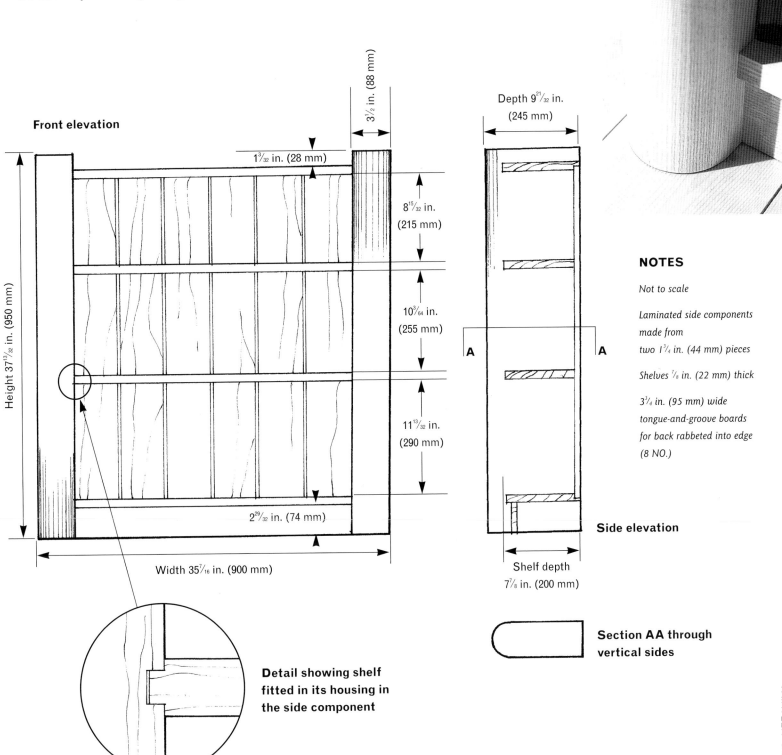

Front elevation

3½ in. (88 mm)

1³/₃₂ in. (28 mm)

8¹⁵/₃₂ in. (215 mm)

10³/₆₄ in. (255 mm)

11¹³/₃₂ in. (290 mm)

Height 37¹³/₃₂ in. (950 mm)

2²⁹/₃₂ in. (74 mm)

Width 35⁷/₁₆ in. (900 mm)

Detail showing shelf fitted in its housing in the side component

Depth 9²¹/₃₂ in. (245 mm)

A A

Side elevation

Shelf depth
7⅞ in. (200 mm)

Section AA through vertical sides

NOTES

Not to scale

Laminated side components made from two 1¾ in. (44 mm) pieces

Shelves ⅞ in. (22 mm) thick

3¾ in. (95 mm) wide tongue-and-groove boards for back rabbeted into edge (8 NO.)

PROJECT 6: BREAKFAST TRAY see page 154

For simplicity, the tray should be made as drawn.
The design has been carefully proportioned for
visual appeal and strength.

Plan

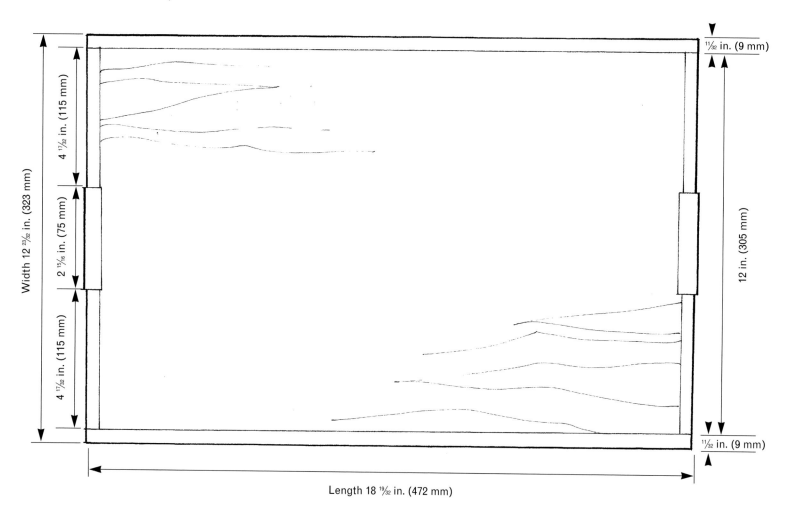

Width 12 ²³⁄₃₂ in. (323 mm)

4 ¹⁷⁄₃₂ in. (115 mm)

2 ¹⁵⁄₁₆ in. (75 mm)

4 ¹⁷⁄₃₂ in. (115 mm)

¹¹⁄₃₂ in. (9 mm)

12 in. (305 mm)

¹¹⁄₃₂ in. (9 mm)

Length 18 ¹⁹⁄₃₂ in. (472 mm)

NOTES

Not to scale

The types of wood chosen for the project make a big difference to the effect of the piece. Thoughtful balancing of the woods selected for the frame, handles, and base will create a pleasing effect.

Side elevation

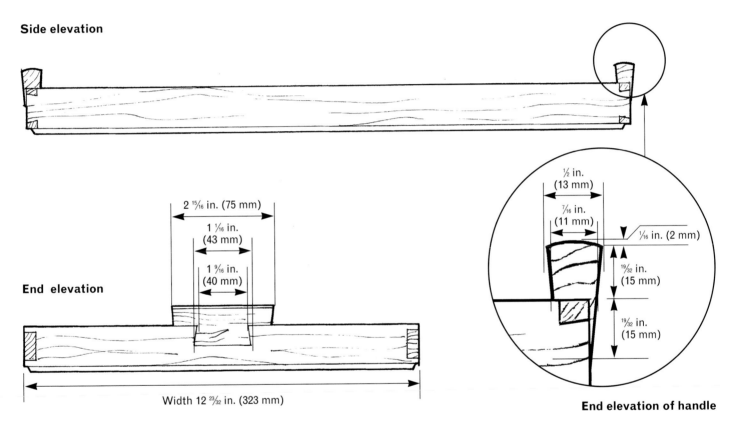

End elevation

2 ¹⁵/₁₆ in. (75 mm)

1 ¹¹/₁₆ in. (43 mm)

1 ⁹/₁₆ in. (40 mm)

Width 12 ²³/₃₂ in. (323 mm)

½ in. (13 mm)

⁷/₁₆ in. (11 mm)

¹/₁₆ in. (2 mm)

¹⁹/₃₂ in. (15 mm)

¹⁹/₃₂ in. (15 mm)

End elevation of handle

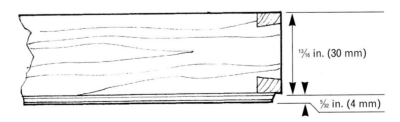

¹³/₁₆ in. (30 mm)

⁵/₃₂ in. (4 mm)

Elevation of dovetail joint. The set in and bevel of the bottom are clearly shown.

PROJECT 7: PARQUETRY SHELF AND WALL MIRROR *see page 175*

The laminated plywood core of this project is lipped in solid wood and veneered in quilted maple with a diamond parquetry pattern of natural and dyed sycamore.

NOTES

Not to scale

Use a bandsaw to produce the wedge-shaped sections and a hand plane to make the lippings flush and prepare the plywood for veneering

Front elevation of shelf

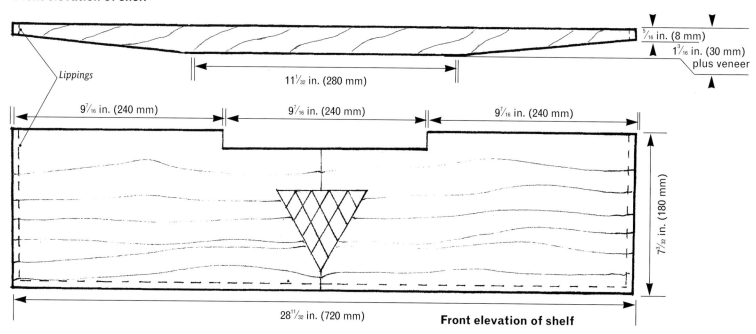

$\frac{5}{16}$ in. (8 mm)

$1\frac{3}{16}$ in. (30 mm) plus veneer

Lippings

$9\frac{7}{16}$ in. (240 mm) $9\frac{7}{16}$ in. (240 mm) $9\frac{7}{16}$ in. (240 mm)

$11\frac{1}{32}$ in. (280 mm)

$7\frac{3}{32}$ in. (180 mm)

$28\frac{11}{32}$ in. (720 mm)

Front elevation of shelf

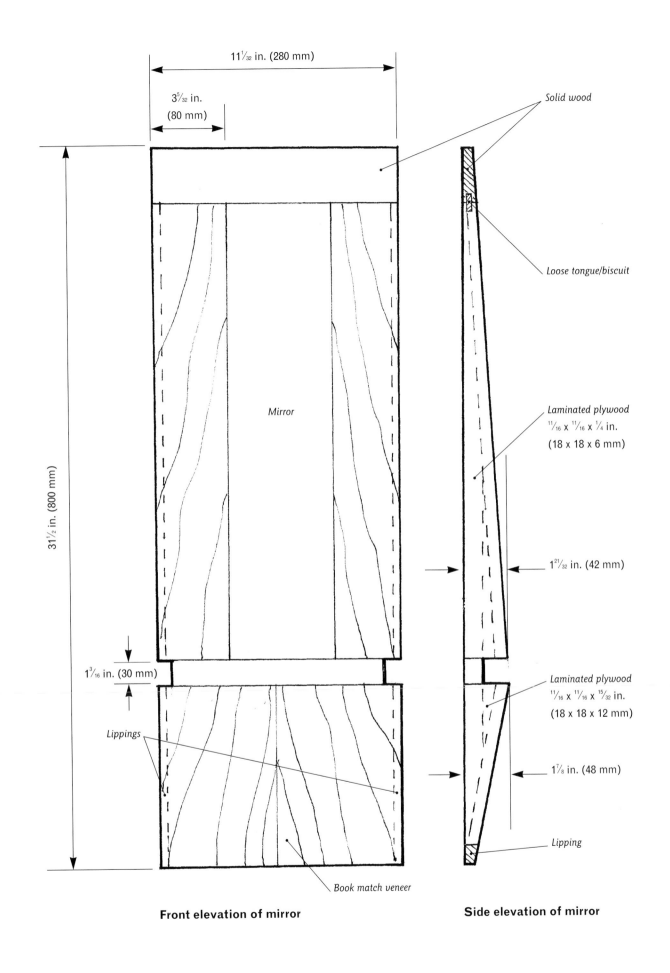

11¹⁄₃₂ in. (280 mm)

3⁵⁄₃₂ in. (80 mm)

Solid wood

Loose tongue/biscuit

Mirror

31½ in. (800 mm)

Laminated plywood
¹¹⁄₁₆ x ¹¹⁄₁₆ x ¼ in.
(18 x 18 x 6 mm)

1²¹⁄₃₂ in. (42 mm)

1³⁄₁₆ in. (30 mm)

Lippings

Laminated plywood
¹¹⁄₁₆ x ¹¹⁄₁₆ x ¹⁵⁄₃₂ in.
(18 x 18 x 12 mm)

1⅞ in. (48 mm)

Lipping

Book match veneer

Front elevation of mirror

Side elevation of mirror

PROJECT 8: TURNED WOODEN BOWL *see page 182*

Turning a small shallow bowl practices the basic techniques and at the same time produces a useful and attractive item.

Cross section of bowl

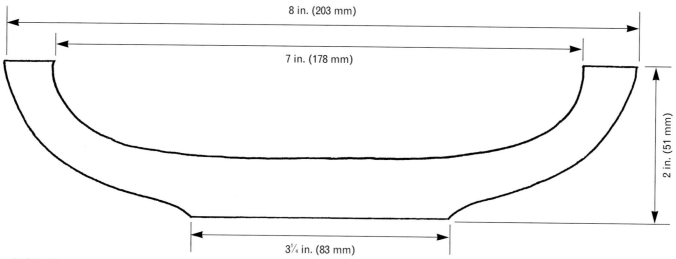

8 in. (203 mm)

7 in. (178 mm)

2 in. (51 mm)

3¼ in. (83 mm)

NOTES

Not to scale

A wide rim gives scope for decoration with concentric curves, radial flutes, or coloring

PROJECT 9: SCALLOP BOX *see page 190*

The natural scallop is one of nature's perfect examples of geometric designs and, over the years, has been a solid foundation for ornamental and classical carvers and sculptors alike.

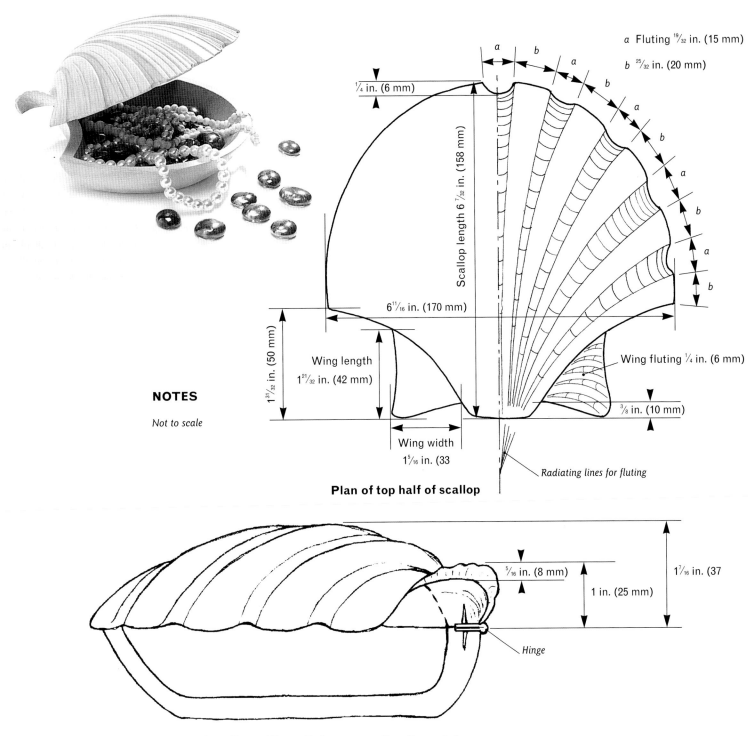

a Fluting $^{19}/_{32}$ in. (15 mm)

b $^{25}/_{32}$ in. (20 mm)

$^{1}/_{4}$ in. (6 mm)

Scallop length 6 $^{7}/_{32}$ in. (158 mm)

$6^{11}/_{16}$ in. (170 mm)

Wing fluting $^{1}/_{4}$ in. (6 mm)

$1^{31}/_{32}$ in. (50 mm)

Wing length $1^{21}/_{32}$ in. (42 mm)

$^{3}/_{8}$ in. (10 mm)

NOTES

Not to scale

Wing width $1^{5}/_{16}$ in. (33

Radiating lines for fluting

Plan of top half of scallop

$^{5}/_{16}$ in. (8 mm)

1 in. (25 mm)

$1^{7}/_{16}$ in. (37

Hinge

Side elevation of scallop with partial cross section through base

Plan detail of back of bottom half of scallop

Hinge cut out

$\frac{7}{16}$ x 1 in.
(11 x 25 mm)

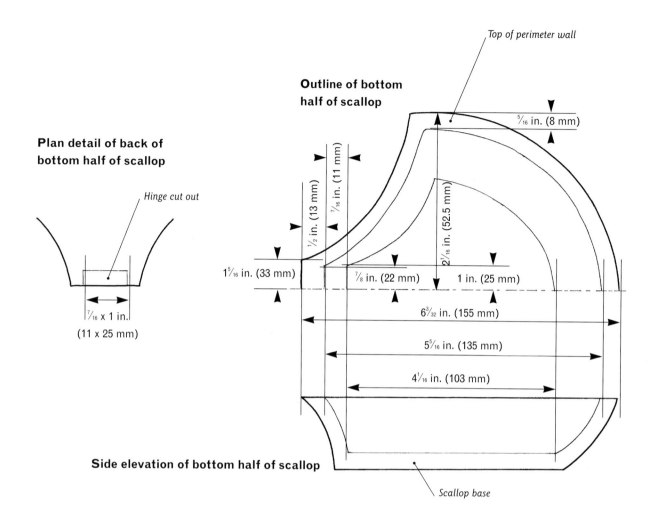

Outline of bottom half of scallop

Top of perimeter wall

$\frac{5}{16}$ in. (8 mm)

$\frac{1}{2}$ in. (13 mm)

$\frac{7}{16}$ in. (11 mm)

$2\frac{1}{16}$ in. (52.5 mm)

$1\frac{5}{16}$ in. (33 mm)

$\frac{7}{8}$ in. (22 mm)

1 in. (25 mm)

$6\frac{3}{32}$ in. (155 mm)

$5\frac{5}{16}$ in. (135 mm)

$4\frac{1}{16}$ in. (103 mm)

Side elevation of bottom half of scallop

Scallop base

Top of scallop supported by cradle

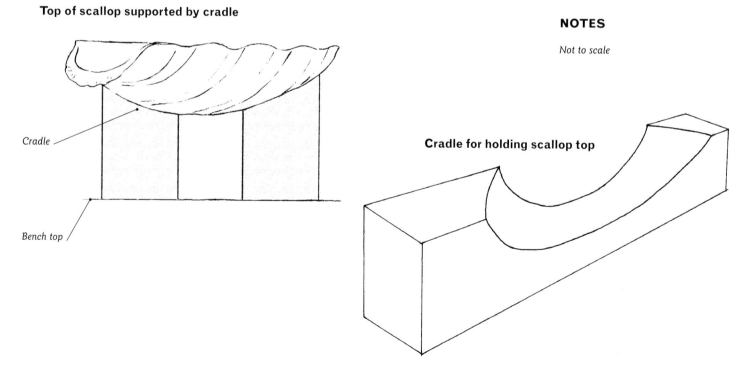

Cradle

Bench top

NOTES

Not to scale

Cradle for holding scallop top

GLOSSARY

Abrasive papers Used for finishing after planing and scraping. Commonly, but incorrectly, called sandpaper and thus the term sanding.

Abrasive papers, aluminum oxide Harder than garnet paper and used both for hand work and for power tools. Very useful for finishing harder lumbers.

Abrasive papers, garnet General-purpose paper, widely used as the initial abrasive when sanding most lumbers.

Abrasive papers, silicon carbide A paper with a zinc oxide powder that acts as a dry lubricant. Ideal for rubbing down hard finishes.

Adhesive, animal Glue made from skin and bones of animals, or sometimes of fish.

Adhesive, contact A glue which is applied to two surfaces, left to become tacky, and then brought together.

Adhesive, PVA (polyvinyl acetate) An emulsion suspended in water that sets when the water evaporates.

Adhesive, UF (urea formaldehyde) A synthetic resin in powder form that sets by chemical reaction.

Air drying see Seasoning, air drying

Aluminum oxide paper see Abrasive papers, aluminum oxide

Animal glue see Adhesive, animal

Arbor The spindle upon which a circular saw is fitted.

Arris Sharp edge formed where two wood faces meet.

Awl Used to mark the center of a hole prior to drilling.

Back iron see Cap iron

Backsaw Saws with a strip of brass into which the blade is set, keeping the blade straight.

Backsaw, dovetail A fine saw, having 16–21 teeth per 1 in. (25 mm), for cutting dovetails.

Backsaw, gents (also beadsaw) A very fine saw, generally with an excess of 26 teeth per 1 in. (25 mm).

Backsaw, tenon Having 13–15 teeth per 1 in. (25 mm). Used for cutting tenons or other large joints.

Balancing Backing veneer glued to the reverse side of manufactured board to prevent it from warping and to balance the face veneer.

Bead A fine strip of wood molded into a convex shape.

Belt sander A hand power tool in which the abrasive paper is a continuous belt running on two cylinders in contact with a pressure plate.

Bench dogs Stops that fit into a series of holes in the top of a workbench.

Bench hook An effective way of holding small-section work while sawing accurately.

Bench saw (also dimension saw) Machine with a circular saw blade protruding from the table which can be raised, lowered, and also canted to an angle.

Bending A traditional way of making curved components. The lumber is steamed, attached to a former or mold and allowed to dry.

Bevel Where a right-angled surface has a slope worked on it at an angle.

Bevel-edged chisel see Chisel, bevel-edged

Biscuit jointer A power tool which makes an oval slot on two joint faces into which an oval plate or "biscuit" fits.

Bits Traditionally, drills used in a brace are called bits, different types being center, auger, and expansion.

Blade guard Protective guard located over the cutter block on a surfacing or overhand planer.

Blank A piece of wood sawn to a disc shape for use on the face plate of a lathe for bowl turning.

Bleaching A method of making wood paler using bleaching chemicals.

Blockboard A manufactured board where the core material is a series of lumber strips faced with constructional veneer.

Book match A decorative effect that gives a mirror image pattern when veneering.

Burl see Burr, lumber

Burr Very thin strip of metal left along the cutting edge after grinding and honing.

Burr, lumber Caused by small growths in tree trunks. When sliced produces whorls in veneers.

Butt hinge Used to hang inset and lay-on doors. Traditionally solid drawn brass.

Cap iron (or back iron) On most bench planes, the cap iron is fixed to the blade and ensures that the shaving curves away from the blade as the plane is used.

Carborundum powder Abrasive powder generally used on the lapping plate to surface a tool. Lubricate with oil or water.

Case-hardened A defect resulting from poorly seasoned lumber.

Catalyst A substance causing a chemical reaction (i.e., to set adhesives).

Caul Sheets of wood or metal used to press the veneer in place.

Chamfer A bevel along the edge of a wooden component, normally at a 45° angle.

Chipboard see Particle board

Chisel, bevel-edged The underside of the blade is flat while the two long edges on the upper face are ground to a shallow bevel.

Chisel, firmer The blade has a rectangular section strong enough to be used with a mallet.

Chisel, mortise A heavier-duty tool with a square-section blade, especially made to be used with a mallet to cut mortises.

Chuck Part of drill into which the drill bit is placed. Can be tightened by hand or with a special chuck key.

Clamp A clamp is used to hold or apply pressure; therefore used to describe a C-clamp or other holding device. (See also Clamp, sash)

Clamp, C- Used to hold work for gluing and assembly. Jaw capacities range from 11/16 in. (18 mm) to 11 13/16 in. (300 mm).

Clamp, sash (or bar) Used to hold work and apply pressure while adhesive sets. At one end there is a screw to apply pressure, while a sliding tail is held in position by a steel pin located in a series of holes along a bar. (See also Clamp)

Collet Tapered sleeve used in a router to hold the router cutter in place at the end of the router spindle.

Combination machine A machine normally combining a disc sander, table saw, horizontal boring machine, vertical drill press, and lathe.

Contact cement see Adhesive, contact

Conversion, quarter-sawn Term to describe planks cut from a log radially (if possible) to expose the best figure.

Conversion, through-and-through The log is cut simply in a series of parallel cuts, and only the center planks will be quarter sawn.

Coping saw Small hand-operated frame saw in which the blade can be turned in any direction.

Counter bore Hole drilled so that the head of a screw lies beneath the wood surface when inserted.

Crosscut saw see Handsaw

Curl Grain effect found in some figured veneers.

Cutter block Used on both hand-held power and machine tools to hold the cutting blade securely.

Cutters, router Specially shaped cutters for the router, which produce many different grooves and patterns.

Cutting back When a finish is applied, the grain is raised or the finished surface itself is uneven, requiring the finish to be smoothed or "cut back" between coats with a gentle abrasive.

Dado (also housing) A channel cut across the grain.

Disc sander A hand-held power tool or machine with a large revolving disc onto which an abrasive sheet is fixed.

Dovetail Woodwork joints composed of a set of tails and an interlocking set of pins to give a strong joint.

Dovetail saw see Backsaw, dovetail

Dowel Simple woodworking joint where small wooden "rods" are inserted into holes in both pieces to be joined.

Drill press Floor- or bench-mounted machine, where various drills can be inserted into a chuck to make holes precisely and safely.

Drills, spur Drills with a central point and outside cutting spur (sometimes called dowel bits) for drilling larger size holes.

Drills, twist Drills make holes and fit into electric and hand tools. Normally used for metals, twist drills are also used by woodworkers and are available in a wide range of sizes.

Drum sander Sander in which abrasive paper is wrapped around a cylinder.

Dying and staining A method of adding color to wood. Available in powder, alcohol or water-based forms.

Escutcheon Protective plate that surrounds a keyhole in a cabinet.

Face edge The second face to be worked when preparing lumber in addition to the face side; all markings taken from these two faces when using squares, rules, bevels, etc.

Face side When preparing lumber this is the first face to be planed; it must be perfectly flat and straight.

Faceplate Used on a lathe for turning wooden blanks into bowls.

Fence Adjustable guide to keep the cutting edge of a tool a set distance from the edge of a piece of work.

Ferrule Metal ring that prevents the splitting of a wooden handle when the tang of a chisel is fixed in position.

Firmer chisel *see* Chisel, firmer

Fleece Resilient abrasive pad of nylon fiber used for cutting back between coats of lacquer. (*See also* Cutting back)

Flitch The prepared log from which veneers are sliced, or the bundle of veneers themselves.

Fluting Groove with a rounded (concave) section; used to add detail to stiles or legs, or in carving.

Forstner bit Used for boring very clean flat-bottomed holes. It is also able to cut holes at the edge of a piece of wood. The cylinder that makes the cuts can either be straight or have a saw pattern on the cutting edge.

French polish Medium-brown finish made from flake shellac. Generally used on furniture until the development of modern-day lacquers and still used in furniture repair and restoration.

Fretsaw *see* scroll saw

Fuming Method of coloring woods that contain tannin by exposure to ammonia fumes.

Garnet paper *see* Abrasive papers, garnet

Gauges Various marking and cutting tools which leave clear, fine lines on the work; they enable the craftsman to mark the lines parallel to a given face. The marking gauge has a simple point that gives a scribe line; the cutting gauge has a small blade that gives a cut line and is most suitable for marking across the grain, while a mortise gauge has two pins that can be set to the width of the mortise which can then be marked in the correct position.

Gents saw *see* Backsaw, gents

Grain The grain direction runs along the length of the tree trunk, so when the tree is converted into planks, it runs lengthways. Different lumber species have grains that vary from very straight (relatively easy to work) to highly convoluted (can be quite difficult).

Grinding The process of initial sharpening by grinding

away metal to specific angles.

Grit The indication of the roughness or smoothness of abrasive papers (i.e., 50 = very coarse, 600 = very fine).

Groove A long narrow channel cut in the direction of, or across, the grain, often used with a tongue to make a joint. (*See also* Tongue)

Groundwork When laying veneer, the substrate to which the veneer will be glued.

Gullet The space between the teeth on saws.

Handsaw Saw for cutting planks or board material by hand. (Examples are ripsaw, crosscut saw, and panel saw.)

Hardwood Lumber harvested from broad-leaved, deciduous trees.

Haunch Part of a mortise-and-tenon joint when used at the corner of a frame to prevent it from twisting.

Hollow-ground The cutting edge of blades on which thickness is reduced toward the center.

Honing After grinding, edge tools are honed (sharpened) on either oil stones or water stones and finally on a leather strop.

Housing A groove generally cut across the grain to accept a fixed vertical partition or a shelf, for example, in a cabinet or bookcase.

HSS (high-speed steel) The cutting edge on machine saws and cutters is made from this to make it harder than the rest of the tool and give a longer cutting life. (*See also* TCT)

In stick Term used when lumber has been converted and is stacked with small wood strips between the boards to allow air to circulate.

Inlays Pieces of material inserted into grooves or recesses which finish flush with the surface.

Jigs Devices made to hold lumber while various operations are being carried out; generally used with machines to enable those operations to be safely carried

out and repetitive operations to be made with precision.

Jigsaw A hand power tool with a reciprocating blade that will cut boards in either straight lines or curves.

Jointer/planer A machine especially designed to plane lumber that has a previously prepared flat and straight face side. The machine is similar to a mangle, and the lumber is passed underneath the cutter block, ensuring a uniform thickness.

Kerf The width of the cut made by a saw.

Kiln Oven for seasoning lumber using a mixture of hot air and steam.

Kiln drying *see* Seasoning, kiln drying

Lacquer, solvent A finish derived from plastics-based chemicals that will set or cure by the evaporation of solvents or moisture, forming an irreversible plastic film.

Lacquer, water Water-based lacquers that do not contain harmful chemicals.

Laminating A means by which curved shapes can be achieved without steaming and bending. Thin veneers are cut, molds are produced, each veneer or laminate is glued to the next and held in position in the mold, so that when the glue has cured, the resulting curve or bend will be stable.

Laminboard A manu-factured board similar to blockboard but with smaller core strips and generally having an extra layer of veneer on the faces which run in the direction of the cores, giving a very stable board.

Lap Simple woodworking joint in which half of the joint area is cut away on each opposing part prior to joining.

Lapping plate A truly flat plate upon which tools can be ground flat.

Lathe A machine on which a motor turns either a face plate or a driving spindle to enable wood to be turned into bowls or spindles.

Lipping Strip of solid wood applied to manufactured boards to protect the edges.

Marking out The basis of all fine work. Accurate marking out with suitable tools is the basis for the finest levels of craftsmanship.

Marquetry An applied decoration using veneers of different species/colors. Generally pictorial or free-patterned.

MDF (medium-density fiberboard) One of the most modern manufactured boards, it has the production advantage of not needing to be lipped since it machines very well and can be stained and polished directly. Very useful for production, but not best used in high-quality work. Concern has been raised regarding emissions of formaldehyde, which is used as the bonding chemical agent.

Miter A joint generally at a right-angled corner with an angle of 45°, normally located with some mechanical means such as tongue and groove, dowel, or biscuit.

Moldings The cutting of decorative shapes, either simple or complex classic.

Mortise A rectangular hole in a piece of wood into which a tenon fits snugly. (*See also* Tenon)

Muntin Generally used to describe a division between two sections of a wide drawer bottom.

Oils A natural material that will build an attractive finish, especially on hard and exotic woods, but without the wearing properties of lacquers. Oils can be linseed, linseed with special driers (Danish or teak oil), or tung oil.

Orbital sander A hand-powered tool which has a base upon which a sheet of abrasive paper fits and oscillates to give a sanded surface.

Panel saw *see* Handsaw

Paring The process of removing very fine shavings from wood with a sharp chisel.

Parquetry Similar to marquetry but using veneers, generally to make geometric patterns or motifs.

Particle board (or chip-board) The generic name for manufactured boards made

from particles or chips of wood. The faces generally have fine chips while the interior has coarser chips. Industrially, this board always needed lipping. (*See also* MDF)

Parting tool Used when turning a spindle either to introduce fine lines or to remove waste at the ends.

Plane blade In hand planes, a sharp blade that gives a very fine finish.

Planer, surfacer or overhand The machine used prior to the introduction of the planer. Properly used, it will produce first a precise face side and then a perfectly square face edge.

Plane, block A lightweight and general-purpose plane that is used one-handed. The blade is set to a low angle and is very useful for planing end grain.

Plane, jack A general-purpose plane for preparing flat planed surfaces.

Plane, jointer A longer plane than the jack, its length makes it particularly suitable for planing long, straight faces and edges.

Plane, shoulder A plane specially made for trimming shoulders both with and across the grain.

Plane, smoothing Shorter than the jack plane, the smoothing plane when finely adjusted is used to put a final finish on the work.

Plunge The up and down movement when using a router.

Plywood One of the earliest manufactured boards, made of a series of veneers, laminates, or plies that always total an odd number, with each veneer at right angles to the one next to it. Depending on the quality of the veneer and the adhesive, a very stable board is produced. It is possible to have grades termed "marine ply" that are impervious to moisture.

Press The modern version of a caul with large steel plates and hydraulic pressure rams, able to veneer large areas and also used in industry to produce high-class laminates or pre-forms.

Punch   A tool that allows panel pins or veneer pins to be punched beneath the surface of the lumber, leaving only a small hole to fill.

PVA glue   *see* Adhesive, PVA

Quarter sawn   *see* Conversion, quarter-sawn

Rabbet   A step formed along the edge of a piece of lumber normally used to insert a panel of lumber or other sheet material.

Rasps, rifflers, and files Normally used in carving where the use of carving tools is not possible or practical. This method of material removal, generally used in metalwork, is used to shape lumber, especially in chair making.

Respirator   Filter used for mouth or nose protection.

Ripsaw   *see* Handsaw

Riving knife   Used on a circular saw, the riving knife is the thickness of the saw kerf, and is fixed behind the blade to prevent the saw cut from closing and gripping the blade.

Roughing gouge   When turning, the tool used to remove a large amount of material quickly before precision work.

Router   A versatile hand power tool which accepts an enormous range of cutters and can make grooves, rabbets, and moldings with ease and precision. (*See also* Cutters, router)

Safety, dust   Dust from woodworking can be harmful to health, and in operations that will generate large amounts (i.e., sanding) a respirator or mask should always be used.

Safety, edge tools   The safest edge tools are sharp ones since they will cut without undue pressure. Care should always be taken.

Safety, machine tools Hand power and machine tools are not inherently dangerous but accidents arising from their misuse can be serious. Always treat these tools with respect and never use them if tired or under the influence of drugs or alcohol.

Safety, noise   Using traditional hand tools there are usually few problems, but when using machine and hand power tools it is essential to have some form of ear protection.

Sanding and sandpaper *see* Abrasive papers

Scraper   Used with certain woods and veneers when it is not possible to use a plane for final finishing. The cabinet scraper is a piece of steel, on the edges of which are formed burrs which will scrape thin shavings from lumber.

Screws, types of   There are two main varieties: the traditional slot-head type which has several types of screw heads (including countersink, raised, and round), a screw shank and a thread; and the Phillips-head, which has a cross- or star-shaped recess for use with a matching Phillips or Pozidriv screwdriver. Generally there is a twin thread that runs from the head the whole length of the screw.

Scribe   A line cut with a knife. Also the method of transferring an irregular line to the workpiece.

Scroll saw   Very fine saw that enables cuts to be made similar to those found in a jigsaw puzzle.

Seasoning, air drying Before the advent of central heating and air conditioning, lumber was normally air dried. After the log has been converted the logs are stacked in stick in the open, but with a cover against rain, to dry naturally. The rule of thumb is one year for every 1 in. (25 mm) thickness.

Seasoning, kiln drying Since man's interior environments have changed, lumber needs to be reduced to a lower moisture content than previously, making drying in a kiln (a large oven) essential. (*See also* Kiln)

Set   Saw teeth are bent slightly to one side, then the other of the blade so that the resulting cut (or kerf) is wider than the blade itself.

Shakes   Faults or defects found in lumber due to poor felling or seasoning.

Shank   Denotes a cylindrical part of either a screw or a nail, or refers to the part of a drill or cutter which fits into a chuck or collet.

Shooting board   A jig that supports the work at right angles to a bench plane.

Shoulder   An edge (as opposed to a face) that will need to connect precisely to another component when making joints (as in mortise and tenon, lap joints, etc.).

Silicon carbide paper *see* Abrasive papers, silicon carbide

Skew   A chisel ground on an angle, right and left hand, to reach less accessible places. Also a specific type of turning tool.

Sliding bevel   An instrument used when it is necessary to mark lines from an edge which are not at right angles. It can be adjusted to any angle and is useful for marking out large dovetails.

Softwood   Lumber harvested from coniferous trees, which usually have needles instead of leaves and do not lose them during the winter.

Soss hinge   A special hinge that is invisible when a door is closed and is set between the door edge and the cabinet side.

Spindle molder   A machine tool with a vertical spindle set in a horizontal table. The spindle takes various blocks with a wide variety of cutters in them, but is usually a production machine. Smaller workshops manage to accomplish most tasks using a router.

Square   Important for marking out, a good square enables precision marking of right angles and is one of the furniture maker's most important tools.

Steel wool   Used as an abrasive to cut down the wood surface. Sometimes used with wax as a lubricant.

Striking knife   A knife specially made for marking cut lines against a set-square or sliding bevel. The most accurate method of marking out.

Tail stock   The part of a lathe at the opposite end to the driving mechanism, used when turning spindles between centers.

Tang   Pointed spur at the end of a chisel or a file that is driven into the wooden handle.

Tannin   The chemical present in oak which causes rust or staining on contact with ferrous metals. All fittings should therefore be of non-ferrous metals, normally brass.

TCT (tungsten carbide tipped)   A very hard deposit applied to the teeth of saws and edges of knives used in machine tools. It will normally stay sharp longer than high-speed steel but can be vulnerable to damage if used carelessly. (*See also* HSS)

Tenon   The end of a rail shaped so that it can fit into a mortise. (*See also* Mortise)

Tenon saw   *see* Backsaw, tenon

Tenting   A technique for accurate paring to a cut or gauge line.

Textures, sand blast Normally used in metal finishing. Interesting effects on lumber can be achieved as the softer grain is removed, leaving a series of grain projections.

Textures, scorch   An interesting textural finish achieved by scorching a softer grained lumber with a blow torch. The burnt surface is brushed with a wire brush which removes the carbon deposits.

Textures, scrub   Some woods can be scrubbed with a stiff brush and caustic soda to give an effect similar to sand blasting.

Through and through *see* Conversion, through-and-through

Tongue   A thin strip of wood (sometimes plywood) that fits into a matching groove in the faces of a joint (either with or across the grain) which reinforces that joint. (*See also* Groove)

Tuning   The process of preparing an edge tool prior to first sharpening and use.

UF glue   *see* Adhesive, UF

Vacuum bag   Used when laminating lumber shapes, its advantage is that only one male mold is needed. The mold plus the package of veneers with adhesive applied are placed in the bag, air is withdrawn using a vacuum pump, and air pressure pushes the laminate firmly down onto the mold surface.

Veneer   Expensive and exotic woods are often best used as thin sheets that are applied to a suitable substrate. Decorative veneers are normally about 3/64 in. (1 mm) thick, while constructional veneers can be up to 1/8 in. (3 mm) thick.

Veneer hammer   In the past, hot animal glues were used to lay veneers. A veneer hammer was used to press the veneers down and remove excess glue.

Viscosity   The amount of flow present in a liquid. In some instances liquid is thinned to allow a faster flow.

Vise   A good vise on a substantial bench is one of the most important pieces of the furniture maker's equipment. There is normally a vise on the front of the bench and often a second vise fixed to the right-hand end of the front of the bench. This arrangement provides the maker with the best control of the workpiece.

Visor   Eye protection for use with machinery and hand power tools which tend to throw out dust or shavings.

Waney edge   The natural edge of a plank which may still have a covering of bark.

Wax   Can be used as a final coat over other finishes, but occasionally used as a finish on its own.

Wetting out   The process of intentionally raising the grain by damping the wood, sanding off, and repeating until the grain is flat.

INDEX

ACKNOWLEDGMENTS

The publishers would like to thank the following for their assistance in supplying equipment and materials for this book:

Alan Holtham, Cheshire
Axminster Power Tool Centre, Axminster, Devon
Crown Hand Tools Ltd, Sheffield, Yorkshire
Elu Power Tools Ltd, Slough, Berkshire
Foxell & James Ltd, London
J Crispins & Son, London
JSM Joinery, London
Morgans of Strood, Strood, Kent
Parry Tyzack, London
Peter Child, Essex
Racal Health & Safety Ltd, Greenford, Middlesex
Wilson Bros., Northfleet, Kent

The publishers and photographers would like to thank all the contributors and project makers for their patient help and advice. Special thanks go to Mark Ripley for his skills and imagination, and clear demonstrations of techniques. Thanks also to the following for their help on location shoots: Gordon Stone, Paul Mitchard, Graham Mills, Gurk, Darren Francis, John Ingram, John Taylor, and Mick O'Donnell.

The publishers wish to acknowledge the help of Nick Chandler for the designs of the bookcase, CD storage box, and glass-topped table projects.

Many thanks to Lucinda Pearce-Higgins for her help in the development of this project.

All photography by Colin Bowling and Paul Forrester for Hamlyn except the following:

Section eleven—Woodcarving
Christie's Images 188 left, 189 below

Section twelve—Woods and Materials
Environmental Images /Herbert Giradet 208 left, 208 below right, /Peter Solness 208 top right
Holt Studios International /Nigel Cattlin 202 below right, /Dick Roberts 202 below left
Oxford Scientific Films /Harold Taylor 195 left, 195 right
Still Pictures /Mark Edwards 208 center right, /Dylan Garcia 201 top right, /Frank Vidal, 194 center, /Martin Wright 194 below

AVAILABILITY

The products detailed below are available through the mail order sources as indicated:

Board Clamps (p. 30): Not yet available in the US, but a very similar product is available from Woodworkers Supply, 1108 North Glenn Rd, Casper, Wyoming 82601 (tel. 800 645 9292).
Wooden Cam Clamp (p. 31): Garrett Wade, 161 Avenue of the Americas, New York NY 10013, and Albert Constantine and Son, 2050 East Chester Rd, Bronx NY 10461.
Japanese Miniature Clamp (p. 31): Garrett Wade (above), Constantines (above) and Lee Valley Tools Ltd. 1080 Morrison Drive, Ottawa, Ontario K2H 8K7, Canada.
Table Saw (p. 36) The model illustrated is not available in the US, but similar machines are manufactured by a number of American companies including Delta and Bridgewood.
Contractor's Saw (p. 37) The model illustrated is not available in the US, but similar American machines include the Delta and the Craftsman 29951 by Sears.
Small Jointer/Planer (p.38): Inca machines available through Garrett Wade (above), Robland machines through Laguna Tools, 2265 Laguna Canyon Rd, Laguna Beach, Cal. 92651, Mini Max (tel 800 292 1850) through agents.
Sanding System (p.43): Not yet available outside Europe.
Lamello Gluing System (p.43): Available throughout the US from suppliers of the Lamello Biscuit Jointer, and by mail order from Garrett Wade (above) and Lee Valley Tools (above). A similar product is available from Constantines.